their country's service, all deserve that their high merits should stand recorded; and never was high merit more conspicuous than in the battle I have described.

The Achille (a French 74), after having surrendered, by some mismanagement of the French men, took fire and blew up; two hundred of her men were saved by the Tenders.

A circumstance occurred during the action which so strongly marks the invincible spirit of British seamen, when engaging the enemies of their country, that I cannot resist the pleasure I have in making it known to their Lordships; the Temeraire was boarded by accident, or design, by a French ship on one side, and a Spaniard on the other; the contest was vigorous, but, in the end, the Combined Ensigns were torn from the poop, and the British hoisted in their places.

Such a battle could not be fought without sustaining a great loss of men. I have not only to lament, in common with the British Navy, and the British Nation, in the Fall of the Commander in Chief, the loss of a Hero, whose name will be immortal, and his memory ever dear to his country; but my heart is rent with the most poignant grief for the death of a friend, to whom, by many years intimacy, and a perfect knowledge of the virtues of his mind, which inspired ideas superior to the common race of men, I was bound by the strongest ties of affection; a grief to which even the glorious occasion in which he fell, does not bring the consolation which, perhaps, it ought: his Lordship received a musket ball in his left breast, about the middle of the action, and sent an Officer to me immediately with his last farewell; and soon after expired.

I have also to lament the loss of those excellent Officers, Captains Duff, of the Mars, and Cooke, of the Bellerophon; I have yet heard of none others.

I fear the numbers that have fallen will be found very great, when the returns come to me; but it having blown a gale of wind ever since the action, I have not yet had it in my power to collect any reports from the ships.

The Royal Sovereign having lost her masts, except the tottering foremast, I called the Euryalus to me, while the action continued, which ship lying within hail, made my signals—a service Captain Blackwood performed with great attention: after the action, I shifted my flag to her, that I might more easily communicate any orders to, and collect the ships, and towed the Royal Sovereign out to Seaward. The whole fleet were now in a very perilous situation, many dismasted, all shattered, in thirteen fathom water, off the shoals of Trafalgar; and when I made the signal to prepare to anchor, few of the ships had an anchor to let go, their cables being shot; but the same good Providence which aided us through such a day preserved us in the night, by the wind shifting a few points, and drifting the ships off the land, except

can I find language to express my sentiments of the valour and skill which were displayed by the Officers the Seamen, and Marines in the battle with the enemy, where every individual appeared as Hero, or whom the Glory of his Country depended; the attack was irresistible, and the issue of it adds to the page of Naval Annals a brilliant instance of what Britons ... ... their service.

... ...

public testimony of my high approbation of their conduct, and my thanks for it. (Signed) C. COLLINGWOOD.

To the Right Honorable Rear-Admiral the Earl of Northesk, and the respective Captains and Commanders.

GENERAL ORDER.

The Almighty God, whose arm is strength, having of his great mercy been pleased to crown the exertion of his Majesty's fleet with success, in giving them a complete victory over their enemies, on 21st of this month; and that all praise and thanksgiving may be offered up to the Throne of Grace for the great benefits to our country and to mankind:

I have thought proper, that a day should be appointed of general humiliation before God, and thanksgiving for this his merciful goodness, imploring forgiveness of sins, a continuation of his divine mercy, and his constant aid to us, in the defence of our country's liberties and laws, without which the utmost efforts of man are nought; and direct, therefore, that

be appointed for this holy purpose.

Given on board the Euryalus, off Cape Trafalgar, 22d Oct. 1805.

(Signed) C. COLLINGWOOD.

To the respective Captains and Commanders.

N. B. The fleet having been dispersed by a gale of wind, no day has yet been able to be appointed for the above purpose.

SIR, Euryalus, off Cadiz, Oct. 24. 1805.

In my letter of the 22d, I detailed to you, for the information of my Lords Commissioners of the Admiralty, the proceedings of his Majesty's squadron on the day of the action, and that preceding it, since which I have had a continued series of misfortunes; but they are of a kind that human prudence could not possibly provide against, or my skill prevent.

On the 22d, in the morning, a strong southerly wind blew, with squally weather, which, however, did not prevent the activity of the Officers and Seamen of such ships as were manageable, from getting hold of many of the prizes (thirteen or fourteen), and towing them off to the Westward, where I ordered them to rendezvous round the Royal Sovereign, in tow by the Neptune: but on the 23d the gale increased, and the sea ran so high that many of them broke the tow-rope, and drifted far to leeward before they were got hold of again; and some of them, taking advantage in the dark and boisterous night, got before the wind, and have, perhaps, drifted upon the shore and sunk; on the afternoon of that day the remnant of the Combined Fleet, ten sail of ships, who had not been much engaged, stood up to leeward of my shattered and straggled charge, as if meaning to attack them,

MILITARY MISDEMEANORS

OSPREY
PUBLISHING

Dedicated to the staff & patrons of the
Café Noir, rue Montmartre, Paris,
and
John Westphal.

ACKNOWLEDGEMENTS

Special thanks to Yves Martin, in particular for the Nelson story;
Anita Baker and Ruth Sheppard at Osprey for their understanding
and continued good humour. Lastly, my wife Sarah for her
continued support and encouragement in what has become
an increasingly all-consuming occupation.

MILITARY MISDEMEANORS

*Corruption, incompetence, lust
and downright stupidity*

TERRY CROWDY

First published in Great Britain in 2007 by Osprey Publishing Ltd,
Midland House, West Way, Botley, Oxford OX2 0PH, UK.
443 Park Avenue South, New York, NY 10016, USA.
Email: info@ospreypublishing.com

Every attempt has been made by the Publishers to secure the appropriate permissions for
materials reproduced in this book. If there has been any oversight we will be happy to rectify
the situation and a written submission should be made to the Publishers.

A CIP catalogue record for this book is available from the British Library

ISBN: 978 1 84603 148 9

Terry Crowdy has asserted his right under the Copyright, Designs and Patents Act, 1988,
to be identified as the author of this book.

Typeset in Adobe Garamond, folio images in DF Primitives
Originated by PDQ Digital Media Solutions
Printed in China through Worldprint Ltd.

07 08 09 11 12   10 9 8 7 6 5 4 3 2 1

For a catalogue of all books published by Osprey please contact:

NORTH AMERICA
Osprey Direct c/o Random House Distribution Center
400 Hahn Road, Westminster, MD 21157, USA
E-mail: info@ospreydirect.com

ALL OTHER REGIONS
Osprey Direct UK, P.O. Box 140, Wellingborough, Northants, NN8 2FA, UK
E-mail: info@ospreydirect.co.uk

www.ospreypublishing.com

Front cover images: 'The hand-writing upon the wall', Library of Congress; newspaper
reporting the Trafalgar victory, akg-images; other design elements from wwwistockphoto.com.
Endpapers: Newspaper reporting the Trafalgar victory. (akg-images)
Title page: The duel of Chevalier d'Éon and de Saint-Georges. (Roger-Viollet / Topfoto)
Design elements on pages 11, 21, 87, 147, 187 and 225 from istockphoto.com.

CONTENTS

ACT III: 'NOT SUCH A GREAT WAR'

ACT IV: 'COLD WAR FALLOUT'

ACT V: 'EVEN IN OUR ENLIGHTENED TIMES?'

AFTERWORD 310

ENDNOTES 313

AN INTRODUCTION ... OF SORTS

'Power tends to corrupt, and absolute power corrupts absolutely.'*

IN the opening years of the 21st century scandals involving the military and security services have come and gone at an alarming rate. Many might feel it is wrong or unpatriotic to criticize the military in any way in the post-9/11 climate; but surely the principal strength of countries with a democratic tradition is the right to question, disagree with, even satirize and lampoon public institutions and figures as we see fit. To remove this right is to remove the very foundation stone of the democratic system and to fall into the abyss of dictatorial totalitarianism.

So then – cruel beings that we are – let us cast scruple aside and feast on the misfortunes and peccadilloes of service folk in peace, wartime and that grey, murky area in between. Alongside movie stars, athletes, businessmen and the clergy, military and secret service personnel – not to mention their political bosses – have provided us with some incredible scandals over the years.

Sometimes appalling, often frankly amusing, these scandals lurch between gross incompetence, sleaze, misplaced megalomania and pure greed.

---

* John Emerich Edward Dalberg-Acton, 1st Baron Acton, 1887.

To begin with, the discerning *scandalista*, the true connoisseur of soldierly sleaze, must learn to distinguish between the *blunder* and the *scandal*. The distinction is subjective, but a good example is found during the arguably pointless Crimean War.

The famous but short-lived 'Charge of the Light Brigade' was as spectacular a blunder as one could hope to imagine. In a moment of madness over 600 British horsemen were ordered to charge into a valley – the wrong valley – which was bristling with Russian guns. France's Marshal Bosquet put it best when he said, as only a Frenchman could: 'C'est magnifique, mais ce n'est pas la guerre.'* The Russian commanders thought the British horsemen must have been drunk.

On the other hand, the despicable living conditions to which troops were subjected in the Crimea were a scandal and public opinion turned against the British government, which many incarnations later still appears to be getting it wrong. During the 2003 Iraq War, a friend in the RAF exclaimed (minus the expletives): 'Third desert deployment – still no desert boots.' His frustration was well placed and by no means unique. With the current vogue for claims and compensation, there was even talk of charging the British government with corporate manslaughter for failing to properly equip its service personnel in war zones. Perhaps the old charge of 'lions led by donkeys' is still relevant today?†

---

* 'It is magnificent, but it is not war.' The French have a well-developed flair for expressing things in such a way.

† This phrase is most famously applied to British soldiers in the First World War, who were slaughtered in droves after being instructed to advance against German machine guns in an orderly fashion. In fact the expression apparently pre-dates that conflict and was used by a London newspaper to describe French soldiers during the Franco-Prussian War (1870–71).

With that, it is time to step back into the pages of history and see how corruption, bigotry, lust, vanity, stupidity and the occasional bout of insanity have coloured the history of conflict in the past.

To err is human, they say. From the evidence you will find presented in the coming pages, you will, I hope, deduce how even the great captains of history were, and remain, very human indeed.

THE PROLOGUE

'INIQUITY IN ANTIQUITY'

THE ONE THAT GOT AWAY

THE first in a duet of ancient outrages takes us to Greece in the summer of 480 BC. The brutality and harshness of Ancient Sparta is legendary. Men were brought up in a bizarre state of pious poverty and extreme discipline, and, when sent to war, were expected – so the saying went – either to return carrying their shield, victorious, or to come back carried on their shield, dead. This is the story of one man who failed to fulfil that pledge.

The story of the 300 Spartans is well enough known. King Xerxes of Persia had invaded Greece and was steamrollering his way through the country when he came to a narrow choke point on the road south at Thermopylae. Here the mountains came very close to the sea, making it an excellent defensive position. In the pass stood guard one of Sparta's two kings, Leonidas, with his handpicked bodyguard of 300 men and an assortment of Greek allies. Against them Xerxes' army numbered into the hundreds of thousands.

For four days and nights Xerxes watched on with incredulity as the Spartans sat combing their hair, waiting for him to attack. When on the fifth day Xerxes saw that this pitiful band had still not fled in terror, he attacked. Unfortunately for Xerxes, the full might of his army was negated by the narrowness of the pass and the skilful soldiery of the Greeks. The invaders were repulsed time and time again with heavy losses.

After a second day of fruitless attacks a Greek traitor named Ephialtes, supposing he would be well rewarded for his treachery, came to Xerxes and offered to show his men a way round the narrow pass. Through the night Ephialtes led a Persian force along a narrow track up to the summit of a mountain overlooking the pass, which they reached at dawn. A force of 1,000 Phocians was protecting the route, but did not see the Persians through the trees until it was too late to bar their passage. The Persians brushed the Phocians aside and flooded down toward the rear of Leonidas' position.*

The doom of the Spartans and their allies had been foretold that morning by the soothsayer Megistias, and also by deserters from the Persian camp. Leonidas had called together his allies and bade them retreat before it was too late. He meanwhile, with the remnants of his 300 men, would defend the pass – come what may.

Along with the other Greeks sent back home were two Spartans who had been dismissed from their camp by Leonidas. They were Eurytus and Aristodemus and both were suffering from an inflammation of the eyes that had rendered them temporarily blind.

However, when Eurytus learned that the Persians had gone round the pass and the Spartans were cut off, he ordered his servant to bring him his armour and then to lead him to where the fighting was taking place. In a display of foolhardy bravery, Eurytus was

---

* At the end of the Persian War, after Plataea, Sparta put a price on the traitor Ephialtes' head. The traitor ran to the state of Thessaly, where he was afforded shelter for some time, but eventually his past caught up with him and he was slain by a man named Athenades, whom the Spartans greatly honoured for his deed.

able to reach the fighting, and died with all his comrades in the pass that day.*

Unfortunately for Aristodemus, his courage gave out and he chose not to follow Eurytus, but left with the other Greeks. In the circumstances, perhaps he would have been excused, but because Eurytus had not allowed the blindness to deter him from fighting, Aristodemus was treated as a traitor. No one would speak to him nor offer him shelter, and everywhere he went he was called Aristodemus 'the Trembler'. His being alive while his king lay dead was an affront to everything Sparta stood for.

Aristodemus did not take his own life but instead set about restoring his reputation among his people. At the battle of Plataea the following summer, in 479 BC, he was given his chance. Rather than a bodyguard of 300, this time the Spartans sent their full army of 45,000 men, including 5,000 Spartan knights – the largest force Sparta ever put in the field. When lining up against the Persians, Aristodemus seized his moment of redemption. He rushed forward ahead of his comrades so that the last of the 300 would be killed before their eyes and the dishonour attached to his name would be removed. By all accounts he fought like a madman and his debt was considered repaid.†

But hang on a minute ... perhaps history has been just a little unkind in singling out Aristodemus. Why didn't Sparta send out its

---

*   Leonidas died surrounded by his men. After the battle Xerxes committed a scandalous act, ordering that Leonidas' corpse be desecrated, by having the head cut off and the body crucified. The Persians were usually quite civilized in their treatment of the enemy dead, but in this case Xerxes was enraged by the Spartans' defiance and the death of two of his brothers, killed in the final attack. Later Xerxes showed himself a man after all and, greatly regretting his action, returned Leonidas' body to Sparta.

†   The story of Aristodemus is told by Herodotus.

full army to support Leonidas in the pass the year before Plataea? Surely, with the Athenian fleet protecting the seaward flank, the full Spartan contingent could have held the pass and the goat track indefinitely – long enough for Xerxes to get bored and leave the expedition to an underling at least.

So why didn't they show up?

It is well known that at the beginning of the war Sparta consulted the Oracle at Delphi. It is believed that the actual oracle was a woman suspended in a chair over a pit of sulphur fumes who – high as a kite from inhaling the fumes – would impart gibberish to a set of priests, whose knowledge was slightly – shall we say – more worldly in origin.

The prediction given to the Spartans was this:

Hear your fate, O dwellers in Sparta of the wide spaces;
Either your famed, great town must be sacked by Perseus' son,*
Or, if that be not, the whole land of Lacedaemon†
Shall mourn the death of a king of the house of Heracles.‡
For not the strength of lions or bulls shall hold him,
Strength against strength; for he has the power of Zeus,
And will not be checked till one of these two he has consumed.[1]

In plainer terms, either Sparta lost a king in battle, or the Persians would sack their city. It was a challenge that Leonidas was prepared to face – and one that may go a long way to explaining why he refused to evacuate the pass and instead chose to meet certain death. But that still does not explain why the rest of the army didn't turn up.

---

* The Persians.
† Sparta.
‡ Leonidas was said to be descended from Heracles.

According to Herodotus, when Leonidas set out with his bodyguard of 300 men it was *in advance* of the main army. This implies that Leonidas expected the rest of the army to follow. Herodotus then goes on to describe how a religious celebration – the nine-day Carneian festival – prohibited the sending of more troops at the time Leonidas set out.

Coincidentally, the Spartans had used the excuse of this religious festival ten years before to explain their inability to aid Athens against the Persians at the battle of Marathon. In reality, it is believed that the real reason Sparta did not send troops to Marathon is that they were busy subjugating an uprising of Helot serfs.

So was the religious festival used as an excuse not to send the main army to Thermopylae because it was not deemed to be in Sparta's interest to fight so far north?

Probably.

With the exception of Leonidas, the rulers of Sparta had no inclination to advance beyond the narrow Isthmus of Corinth, the natural line of defence of the Peloponnesian states. If that is the case, one wonders whether the fabled oracle's message was in fact a very clever put-up job to get rid of Leonidas? In which case Aristodemus' inclination towards self-preservation at the expense of honour was not the biggest scandal at Thermopylae!

HE CAME. HE SAW.
HE WAS CONQUERED!

Eclipsing all others in the outrage stakes was one of the great commanders of the Ancient World. In terms of scandal, Julius Caesar had few peers, which is saying something in the corrupt, festering pool that Rome had become at the end of the Republican era.

His conquests were by no means limited to the battlefield, for our Julius was a notorious and serial adulterer. His most famous mistress, Cleopatra, was only one of a number of high-profile bedmates. It also appears that Julius was saddled with the baggage of an embarrassing and very public homosexual affair in his youth. He was, according to one commentator: 'every woman's man and every man's woman'.[2]

Our main source for this prime, rare, juicy gossip is Suetonius, the former soldier turned historian and author of such salacious – but now unfortunately lost – gems as the *Lives of Famous Whores*. Although widespread in the Ancient World, homosexuality was not entirely without stigma. Even though it was common for Roman men to take young male slaves for lovers, it was unacceptable for a Roman not to be the dominant partner in the act. In the macho world of Roman society, to indulge thus was seen as unmanly in the extreme. Caesar therefore invited ridicule by doing just that when he became an object of love to King

Nicomedes III of Bithynia, a state on the Black Sea, which in modern times forms part of Turkey.

Caesar crossed this sexual Rubicon on his first military campaign, serving on the staff of Marcus Thermus, Roman governor of Asia Minor. History books tell us that Caesar showed such bravery at the siege of Miletus (80 BC) that he was awarded the *corona civica* – an oak crown awarded only to those individuals who had bravely saved the lives of fellow Romans. Such was its prestige that even senators were required to stand and applaud the holder.

During the same campaign Caesar was sent to Bithynia to collect a fleet. His absence was so prolonged rumours grew that his relations with King Nicomedes had become 'improper'. These rumours increased when Caesar made a brief reappearance in the Roman camp, only to announce that he was immediately returning to Nicomedes.

His relationship with the Bithynian king tarnished his reputation for life. According to Suetonius Caesar was dubbed 'the Queen's rival' and 'the inner partner of the royal couch'. Some labelled him 'the Queen of Bithynia'; others charged that Caesar had acted as a cup-bearer to Nicomedes and 'his wantons' at an enormous dinner party. At one crowded assembly an obviously drunken Roman saluted Gnaeus Pompeius (Pompey the Great) as 'rex' then saluted Caesar as 'regina' (queen).

Perhaps worst of all, word of Caesar's actions spread among the ranks where he became the subject of bawdy marching songs. Suetonius recorded a few lines of a song referring to his fling with Nicomedes sung by the soldiers as they followed the chariot to military immortality after Caesar's famous conquest of Gaul (58–50 BC):

> All the Gauls did Caesar vanquish, Nicomedes vanquished him;
> Lo! Now Caesar rides in triumph, victor over all the Gauls,
> Nicomedes does not triumph, having subdued the conqueror.[3]

From the same era another popular soldiers' ditty on Caesar went as follows:

> Watch well your wives, ye citizens, we bring a blade,
> A bald-pate master of the wenching trade.
> Thy gold was spent on many a Gallic whore;
> Exhausted now, thou com'st to borrow more.[4]

It is true that Caesar had a long string of female lovers and he was rumoured to have seduced many illustrious women. Suetonius lists the names Postumia, Lollia, Tertulla and Mucia before declaring Caesar's love for Servilia Caepionis, mother of Marcus Brutus – one of his eventual assassins. In his first consulship, Caesar is believed to have bought her a pearl costing 6 million sesterces and during the civil war sold estates to her at bargain prices. It was even believed that Servilia prostituted her daughter Tertia to Caesar. Their affair became public after Caesar was caught reading a love letter from Servilia in the Senate.

He had love affairs with queens too, above all with Cleopatra who famously presented herself to Caesar rolled up in a Persian carpet. It is said that he often feasted until daybreak with her and that he would have gone through Egypt with her in her state barge as far as Ethiopia, had not his soldiers refused to follow. He took Cleopatra to Rome and showered her with gifts. In turn she bore him a son, although this was officially and strenuously denied.

It will not surprise you to learn that when the shoe was on the other foot, Caesar would not tolerate infidelities against him. He divorced his second wife, Pompeia, after a man was discovered in Caesar's house dressed as a lute girl during the nocturnal festival of the goddess Bona Dea. Although Caesar could offer no evidence of wrong-doing, he said he divorced her because: 'I thought my wife ought not even to be under suspicion.'

It was this sort of vain hypocrisy that led Caesar to declare himself dictator for life in 48 BC and it was no wonder that a few years later 60 senators stabbed him to death.

Caesar … it seems you had it coming.

ACT I

'OUR INGLORIOUS PAST'

THE INFAMOUS LIEUTENANT BIRD

IT is time to leapfrog forward in history, to reach the beginning of modern times, when the proliferation of newspapers and popular journals, along with an increase in the literacy rate, meant that scandals were propagated en masse. As the 18 centuries since Caesar's untimely end peel back like the skin of a rancid banana, some of the more unsavoury moments of history are exposed once again.

This first port of call is London in the early 18th century during the reign of King George I. Our opening miscreant is not one of the great names in history; he never obtained anything but modest rank and never made a name for himself by courageous daring-do in war. In truth, if it had not been for his dastardly crime, Lieutenant Edward Bird might have been forgotten by history altogether.

Bird was born at the town of Windsor to respectable parents – by which we mean that they were not of the aristocracy, but were wealthy enough to be tolerable to them. They sent their son to Eton, the school with playing fields that would one day produce the victors of Waterloo. In the case of Edward Bird, however, Eton produced nothing more than a self-centred, whoring murderer.

After Eton Bird did the Grand Tour of France and Italy. Much like the sons and daughters of the modern-day rich, he was sent abroad to sully other people's doorsteps with his youthful exuberance and ensure that any 'mistakes' were not committed in his own backyard. However, this stint on tour did not exhaust Mr Bird's proclivities, but only served to educate him in sin and make him hungrier for more of the same. When he returned to England and was favoured with a commission in His Majesty's cavalry, his bad habits followed him like a shadow. And now we come to his crime…

On the evening of 25 September 1718, Lieutenant Bird arrived in a coach at a *bagnio* in Silver Street, London. In its original sense, a bagnio was a coffee house where a patron could enjoy a Turkish bath. However, by the 1700s it increasingly referred to a place where bedrooms could be had with no questions asked and where the guests rarely stayed for breakfast.

This particular house of ill repute was managed by the appropriately named Mr Seedwell. Bird and his 'companion' arrived with a bottle of champagne* and were shown to a room by their 'waiter' for the evening, Samuel Loxton. Nothing more was heard from the couple until 2am, when Loxton heard a knocking from Bird's room. He went upstairs to investigate.

As he entered the room, Bird and companion were still in bed. The lieutenant demanded that a bath be brought to the room. Loxton replied that he was in the middle of bathing a 'great gentleman' and would attend to Bird as soon as he was done.

---

* *Champain Wine* in the original text. As a note of trivia, it is commonly thought that champagne was invented by the Frenchman Dom Pérignon. There is, however, a growing belief that it was the English who invented the process of double fermentation which gives champagne its fizz several years before the French. Key to making champagne was the stronger glass bottle, which was invented by the English. If it is too hard to believe that the French were taught winemaking by Englishmen, there is more evidence that they were taught to cook by the Italians. By all accounts French cooking was nothing to write home about until after the arrival of Caterina de' Medici in 1533. In her retinue were Florentine cooks who introduced many recipes, including onion soup and the concept of eating food in courses, rather than having it all served on the table at once.

Bird was not about to put up with this kind of insolence. He told Loxton to damn the gentleman and bring him a bath at once – either that or he would kill him.

Off Loxton went to make arrangements. Having taken leave of the 'great gentleman' Loxton sent another servant up to Bird's room to tell him the bath would be forthcoming. Loxton did not go himself because he was scared.

Thomas Baberton, or 'Vernassel' as he was better known, went to Bird's room and assured him the bath would be ready in 'the eighth part of an hour'. This was not good enough for Bird who told the servant: 'God damn you Sir, I will have it this moment.' He jumped out of bed, grabbed his sword and began lunging with it at Vernassel, who was fortunately close enough to the bedroom door to shield himself behind it. He shut the door and waited. A moment later he heard the sound of the sword being dropped and, being a glutton for punishment, went back into the room to try and pacify Bird. The fiery lieutenant chased after Vernassel and, catching him, threw him down the stairs.

All this commotion brought the attention of the mistress of the house, Mrs Seedwell. Seeing Vernassel at the foot of the stairs clutching what he suspected were broken ribs, Mrs Seedwell sent a maid to the room to ask Bird what he was doing, trying to kill the servants. Bird's reply was predictable enough: 'God damn you for a bitch ... I would stick you first.'

At this, Mr Seedwell joined the fray. He, his wife and Loxton went up the stairs to confront Bird – Loxton carrying a brass candlestick holder. Seedwell didn't really want trouble. Well-managed houses of ill repute rely on peace and quiet to retain their discretion. He told Bird: 'For God's sake, Sir, what have my servants done? If they have [done wrong], I will punish them before your face [and] you shall have accommodation in my house. But if you cannot [give me a reason] I will provide you either coach or chair to go as you please.' Bird was outraged. He took up his sword, jumped out of bed and lunged. The blade of Bird's sword pierced Loxton's side, passed through his ribs and 12 inches into his body. The servant staggered forward for an instant, then fell down dead without uttering a word.

As the Seedwells looked on in horror, Bird told them: 'God damn you, I'll kill you all.'* There was then a fierce struggle in which Bird was restrained by Seedwell long enough for the arrival of a constable and watchman who took the lieutenant into custody and committed him to Newgate prison.

Bird was sent to London's Old Bailey for trial on 15 January 1719, accused of the murder of Samuel Loxton. In his defence Bird claimed he had stayed at the bagnio because he had to make an early start next day and did not want to inconvenience his family by getting up at such an hour. He claimed that he had asked for a bath, but that this had been denied to him and that he had been locked in his room. The staff had then forcibly tried to eject him – he had drawn his sword to protect himself, and the man Loxton, with whom he had no complaint, accidentally fell onto the sword.

Of course, this explanation did not wash with the jury, who found the 27-year-old lieutenant guilty and sentenced him to death by hanging. His execution was set for 23 February at Tyburn, a village then on the outskirts of London with a gallows – the 'Tyburn Tree' – erected in the middle of a crossroads.†

---

* It is a well-known fact that the British used the oath 'God damn' so often that one of the French nicknames for Britons was *les goddams*.

† It was considered important to hold executions at crossroads in order to confuse the ghost of the departed.

On the eve of his execution Bird attempted to cheat the hangman by taking poison, but it failed to work. Next he tried to stab himself several times, but again without the desired result. Instead he was taken to Tyburn, not in the normal cart, but riding with his mother in a funerary mourning coach. Arriving at the village he was obliged to wait for an hour before being transferred into the cart that would take him up to the gallows.

Executions were a very public affair at the time, and certainly events worth attending. Apprentices would be given the day off to make the journey to watch the executioner – Tyburn's 'Lord of the Manor', as he was known. If the victim failed to put on a good show and met death whimpering or begging he or she would be heckled and booed by the crowd. In Bird's case, because he was not your usual riffraff, but an officer of the king, he could be expected to put on a fitting performance.

In part atoning for his dreadful crime, Bird did at least please the crowd and perform as well as could be expected. Climbing into the cart he nonchalantly asked for a glass of wine, but when none was forthcoming he managed to beg a pinch of snuff from someone when he reached the gallows. He took the snuff, wishing everyone around him good health and, after reciting the Apostles' Creed, was launched through the trap door into the pages of history.[5]

Good riddance to you, Sir.

A VICTIM OF THE PRESS

IT is well known that the British Navy once relied on press gangs to recruit its sailors against their will. It was a villainous system, but despite attempts to outlaw it as far back as Oliver Cromwell's day, no suitable alternative had been found.*

The process generally followed a set routine. In times of war the navy would require an enormous boost in manpower – preferably trained sailors. Ideally these sailors would be taken from the merchant fleet and retained by the navy for the duration of the war, or until they were maimed, blinded, otherwise disabled, killed, or became too sick from disease or neglect to be of any further practical use to His Majesty's Service.

To activate the press – a term that originated from the word 'prest', namely a payment made to a sailor on enlisting – the government would first grant licences, or press warrants, for forced recruitment to take place. The territory would be divided up and officers – normally grizzly old lieutenants – sent out to round up a crew.

The lieutenant would set up a rendezvous point, usually in a tavern or any other establishment serving alcoholic beverages, and then post recruitment posters inviting the locals to join voluntarily.

---

* The system of impressment ended in practice at the end of the Napoleonic Wars. The next big crisis was the First World War of 1914–18, by which time conscription had been introduced.

At this point some men would be forthcoming. Some volunteered because they thought a life at sea would be somehow a great adventure; some joined because they were the very living dregs of humanity and could not believe the navy would be in any way worse than the life they already led, and because, if nothing else, they would be fed at the king's expense.

Others were begrudging volunteers because they knew they would probably be targeted by the press gang anyway if they didn't come forward now. By volunteering they qualified for quite a generous bounty and saved themselves a few bruises and a bloodied nose in the process.

Once the supply of volunteers was exhausted, if the recruiting officer was not satisfied, he would let loose the press gang to abduct suitable candidates. They would go out, often armed to the teeth, not to threaten and coerce people into coming with them – although the clubs did help persuade most individuals – but to protect themselves from the population. It was not unknown for the population to fight back once the gangs appeared and started dragging men out to sea.

Officially the gangs were not meant to target landlubbers, by which we mean people sensible enough not to make their careers on a boat. It took years to become proficient in the ways of the sea, so the navy preferred experienced seafarers, or lads who would grow up learning the ways of the sea. A bow-legged, toothless shopkeeper pulled off the foul streets of London was little use to the navy, though that is not to say that recruiting parties did not occasionally chance their arm and abduct such people anyway.

In times of hardship, or through over-zealous attention to duty, press gangs did occasionally run amok against the population at large. Such instances were known as 'hot presses', when all the usual exemptions were considered not to apply. When they occurred, normal everyday folk would find themselves waking up in a groggy haze on board a floating nightmare.

Legally speaking, there was little anyone could do when pressed. True enough, the press was not a legally instituted system; but then again, neither was it illegal. Then, as now, British law worked mainly on precedent, and in 1743 a judge had found that, although the press was harsh, the king had a right to demand it whenever public safety called for it.[6]

In 1755 such a call was made. Trouble in America and impending war with France saw the British fleet put on a war footing. On 23 January a bounty of 30 shillings was set for all able seamen to come forward. On 8 February the bounty was raised to £3, with a £2 reward to informers who would reveal the whereabouts of sailors in hiding. The call for sailors was so great that the prisons were searched for willing hands and the law was changed to allow greater numbers of foreigners to serve on His Majesty's ships. But still this was not enough and so the government announced a 'hot press'.[7]

Although the authorities accepted that the press gangs had a job to do, there was a limit beyond which the law of the land would not accept impressment. In the annals of Newgate prison there is an example of one man who made a lucky escape from the 'hot press' at work in London during that year.

According to the records, Midshipman Robert Alsop and six sailors sparked off a riot in the City of London when they burst into the house of the cooper William Godfrey. Perhaps it was Godfrey's skill at barrel making that they thought might come in useful, or perhaps he was simply in the wrong place at the wrong time. The cooper evidently resisted his abduction, for he was knocked unconscious and then dragged through the city

29

streets before being unceremoniously dumped on one of His Majesty's ships moored on the River Thames.

When he came to, Godfrey found himself in what must have appeared to be a low, dimly lit, rolling and pitching dungeon. As he came to his senses he noticed he was missing a shoe. It had probably fallen off while he was dragged through the streets. Then, as his eyes adjusted to the darkness, he noticed all the other victims who, like him, had until very recently been going about their daily business without a thought for a life on the ocean waves.

About then he noticed the smell.

It stank.

The air was so awful that Godfrey felt as if he was suffocating. For the next 12 hours that he spent in that foul-smelling hold, Godfrey could do nothing to allay the assault on his olfactory senses. All he could do was fear for his future and his life. Never before had he been exposed to such appalling conditions.

This ship was what they called a 'pressing tender'. Although theoretically a victim of the press was taken back to the rendezvous and examined by a Regulating Captain to ensure he was not exempt from service at sea, whenever possible press gangs preferred to get their men onto boats as swiftly as possible. It was of course much harder for the person to escape, or for his family and friends to mount a rescue attempt, if he was already floating off into the sunset.

Fortunately for Godfrey, in this case his struggle had not gone unnoticed and an account of his scandalous treatment was taken to the Lord Mayor. His Lordship arranged for the cooper's release and saw to it that the riotous miscreants passing themselves off as a recruitment party were arrested.

Along with Robert Alsop, William Sturges, John Dodsey, Frederick Offler, James Williamson, Charles Powell and Benjamin

Tidsdale were indicted and committed to Newgate prison. Being brought to trial at the Guildhall of the City of London, Sturges and Dodsey, having previously surrendered themselves and pleaded for mercy, were acquitted. The others were found guilty.

However, as the court was deliberating on the punishment to be inflicted on the riotous mob, some naval officers interceded on behalf of the government. Pointing out that the country was at war with France and that the services of such men were greatly in need, the officers had the press gang plead on their knees for Mr Godfrey's forgiveness – which he generously gave.

The judge was not entirely forgiving. War or no war, the riotous behaviour of Alsop and co. deserved to be punished and so the guilty men were each sentenced to ten days in prison. Compared to the lifetime at sea they had tried to inflict on poor Godfrey, and the harshness of judicial system of the time, the sentence was no more than a token slap on wrist. Within a fortnight Alsop and his mates were no doubt back on the streets of London plying their villainous trade again, dragging men from their homes and families out to sea.[8]

BOLDLESS BYNG

Part of the success of the British Royal Navy through history was the willingness of its commanding officers to – as a later seafarer would say – put themselves in harm's way. When Britain ruled the waves, it was because they often waived the rules of naval combat, and, instead of fighting in neat lines of battle, boldly and aggressively sailed straight at the enemy, put their ship alongside that of their foe and engaged in a life or death struggle.

Although British sailors could look back to the days of Sir Francis Drake for inspiration in aggressive boldness, it was perhaps not the need for success that drove them on, but the dreadful fear of failure and the example of what happened to Admiral Byng.

Let us return, then, to the year 1756, when Britain was engaged in the first true world war – the Seven Years' War, better known to our American cousins as the French and Indian War.

In the first year of the war, France invaded the Mediterranean island of Minorca, which had been in Britain's possession since 1708. Under the command of the Duke of Richelieu the French force of 14,000 troops quickly overran the whole of the island, except the fortress of St Philip, in which a small British garrison under General Blakeney held out under siege.

If St Philip was allowed to fall, not only would it be a dent in Britain's military prestige, it would be very bad for business. Already losses in the American colonies were harming trade and the City of

London was very concerned that the French were ruining British commerce in the Mediterranean. The City presented a petition to King George II, pointing out what it perceived as his government's incompetence in handling the war. Stung into action, the government announced that it was going to relieve Minorca, and handed the poisoned chalice of that operation to Admiral John Byng.

A squadron of ten ships was assembled for the task. Byng became immediately concerned when, to make room for the infantry he was carrying to relieve Blakeney's garrison, his marines were taken off the ships. If, after landing the relieving force, Byng encountered the French, he would be severely undermanned in battle without any marines. He therefore set off for Gibraltar under a cloud and suspecting that the enterprise was doomed to failure from the start.

When he arrived in Gibraltar on 2 May of that year, his problems were exacerbated further. He learned that a squadron of French warships, which the government had believed was intending to sail for America, was actually cruising off Minorca protecting Richelieu's army. On 4 May Byng communicated this intelligence to the Lords of Admiralty in London, and took the opportunity to point out what a deplorable mess he had found Gibraltar in.

The ships he had been given were in a poor state. There was not much he could do to refit them because Gibraltar was also in a mess. The stores and magazines were empty and, even if they had been full, there were too few wharves and docks for his squadron to be repaired. Worse was the news that Byng had received from some engineers and artillerymen who had recently come from Minorca. They told him that he was on a fool's errand and that there was nothing that could be done to save the island. Byng wrote that he would go to Minorca anyway, but if he felt that nothing could be done he would return to protect Gibraltar.

In short the letter was a damning indictment of government mismanagement, warning that the expedition was likely to end in failure. It was not the sort of letter that governments enjoy receiving, and Byng's frankness would ultimately cost him his life.

Despite serious misgivings, Byng set sail for Minorca on 8 May, arriving nine days later. As he sent two frigates to open communications with the British garrison, the French squadron appeared. Byng recalled his frigates, and for the rest of the afternoon his and the French ships eyed each other warily, before withdrawing for the night.

The following afternoon the two squadrons engaged one another. The British actually had an advantage in ships over the French; having received an additional three ships at Gibraltar, Byng had 13 vessels, while his opponent, La Galossonière, had 12. Amazingly though, because the convention was to fight in line, one ship facing the other, Byng ordered the *Deptford* out of his line to even the two forces up.

About 2pm then, on the afternoon of 20 May, the two lines began to converge and the battle was opened. Despite the winds being in his favour, Byng's line was not parallel with the French line. Although the ships at the front of the line were engaged, those at the back of the line – Byng's included – were too far out of range to do anything.

The battle turned into a fiasco when the sixth ship in the British line, *Intrepid*, lost a mast owing to French fire. The steering collapsed and the ship spun round and lay across the path of the remaining ships. The next ship in line, the *Revenge*, ought to have passed between the *Intrepid* and the French line, but instead the captain tried to go the long way round. Realizing there was about to be a collision, the *Revenge* was forced to back off, as were the vessels behind her.

With the British line broken in two, Flag Captain Gardiner advised Byng that if he broke out of the line, he could still bring the French under his guns. Byng refused to do anything so bold, and thus allowed La Galossonière to get away.

Byng sailed off Minorca for four days without making any attempt to communicate with Blakeney, who was under heavy artillery fire from French siege batteries. At the end of this period he called a council of war, announced that it was useless to remain and returned to Gibraltar, leaving Fort St Philip to its fate.

With the British squadron gone, the French redoubled their efforts to take the fort, which finally surrendered on 29 June. Blakeney was allowed the honours of war and permitted to return to Britain with the surviving members of the British garrison. He had done all he could; but could the same be said of Byng?

When news of the 'battle of Minorca', as the naval engagement of the 20th was known, reached England there was uproar in the country. In London Byng was hanged in effigy by an angry mob. The City of London, the body which had called for the expedition, now called for Byng's life. Although under fire, the government of the day did nothing to quell the unrest, for in Byng they had found a most suitable scapegoat for their own mismanagement.

Byng was recalled from Gibraltar and placed under close arrest in Greenwich Hospital. He actually welcomed the prospect of a court martial because he was convinced he had done no wrong. In believing this Byng had failed to gauge the public mood at the time. He might have changed his opinion when he was transferred from Greenwich to Portsmouth, where the trial was set to begin on 17 December, on board the *St George*. Escorted by a strong body of horse guards, as Byng passed through towns and villages on the way to Portsmouth he was met everywhere by insults and angry mobs.

At his trial he was accused, not of cowardice, but of not doing his utmost to destroy the French squadron and to relieve Blakeney. This, the court martial heard, was in breach of the 12th Article of the Laws for the Government of His Majesty's Navy. It was pointed out to Byng that war was, by necessity, a hazardous enterprise and that his actions had set a dangerous precedent. What would happen in future if other commanders declined to fight because of the hazards?

Sentence was passed on 28 February 1757. It found that the admiral had not done his utmost against the enemy and was in breach of the 12th Article. He was therefore guilty of negligence and as such had to receive the only sentence they could inflict – death by shooting.

Byng was amazed by the decision, but kept his composure. He bowed to the court and retired. He had been so certain he would be acquitted that he had even ordered his carriage to come to pick him up at Portsmouth after the verdict was given. But now he faced execution.

There was still the chance that the king might pardon him and many in the Admiralty lobbied for mercy to be shown. However, so strong had been the feeling of outrage, that the king had been led to believe that the country demanded Byng's death to appease the fury of the populace.

And so, on 14 March 1757, Admiral Byng was taken on board the ship *Monarque* to have his sentence carried out. Every ship in the squadron at Spithead sent a boat with the captain, his officers and a detachment of marines to watch and learn from this display of His Majesty's justice.

At noon Byng walked out onto the quarterdeck to face a firing squad of marines. At first Byng wanted to face the marines without a blindfold, but his friends convinced him he might put off their aim by doing so.* Understanding their request, Byng threw off his hat and knelt on a cushion. He tied one white handkerchief round his eyes and held a second aloft in his hand. After a moment's pause, Byng let go of the handkerchief and, in doing so, let go of the world. The firing squad fired as one and Byng was struck by five balls that passed clean through his body, which slumped down lifelessly onto the deck.

His body was placed in a coffin and handed over to his family for burial at Southhill, Bedfordshire. The inscription on his tomb reflected the growing realization that Byng had been the victim of unscrupulous political intrigue rather than cowardice in face of the enemy. His epitaph reads:

> To the perpetual Disgrace of public Justice, the Honourable John Byng, Admiral of the Blue, Fell a Martyr to Political persecution on 14th March in the year 1757, when Bravery and Loyalty were insufficient Securities for the Life and Honour of a Naval Officer.[9]

---

* It is well recognized that blindfolds are given not for the benefit of the victim, but for the sanity of the men in the firing squad, who might otherwise have to see the emotion in their victim's eyes.

THE TRANSVESTITE KNIGHT

I N 1777 a bizarre case came to the London courts. It concerned a wager between two men over the true gender of the Chevalier d'Éon. A certain Mr Jaques had taken out an insurance policy in order to pay a Mr Hayes 700 guineas if he could prove that the French knight was in fact a woman. Theirs was not the only wager on the subject – it is even said that similar bets exchanged hands on the London Stock Exchange. Therefore many a punter was eagerly awaiting the official pronouncement from the courts.

This is perhaps one of the most bizarre cases of gender confusion in history. It is the true tale of Charles-Geneviève-Louis-Auguste-André-Timothée d'Éon de Beaumont (1728–1810) and the scandal in which he became embroiled. In his time d'Éon was a dragoon war hero, a champion duellist and a lady in waiting to the Empress of Russia. He entered service for France in 1749, when he was made royal censor for history and humanities by Louis XV. He was soon initiated into the *secret-du-Roi*, a sort of clandestine cabinet which the king maintained separate from the government. The object of this *secret* was to gain Louis' brother, the Prince of Conti, the throne of Poland. The principal stumbling block to this was Russia, which appeared to favour Britain over France. D'Éon was sent to facilitate a secret dialogue between the French king and Empress Elisabeth.

It is thought d'Éon began wearing dresses at a young age. By his mid-twenties he could easily pass himself off as a young lady – quite a charming one at that. Posing as a lectrice named Lia de Beaumont, he secured a position in Elisabeth's court. He found that the empress was quite open to a dialogue with France and that it was her Anglophile ministers who were preventing her from starting one. It appears that the empress knew about d'Éon's true gender, but played along with the charade and gave him a letter to take back to Louis XV. In 1758, d'Éon returned to St Petersburg, this time as secretary to the French ambassador, posing as Lia de Beaumont's brother.

His undercover work ended in 1760 when d'Éon entered service as a captain of dragoons in the Seven Years' War (1756–63). During this conflict, he earned a reputation for bravery and was twice wounded. At the end of the war he was sent on a clandestine mission to London. In September 1762 d'Éon arrived in Britain as secretary to the Duke of Niverais, to uncover the terms under which the British would accept peace proposals. D'Éon was successful in this mission, having examined the contents of a briefcase belonging to the British Undersecretary of State, whom he had plied with wine.

The legendary duel between d'Éon and de Saint-Georges. D'Éon, banned from wearing male clothing by Louis XVI, fought in a dress. (Roger-Viollet/Topfoto)

At the end of the war in 1763, d'Éon saw himself very much as a player on the international scene. Unfortunately all this hobnobbing with high society was hurting the chevalier in the purse and he was dangerously near to bankruptcy. When it appeared that he was about to be recalled to France, the chevalier blackmailed the King of France, Louis XV. In the course of his secret work, d'Éon had learned that the French king had signed the peace treaty with London in order to buy time for him to plan an invasion of England. By publishing a book that hinted at scandal in high places, d'Éon was granted an annuity in 1766.

After the death of Louis XV in 1771, d'Éon tried to negotiate his return to France. In return for certain secret papers in his possession, the chevalier wanted a pension and an invitation to come home.

He also wanted it recognized that he was a woman.

Even in an age of fabulous and opulent decadence, d'Éon was an oddity. Although rarely seen out of his beloved dragoon uniform, there had been continued speculation that he was in fact a woman disguised as a man. Rather than play it down, d'Éon appears to have encouraged the scandalous rumour and speculation on his gender reached fever pitch, culminating in a betting spree that led to the court case between Jaques and Hayes. During the proceedings two French gentlemen testified that d'Éon was definitely a woman and so the courts found in favour of Hayes.

The reason this testimony was given is that in 1775, d'Éon's wish to return to France was granted by the new French king, Louis XVI, on one condition: from thenceforth d'Éon was to dress only in female attire! D'Éon begrudgingly gave up his uniform for a frock and, as rumour has it, was attended to by dressmakers appointed by Queen Marie Antoinette herself. It was only in 1810 when the chevalier died that the matter was settled. He was completely anatomically male.[10]

IN THE DOCK, THEN
OFF THE HOOK

WHILE London society was scratching its head over the case of the chevalier's gender, wicked, evil things were afoot in the self-appointed greatest city of the known world. Robert Jones was a captain of artillery, but was perhaps better noted for his work on fireworks and ice skating.* It was Captain Jones' idea to attach the skate to the shoe by a screw, thus making it an integral part of the foot. Until this innovation, skaters had relied on strapping the skate to the foot and spent much of their time sitting on their backsides after the strapping had come undone. He was a well-liked individual, witty, an excellent conversationalist, and in 1772 was about to marry. All this until Captain Jones was exposed as a pederast – a paedophile with a penchant for young boys.

In this case the young boy was Francis Henry Hay, a 13-year-old apprenticed to his jeweller uncle in Parliament Street. A trial at London's Old Bailey heard how Jones committed a 'detestable and abominable vice'. Giving evidence, Hay described how in St Martin's Lane he had encountered the captain, who told him he had a buckle to repair. Knowing the captain was a regular customer, Hay followed him to his lodgings over a shop where he was sexually assaulted – or, to put it more bluntly, raped. Hay had little idea what was going on,

---

* Some reports say that he was a captain in the artillery train, others that he was a lieutenant.

but out of nervousness complied with the captain's orders and did not cry out, even though he knew he was not alone in the building – the shopkeeper and landlady being downstairs.

After the act, Jones gave Hay some money, warned him to keep quiet about it and told him that he should come back again for more. Out of shame, Hay did not tell his uncle and returned to the captain's home again over the next two days – telling the court that he did so in order to protect his uncle's trade.

Finally the lad had enough and refused to go back to the captain's lodgings. A week later the captain visited the shop and ordered a shirt buckle. When Hay's uncle told him to deliver it to the captain, the lad refused. Ashamed to tell his uncle why, he told another jeweller, a Mr Rapley of Tottenham Court Road. After hearing the boy's story, Rapley told the uncle that he believed Captain Jones had attempted to 'commit buggery' on the boy. Fearing that the lad would be too embarrassed to talk to him directly, the uncle asked another colleague, a Mr Brest, to talk with the boy. Mr Brest explained to the lad that, if what he said was true, the crime was so serious that Captain Jones would lose his life. Hay said that he understood this but that he stood by his story. Within a week, Jones was arrested and committed to Newgate prison.*

In his defence, Jones claimed an 'attachment to women' and called on a succession of ladies to prove that his tastes were quite natural. It did him little good. After hearing the evidence, the jury retired and found Jones guilty after just five minutes of deliberation. Jones remained composed when the death sentence was read out and continued to insist on his innocence.[11]

---

* It is interesting that much was made of Hay's age. If Hay had been over the age of consent (which was then 14 for males) he too would have stood trial and possibly faced the death sentence.

Full details of the trial appeared in the newspapers of the age. Most were rightly outraged by Jones' behaviour and supported the death sentence as a deterrent to others. At the same time, the press revelled in the story, for nothing sells newsprint like a good scandal. Although the crime was of the most serious nature, much of the reporting was heavy in tasteless innuendo. Take for example the following piece published in the *Morning Chronicle* on 4 August 1772 – apparently penned by a Dr Last, of Gregg's Coffee House in York Street.

On an Officer in the Artillery, now under sentence for a most
detestable crime.[12]

Though the Captain (it plainly appear'd) did partake
Of a dish he was fond of, suppose a *rump-steak*,
'Let us hope (say his friends) the King's mercy he'll reach,
As his crime it was only, ye *batter'd in br–ch*;
And when foes turn their backs, it is *en militaire*
For a soldier to make an attack in the *rear*.'
With such engineers would our laws were this plan on,
Instead of the halter, to spike up their *cannon*.
To be then, explicit, this remark I'll add more,
When the fox you have caught, *nail his brush on the door*;
And this punishment may these vile wretches endure,
Which I here recommend as a *radical* cure.

As hinted at in the above verse, speculation in the media began to mount that Jones would be pardoned by the king. Behind the scenes much was being done to discredit the boy. A petition signed by all the officers in the artillery corps had been presented to the monarch on Jones' behalf. How could the boy's word be trusted against the testimony of so many officers? Hadn't the boy gone back to the captain's of his own free will? Despite this glimmer of hope, Jones was grudgingly administered the holy sacrament in preparation for his execution on Tyburn Hill.

After the officers' intervention, the faint glimmer became a blazing beacon of hope for Jones. On 4 August the execution was postponed until Tuesday 11th in order for more deliberations. Late on the eve of the new execution date a further respite came, holding off the execution pending his Majesty's pleasure.

Robert Jones was discharged from Newgate prison at the end of October on the condition that he left the country within 14 days. He had been found guilty of the most heinous crime; yet because of his brother officers, he served less than three months.

Scandalous!

THE ONE ABOUT THE CAT

VIEWERS of the long-running hit TV series *M*A*S*H* will no doubt remember the outrageous antics of Klinger, the corporal who dressed in women's clothes in order to gain a psychiatric discharge. Such desperate measures have been known throughout the ages in order to avoid the call of the drum. Perhaps the most extreme – the most awful and shocking – is found in the memoirs of the French general Baron d'Hastrel. Dating from the War of the French Revolution, the piece tells of Klinger's 18th-century French equivalent: a man whose fetish so scandalized the commissioners of a discharge board that they ejected him from the army immediately. Lovers of feline-kind may prefer not to read the account.

We were confined with the 3rd battalion of Ain, in which there was a soldier who ate live animals. He called himself Kerrere, and he was born at Tarare, in the department of Saône-et-Loire; he was only twenty-two years old. He was presented at a hearing, and, in the presence of the commissars charged with examining the men put up for discharge, was given a live cat. He seized it by the neck and the four legs and gnawed the claws, the feet and the legs. After this preliminary operation, he bit off the lower jaw, and then the upper, swallowing it all. Then, grabbing his victim by the head and by the rear, he started on its back with an appetite which disgusted the assistants, and they dismissed him. But he did not want to give up his prey; he put it in his bag, promising to finish it for his supper.[13]

THE BONEY MAN

BORN in Corsica to aristocratic Italian parents and trained in the French royal academies, Napoleon Bonaparte leapt on the French revolutionary bandwagon, hijacked it, crowned himself emperor and led France on a series of wars that cost the country a million dead and countless others lame, bankrupt and destitute. Of course, he was without doubt the greatest general of his age – perhaps all time – but as a human being he really did come up short.

This statement is not intended to demonize Napoleon out of hand, nor to make light of his diminutive height, but merely to offer a flip side to his glorious reputation. We are told that he did accomplish some positive things during his reign; however, his career as a politician and soldier was tarnished not only by his final defeat at Waterloo, but by his egotistical and dictatorial management of France, not to mention the placing of siblings and favourites on the foreign thrones which his armies had invariably made vacant.

There is a popular legend – probably an old wives' tale – that Napoleon's name was corrupted to form the word 'Bogeyman'. In Britain people shortened Napoleon's surname, Bonaparte, to 'Boney', which developed into Boneyman – a phrase which was used to scare children into going to bed early. This in turn became Bogeyman and so on...

Napoleon's name is perhaps most associated with his supposed bedside remark to his first wife: 'Not tonight Josephine'.* Although the origins of this phrase may be nothing more than an anachronistic vaudeville quip, they do suggest a certain lack of libido in the man who once ruled most of Europe. It is a quip that should be consigned to the dustbin for ever. Napoleon was, like Caesar, a passionate adulterer.

For that matter, Josephine was no shrinking violet herself. Thrown into prison after the execution of her aristocratic first husband in 1794, she, along with everyone else in the crowded cells, lived every day as if it were her last, with what few pleasures came readily to hand. Although no doubt very elegant in manner, Josephine was careful to hide her teeth, which, according to one English caricature, were so rotten they looked like cloves. When, in a sibling row with his brother Lucien, Napoleon called his brother's wife a whore, Lucien's acidic reply was: 'At least my whore is young and pretty!'[14]

Miraculously Josephine survived long enough to see out the infamous Reign of Terror and, in search of funds, attached herself to the politician Paul Barras. When Barras eventually tired of his mistress, he set her up with a young protégé of his – Bonaparte.

Their marriage ceremony on 9 March 1796 was a complete farce. Napoleon turned up three hours late. The man who performed the civic ceremony was not legally entitled to do so and both Napoleon and Josephine lied about their ages – to appear older and younger

---

* Napoleon's life and career have taken up more space in print than those of any other person in history. For readers in too much of a hurry to delve into the Corsican's life and times further, perhaps the following brief epitaph will suffice. In a line delivered in the 1989 film *Bill and Ted's Excellent Adventure*, Napoleon was referred to as: 'the short, dead dude'.

respectively. Forty-eight hours later Napoleon bade his bride farewell and went off to war.

As if to give his blessing to the union, Barras had promoted Bonaparte to command the Army of Italy. This appointment caused quite a scandal in itself. Firstly there was a question of 'Napoleon who?' There were many more high-profile, deserving generals than Bonaparte in line for an army command, which was in itself a veritable licence to print money – or at least loot everything in sight. Paris gossipers concluded that the appointment was in fact Barras' dowry to get rid of his mistress, Josephine.

Napoleon appears to have been genuinely smitten with Josephine. When conquering Italy he actually spurned the advances of Madame Grassiani, a noted Italian opera singer. That said, he grew increasingly frustrated that his wife would not visit him in Milan. Josephine told him she could not leave Paris because she was pregnant, but then altered her excuse to illness. Bonaparte grew so frustrated that he actually threatened to desert the army if she would not deign to visit him in the field. To avoid this catastrophe Barras had Josephine bundled into a carriage and sent to the front.

With his wife by his side, the campaigns in Italy went very well for Napoleon. Even so, he wanted more. In 1798, he thought he would follow in the footsteps of Alexander the Great and conquer Egypt. Perhaps he too would be proclaimed a god as Alexander was before him. More than anything he desperately wanted Josephine to come to Egypt with him and share in his glory – to witness his triumph. But she was somehow reluctant – subject to fainting fits and otherwise indisposed to make such a long, dangerous sea voyage.

Unknown to her husband, Josephine's reluctance was more to do with an intense affair with a certain Captain Hippolyte Charles, a man of such wit, elegance and sophistication that he was said to tie a cravat like nobody else. Josephine's affair with Charles had been going on since Napoleon had left for Italy, but he had no idea of his wife's infidelity ... yet.

Napoleon set sail for Egypt without his wife and was doing very well, having beaten the Mamelukes and taken Cairo, when a certain Horatio Nelson smashed the French fleet at anchor. It was bad enough that Napoleon and his army were marooned in a land without wine, but worse news was to follow. One of Napoleon's aides let slip about Josephine's infidelity with Charles. A black cloud came over our conquering hero and it was said that from this moment on his tyrannical qualities emerged.

Napoleon's revenge was swift. A number of French women had followed the expedition to Egypt, including Pauline, the 20-year-old wife of Lieutenant Fourès. Bonaparte took Pauline as his mistress and had her husband sent on a mission to Paris to keep him out of the way; if he was killed or captured en route, all the better.

Alas, as was so often the case, the British spoiled Napoleon's fun. Lieutenant Fourès was captured not long out of Alexandria harbour and was mischievously freed by the perfidious Albionites and sent back to Cairo. When Fourès returned to the Egyptian capital and found out what had happened to his wife, to say he was unhappy is at best an understatement. Ignoring the protocols of rank, he went to Bonaparte's residence and demanded that his wife come home with him. Pauline refused and asked for a divorce. The husband tried to strike her but was restrained and that was the end of the matter. Napoleon organized the divorce and told Pauline he would marry her – if she produced a child.

One must remember that all this was happening in front of Josephine's teenage son, Eugène Beauharnais, who was an aide to his stepfather, Napoleon. Before we sympathize too much with the future Viceroy of Italy, it should be pointed out that he was too busy expending his energies elsewhere to concern himself with domestic disputes. According to a 'warts and all' memoir of one expedition member, Eugène was bragging about a scam to get girls at a bargain price. He advised the uniform procurer François Bernoyer to go to the home of the Capuchins and ask for Father Felix, who would get him a nice Christian girl if that is what he preferred![15]

In February 1799 Napoleon set off on an expedition into Syria, where a number of his deeds were considered scandalous in the extreme. Perhaps the most infamous of these was the massacre of prisoners at Jaffa on 10 March. Napoleon's apologists claim he had no choice but to order the massacre of prisoners taken in the siege of Jaffa because he did not have enough men to guard them, nor could he offer them parole, because some of them had broken an earlier one. Probably in excess of 3,000 prisoners were led out onto the beaches near the city, where they were broken up into small groups and bayoneted or shot by French soldiers. Whatever the excuses given, it was an atrocity of the first rank.

While at Jaffa, Napoleon's army was exposed to an outbreak of bubonic plague. Nevertheless, Bonaparte pushed on. Between 18 March and 20 May his army unsuccessfully besieged the port of Acre. Breaking off the siege because of heavy casualties, dwindling supplies, the continued presence of the plague and the arrival of Turkish reinforcements, Napoleon made another controversial decision by authorizing the poisoning of his terminally sick and wounded with a broth laced with a lethal dose of opium. Again, his apologists say he did the right thing, as the men were too sick to move and were terrified of falling into Turkish hands; but it reduced the army's morale considerably.

On 14 June, Napoleon and the remnants of his army arrived in Cairo amid much fanfare but little cheer. To add to his woes, he found that Pauline (nicknamed Cleopatra by the troops) had not produced a child – a problem she claimed was not her fault. As Napoleon saw it, there was nothing for it but to return to France and start on the glory trail afresh.

On his return, Napoleon's first business was a small domestic matter: dealing with his wife. When Josephine learned that her husband had landed she flew into a panic, jumped into a carriage and sped off to meet him. She had to reach her husband before his family revealed the extent of her infidelity. Unfortunately she took the wrong road.

Napoleon returned to his Paris home and found the building empty. From this he drew the most obvious conclusion about his wife's guilt. Despite his diminutive stature, Napoleon's rage was such that he

A cartoon depicting how Barras enticed Napoleon to take Josephine off his hands. Engraving by James Gillray, 1805. (Library of Congress)

51

could bring tears to the most battle-scarred grenadier. He dumped his wife's possessions in the street and, in a raging sulk, locked himself in his bedroom ready to repel Josephine's excuses and entreaties.

But even Napoleon had his weaknesses. When his brothers came to visit him the morning after his arrival, they found him snugly tucked up in bed with Josephine. After enduring hours of her wailing at his bedroom door the night before, Napoleon had finally given up sulking and let her in. By suggesting that he could well do without the scandal of a messy, public divorce so soon after arriving from Egypt, Josephine proved herself as good a politician as her husband.

Napoleon's family were aghast. They had been trying to get rid of Josephine from the start. Alas, however, things would never be the same in the Bonaparte household. In 1800, Bonaparte did not spurn the advances of Madame Grassiani a second time. Soon after the battle of Marengo, General Berthier arrived for a breakfast meeting with Napoleon and found the general happily ensconced in bed with the opera singer. She followed him back to Paris and continued the affair.

Then there was the famous actress Mademoiselle Georges, whom Napoleon took as a mistress. One night, while in the throes of passion, Napoleon was taken ill. The actress thought she had caused him to have a heart attack and woke the house with her screaming. Napoleon thus suffered the humiliation of a houseful of people – Josephine included – piling into his bedroom to find the cause of the screams.*

---

* One should add a small point of interest before continuing. While Pauline 'Cleopatra' Fourès went on to have an affair with General Kléber, Mademoiselle Georges and Madame Grassiani are both said to have become mistresses of Napoleon's eventual nemesis – the Duke of Wellington.

In 1804 Bonaparte decided to take up the crown of France, giving the wonderful excuse that he did so only to prevent the return of the exiled Bourbon monarchy! Before his coronation on 2 December 1804, Bonaparte had one last dastardly plan to enact. There had been several attempts on his life by royalist plotters. Understandably upset by this, Bonaparte decided to give the exiled Bourbons a very clear 'back off' signal. French agents kidnapped the Bourbon Duke of Enghien from the neighbouring state of Baden and took him to the Château de Vincennes, near Paris. After a secret trial, the duke was executed by firing squad on 21 March. It was so dark when the execution took place that they made the doomed duke hold up a lantern so the soldiers could see what they were shooting at! This act caused outrage throughout Europe.

With a crown, Napoleon just needed a successor. Eager to prove that it was not Napoleon's fault Josephine had not produced children by him, his sister Caroline set up another mistress with the express intention of producing a child, albeit an illegitimate one. The guinea pig 'conscripted' into service was 18-year-old Catherine Eléonore Denuelle. Caroline set aside a wing of her house for Napoleon to visit as often as he could.

Eléonore did not look forward to Napoleon's visits. She found him as abrupt in bed as he was in other forms of social interaction. In order to shorten his visits yet further, she would set the clock half an hour forward when he visited. When she actually became pregnant and had a son, Charles Léon, in 1806, Napoleon was relieved, but not entirely convinced he was the father. The emperor believed that Caroline's husband, Marshal Murat, must have found his way into the bedchamber. Murat had in fact done this, but as the child grew up and came to resemble Bonaparte, Napoleon did recognize him in his will.

Among a number of other suspected Napoleonic bastards, the most famous was Alexandre Walewski (1810–68). Fresh in the knowledge that Eléonore had borne him a son, Napoleon set his sights on the Polish countess Marie Walewski. Despite initial resistance, Napoleon told Walewski that if she succumbed to his wishes he would ensure Poland benefited from his favour. The gullible Countess laid herself down for her country, left her husband and young son and set herself up as a mistress to the French emperor.

With the question of Napoleon's potency satisfactorily answered, the writing was on the wall for Josephine, who had not produced the desired heir. With the illegal irregularities of their wedding as a convenient excuse, the marriage was annulled on 10 January 1810. Napoleon remarried the following year. The emperor could have married Walewski, but instead decided to cement his relationship with the Austrian emperor by marrying his daughter Marie Louise. At last she produced for Napoleon the legitimate heir he had waited for.

It was all in vain of course. Four years later Napoleon's empire went the way of the dodo and although his son, Napoleon II, is officially recognized as having briefly reigned in France, the reality was that his mother would not let him anywhere near the sight of his father, let alone the throne of France.

'ABDALLAH' MENOU

ALTHOUGH Napoleon must have been the favourite of contemporary rumourmongers, many of his generals and sidekicks provided ample fodder for gossip. Some were slightly mad, and more than a few had women on the side. But above all in terms of scandal – Bonaparte excluded – perhaps the darkest star of them all was not Marshal Murat, Lannes or Ney, but General Jacques-François Menou.

Menou was never among the top echelon of Napoleon's glitterati – for although the emperor was sometimes generous in his appointments he was not known for his profligacy. Nonetheless, Menou featured highly enough and was shown favours far in excess of his capabilities, which were limited in the extreme.

Of this man Napoleon said: '... although abounding in courage, business talent, and goodwill, [Menou] was of a disposition wholly unfit for military command'.[16] So what was he doing as a senior general? Like so much else that was wrong with Napoleon's career, the answer dates back to Egypt.

On 23 August 1799 Napoleon quit Egypt with a select few companions and returned to France. His critics will tell you that by doing so he was guilty of deserting his army in the field. On the other hand, his apologists will sing his praises and tell you he only went home to get help. Believe it how you will, but one thing is for sure: the majority of his men were glad to see the back of him.

55

The problem they had with Napoleon is that they saw little chance of going home while he was in charge. As one of the expedition members put it: 'If Napoleon had not seen the opportunity to seize supreme power in his adopted country he would have remained in Egypt, where he would have created an independent state, but at the cost of our blood. Like Caesar, he would prefer to be first in Cairo rather than second in Paris.'[17]

What was truly scandalous about Napoleon's abrupt departure was the way he appointed his successor. General Kléber was the physical antithesis of Napoleon. He was a giant of a man – a veritable Mars in boots – and was loved by the troops. Kléber had also spoken out against Bonaparte's mishandling of the siege of Acre and it was probably this that stopped him being invited back to France.

While Napoleon quietly plotted to leave, he tricked Kléber into being absent from headquarters at the time of his departure. When Kléber returned he found instructions ordering him to take over control of the army. Kléber went berserk; when asked how he would break the news to his men, he apparently exclaimed: 'That bugger has left us here with his breeches filled with shit! We will return to Europe and rub them in his face!'[18]

Unfortunately Kléber was denied this showdown. A year later, on 14 June 1800, while Bonaparte was having a lucky escape at Marengo – the battle that was said to have put the crown of France on his head – the thunderous Kléber fell victim to an assassin's dagger in Cairo. The devil, they say, protects his own.

Kléber's successor was General Jacques-François Menou, a former nobleman who had embraced the French Revolution and served in the Republican armies. He didn't really aspire to be commander-in-chief, but following the exodus of generals with Napoleon to France he was the senior man next in line.

His first act as commander-in-chief was to oversee the execution of Kléber's murderer, Soluman El-Halaby. With unusual sensitivity to local customs, the French granted the assassin a traditional local execution. This involved slicing off one of his hands and then impaling him on a pole like a giant shish kebab. For good measure the French also beheaded three local leaders for not warning them of the plot.

Kléber was a hard act to follow and Menou's appointment offered his soldiers little hope of an early return to France. You see, Menou quite liked it in Egypt. He liked it so much he had converted to Islam and married a girl from Rosetta, Zubayda El-Rashidiya. This rejection of his native Catholicism caused equal servings of outrage and mirth among his troops – particularly when he added the prefix 'Abdallah' to his name.

True, Napoleon had earlier converted to Islam – after a fashion. The main difference between Napoleon and Menou on this matter was that Menou appeared to be genuine. Old Boney had tried to trick the Egyptians by claiming he was a Muslim. Distancing himself from earlier European invaders, Napoleon pointed out that he had attacked the Vatican and defeated the crusader Knights of St John at Malta on his way to Egypt.

As ever, Napoleon never knew when to stop: having given these almost plausible proofs of his sincerity, Napoleon ordered a group of Cairo clerics to issue a fatwa to the effect that his coming had been predicted in the Koran!

It was at this point that Cairo exploded into revolt and from then on the French commander's days in Egypt were numbered.

Partly from the stigma attached to his religious conversion, Menou has suffered from a very bad press over the years, and although many of his critics are often biased in one way or another, it is rarely the case that there is smoke without fire.

General Marmont – the Duke of Raguse to give him his lofty and perhaps ill-deserved Napoleonic title – had some very interesting things to say about Menou when writing his memoirs. Apparently Menou was: 'Spirited and cheerful, an agreeable storyteller, a terrible liar, although not lacking in a certain education: his character, the most peculiar in the world, approached folly ... He was extravagant, insane, sometimes amusing, but a plague to anyone depending on him.'[19]

Marmont cited several examples where Menou appeared brazenly unwilling to do or unconcerned with his duties. His first example dated from 1799, when Bonaparte left for Syria. Apparently he left Menou in command of Cairo during his absence. Although Bonaparte was then away for five months, Menou only arrived in the Egyptian capital to take his post eight days before his return. Equally, on his return to France, Menou somehow managed to remain in Marseilles for four months doing absolutely nothing before reporting to Napoleon in person.

The timing of Menou's eventual arrival in Paris was superb. According to the memoirs of Napoleon's secretary Bourienne his arrival had just been preceded by the re-establishment of Catholic worship in France, which had been suspended during the Revolution. Just as it looked as though France was returning to the religious fold, out popped a senior general who was a convert to Islam!

Despite losing Egypt, Menou was well received by Napoleon, who appointed him governor-general of the Piedmont region in northern Italy. Napoleon granted such a favour because of Menou's steadfast loyalty to him while commander in Egypt. Yes, Menou might have been a lunatic as Marmont suggests, but he was Napoleon's lunatic. It was such judgements of character that eventually landed old Boney on a semi-deserted rock in the middle of the Atlantic.

Menou did not appear too bothered about his new appointment. Apparently he put off travelling to Piedmont every day for six months. It was only when a carriage with post horses attached was put outside his door that he allowed himself to be cajoled into making the journey across the Alps.

The Italians had initially welcomed the French, and Bonaparte in particular – for, although of Corsican birth, he was of Italian descent. This enthusiasm stemmed from a desire to share the freedom of the French Revolution and Napoleon was seen by many as the chosen one who might grant them their liberty. Fat chance.

Instead they got war, devastation and lots of taxes. They were also robbed utterly by the French, who stole cartloads of Italian art including the Venus de Milo and the Horses of Saint Mark from Venice. One French general – Philibert Duhesme – proved himself so adept at looting that he was actually put in chains and carted back to France. The only reason he got off without further punishment was the realization that if the government penalized one general for looting it would have to punish the whole lot of them.[20]

As governor of Piedmont, Abdallah Menou's debauchery knew no bounds. According to one scurrilous, yet highly plausible account, alongside his Egyptian wife the French general added an Italian and two French girls of dubious standing to his harem. Although polite sources report that the girls were ballerinas, they provided themselves with an income by selling their influence and protection – as well as their bodies.[21]

Menou's 'hotel' in Turin doubled as a casino with gaming tables at which people seeking his favour could make large enough deposits without resorting to outright bribery. He reputedly never paid cash for anything. In fact, he and his entourage rarely paid for anything at all. Anyone impertinent enough to pester the general for payment would find himself under investigation by one of the special tribunals he had set up in every town, and against the decisions of which there was no appeal. The same fate awaited any traders brave enough to refuse him credit, for his temper could be violent. According to Marmont, Menou killed one supplier after hitting him with a lump of wood when the impertinent devil came to his Turin home looking for payment.[22]

To supplement his income, Menou ran a protection racket alongside the regular collection of taxes. People were charged according to their wealth and, when the tax farmer came calling, a little premium was added to the regular payment, which of course the victim was forced to pay, lest the next visitor was from the tribunal.

Having proven his incapacity to govern in Piedmont, Menou was transferred by Napoleon to Venice. When he quit his offices in Piedmont Marmont recalled that aides found 900 letters in his office which had not been opened. Some administrator!

As governor of Venice, Menou fell passionately in love with the famous Spanish singer Isabella Colbran, who would go on to marry the composer Gioacchino Rossini in 1822. He made himself a laughing stock, chasing after her from one Italian city to another, always arriving just after her departure.[23]

Menou was constantly in debt – often heavy debt – and was bailed out by Napoleon several times. His business acumen – which Napoleon applauded at the beginning of this piece – was in fact a sham. Marmont believed that for ten years Menou had relied on his manservant to handle his accounts.

In the end, in 1810 Napoleon had no option but to dismiss the troublesome Menou from his service. Within a month Menou had died of a stroke.

MUTINY AND MURDER AFLOAT

Perhaps the most famous sea mutiny on record is that of the *Bounty* in 1789. The villain of the piece – one Lieutenant Bligh (cast as 'Captain Bligh' in the movies) – was sent on a mission to transport breadfruit from Tahiti to the West Indies where it was going to be used to feed slaves. When the ship reached Tahiti on 26 October 1788, it remained there six months while the breadfruit seedlings were collected. It was an idyllic time for the crew, who enjoyed the hot climate, the food and, most of all, the local women.

Bligh did have a certain manner that offended people, but he was no more a tyrant than many ships' captains of the day. However, tensions between him and his crew steadily increased as the day to sail approached. While still on Tahiti three crewmen tried to desert. They were recaptured and, according to naval regulations, flogged.

Matters finally came to a head after *Bounty* made sail on 4 April 1789. Bligh fell out with his first mate, Fletcher Christian, in an argument over coconuts. Bligh accused Christian of stealing his coconuts and gave him a sharp dressing down and cut the grog ration for the crew. This sparked a mutiny on 28 April, after which Bligh and a good number of crewmen who wanted nothing to do with Christian's uprising were set adrift.

Bligh survived the incident, got his motley crew back to civilization and saw to it that some of the mutineers were rounded up and swung from the yard arm. In recognition of his celebrity, Bligh became known as 'breadfruit Bligh' or, perhaps less charitably, 'that *Bounty* bastard'.

From that point on scarcely a mutiny went by without Bligh somehow being involved. In May 1797 Bligh was again tipped off his ship, this time the *Director*, which was at the Nore on the mouth of the Thames undergoing a refit.* The Nore mutiny was one of two 'great' mutinies that year. We have already seen how the British system of recruitment was infamous at best and you will remember that when men were pressed it was for the duration of the war. By 1797 war with France had dragged on for four years. Men were tired and conditions on board ship were as horrible as ever.

The mutiny at Spithead began in February, when sailors complained that they had not had a pay rise in more than a hundred years. They had a fair point and, by and large, their grievances were listened to if not actually met.

At the Nore mutiny, however, things were a little more politically motivated. It began on 12 May when the crew of HMS *Sandwich* seized control of their ship. Rather than rates of pay, the mutineers on the *Sandwich* started talking about issues such as living conditions and modifications to the conditions of service. Before long they were discussing social revolution – and that got the Admiralty and government very worried. When the mutineers attempted to blockade

---

* In 1805 Bligh was given the governorship of New South Wales in Australia with a mandate to get tough and stamp out what London perceived to be rampant corruption in Sydney. Again Bligh's manner failed to win over his subordinates. On 26 January 1808 he was deposed in a mutiny known as the Rum Rebellion by Major Johnston of the 102nd Regiment of Foot – thus Bligh was the victim of the only armed coup in Australian history. Once, unlucky ... but three times a victim of mutiny? The man obviously had issues with social skills.

the River Thames things turned nasty. At the end of it, rather than receiving the pardons given out after Spithead, 29 of the worst offenders were hanged.

But, without a doubt, the most serious of all the mutinies that year occurred on the 32-gun frigate *Hermione*. While the *Bounty* story makes for a good bedtime yarn, the fate of Captain Pigot and his fellow officers is not one for the faint hearted.

On 21 September 1797, the *Hermione* was cruising off the island of Puerto Rico. The ship's captain, Hugh Pigot, was by any estimation a foul-mouthed, tyrannical sadist of the first order. If he had been commanding the *Bounty* rather than Bligh, Fletcher Christian and his chums really would have had something to complain about.

Pigot was impatiently watching his crew reefing the ship's topsails. Dissatisfied with what he saw, he bellowed for his sailors to come down off the rigging and shouted that the last man off the mizzen-top yard would be flogged. Knowing the captain to be a man of his word, the sailors literally climbed over one another to get down the rigging.

The two outermost men on the mizzen-top yard were at an unfair disadvantage in this race. With furthest to go it seemed they were the ones most likely to suffer the bite of the lash. So desperate were they to avoid this that they tried to jump past their comrades. Losing their footing on the ratlines, both men fell to their deaths, their bodies crumpling in a loud and sudden rendezvous with the quarterdeck upon which Pigot was standing.[24]

If fate had been kinder, perhaps one of those poor wretches would have landed on the captain and spared everybody what was to follow. Pigot was avoided such an unusual ending, but only that he might receive one even more villainous. The captain's reaction to

63

the crewmen's death was callous in the extreme: 'Throw the lubbers overboard' was his only epithet. He then began bawling at the rest of the crew and threatened them with every known punishment beneath the sun.

But as that sun began to fade in the sky the first signs of mutiny were felt. Someone let a double-headed shot loose on the deck. As the ship pitched and rolled, the shot could be heard rolling back and forth along the wooden planks. If by chance it had met an unsuspecting human leg on the way its momentum and weight would have been enough to smash the bone to pieces.

Then the murmuring began.[25] When the first lieutenant went to investigate the disturbance on deck, his enquiries were met with violence. One of the crewmen embedded a tomahawk in his arm. As the officer fell helpless on the deck, a well-handled knife slit his throat, followed by a dozen or more stabs to the body. The officer's corpse was thrown over the side and the mutiny burst into noisy life.

Pigot came out of his cabin and onto the deck, but was met with repeated blows. Badly wounded, he staggered back into his cabin and fell back on his chair. Seizing the moment, the ship's coxswain and three others coldly butchered him with their knives. His bleeding body – still alive – was hauled off the chair and forced out of the cabin window into the dark waters below. Thus, in a fitting manner, ended the life and career of one of the Royal Navy's most detestable characters.

Now the crew's blood was up and they ran about the ship hunting Pigot's commissioned officers like rats caught in a barrel. Before the night was out, eight more were cut down and murdered including three lieutenants, the purser, surgeon and clerk, one midshipman, the boatswain, and the marine lieutenant. It is said that many of the officers pleaded for their lives pitifully – and vainly – for the sake of their wives and children. It is believed that the boatswain was thrown to the mercy of the ship's boys. Their age was no bar to cruelty and they killed him slowly by scraping the flesh off his bones with their tools.[26]

In control of the ship, the mutineers headed for the nearest Spanish port at La Guayra and surrendered to the authorities there. The mutinous crew remained silent on the murders and claimed they had turned the officers adrift in one of the ship's boats. Without much regard to scruple the Spanish accepted their version of events and gladly welcomed the British frigate into their own navy.

When the truth of the mutiny reached the British commander in the West Indies, Sir Hyde Parker, he sent under the flag of truce a true account of what these mutineers had done and called on the Spanish to act honourably and turn over the murderous crew so they might receive justice.

The Spanish cared not a jot how this ship had come into their hands, and were unwilling therefore to deliver the very generous men who had gifted it to them back into the hands of the godless and perfidious British. Would the British have done the same? Of course they would.

From that moment forth it became a point of honour for the British to recapture the frigate and crew from the Spanish. Thus the 25th day of October 1799 goes down in the annals of British naval history as a great day, for the *Hermione* was recaptured by the aptly named HMS *Surprise*. In all 33 mutineers were captured and 24 hanged.

BARON CROCODILE

IGNORING the calamities of past pages, Britons are generally proud of their naval heritage, and of all their heroes they revere none more than Horatio Nelson. It was Nelson who saved old England from Napoleon, they say: leading by glorious example, paying for the victory at Trafalgar with his life. Nevertheless, he was also an adulterous so-and-so whose scandalous private life puts even Napoleon's in the shade.

It is a recurring theme, but true nonetheless ... it all began in Egypt. We have already mentioned that Nelson sank the French fleet off Egypt, in the so-called battle of the Nile in 1798. From there the victorious – and badly wounded – Nelson made sail for the allied port of Naples. Waiting for him there in enthusiastic expectation was Emma, Lady Hamilton.

It is difficult to know where to start with Lady Hamilton. Napoleon's Josephine had a notorious enough reputation, but one suspects that even she would have been upstaged by Lady H if the two had ever come face to face.

She was the daughter of a blacksmith who, by the age of 12, moved to London and worked as a maid in the house of the composer Thomas Linley. It is said that by the time she was 16 she was engaged to a market fruit dealer before ending up working in a brothel on Arlington Street run by the madam Mrs Kelly who went by the lavish title of 'The Abbess – a devotee of pleasure'.

This rude apprenticeship served to get Emma noticed and she found herself performing in the bizarre world of James Graham, a quack fertility doctor who created a 'Temple of Health and Hymen'. It also put her in contact with high society and she became the lover of Sir Harry Featherstonehaugh, who took her to his family estate at Uppark in Sussex, then sent her back to London with five pounds in her pocket and a baby daughter on the way.

Parties at Sir Harry's had been extravagant in the extreme. Emma was said to have danced naked on the dining room table for his guests, one of whom, Charles Greville, bailed her out next. In April 1782 Greville introduced Emma to the artist George Romney, who became absolutely besotted by his new muse. He became so obsessed that he featured Emma in over 60 paintings, much to the detriment of his regular commissions.

When Greville decided he should marry, he had no qualms about off-loading Emma on his 62-year-old widower uncle, Sir William Hamilton – Britain's man in Naples and an authority on volcanoes to boot. Hamilton invited Emma to Naples where she became a hit sensation for performing what she called her 'attitudes'.

For the benefit of the uninitiated, these 'attitudes' were a sort of performance art where Emma would pose as famous mythological and historical figures, or even ideals. She would hold her pose as still as a statue and then, with the clever and tantalizing use of draped shawls, metamorphose into a new form. It was a technique she had performed while modelling in Romney's studio.

Hard as it may seem today, the Neapolitan court was amazed by these performances and they became talked about all over Europe. There was, after all, no television in the 18th century.

In 1791 Sir William took the unexpected step of marrying his mistress. Although Emma was known by the royal court, she could not formally appear in it until marriage to Sir William legitimized her. Lady Hamilton was now able to cultivate her friendship with the Neapolitan queen, Maria Carolina, and become a person of some importance.

In 1798, threatened by the incursion of French forces into Italy, Naples went mad with delight at the news of Nelson's victory on the Nile. An arch-thespian, Emma is said to have fainted at the news of his victory. Hearing that Nelson was on his way to Naples, Emma went into overdrive, writing to him in the most gushing terms. When in September 1798 Nelson arrived in Naples he was greeted in spectacular fashion. When Emma saw her hero she is said to have uttered 'Oh God, is it possible?' and then, in one of her trademark swooning fits, collapsed onto Nelson's one remaining arm.

Nelson was left in an interesting position. Taking a mistress was nothing new to him. He had already dipped his toe in the ponds of infidelity with an opera singer, Adelaide Correglia, with whom he had an on/off two-year affair.

Faced on one hand with a raft of letters from his wife Fanny about the inanities and drudgeries of daily life in boring Norfolk, and ravishing Emma's semi-religious hero worship on the other, Nelson made up his mind.

Emma rewarded his attention by bestowing on him titles and honours of her own. Nelson had been made Baron of the Nile after Aboukir. To Emma he became 'Baron Crocodile', 'Viscount Pyramid', and so on.

What is truly perplexing about Nelson and Emma's affair is the role of Sir William in the trio. Surely Hamilton knew what was going on between the two of them – and if so, why did he go along with it? The answer may be that the elderly gent truly did not care any more, provided he was left alone to pursue his active interest in volcanology.

By all accounts he thought Nelson was a thoroughly decent chap – a sentiment reciprocated by the sailor.* The mind boggles at it all.

Perhaps suffering from his wounds – he had almost been scalped by a fragment of cannon shot at the Nile – and certainly distracted by Lady Hamilton, Nelson started to court trouble. First he ignored orders from his naval superior Lord Keith, who wanted him back on the move and in action again. Then he began to cause the first rumblings of scandal back in London by taking a very active role in Neapolitan politics. The scandal began to increase when news of his affair with Lady Hamilton and the bizarre ménage-à-trois became public knowledge.

Poor old Fanny. Nelson's wife tried writing to her husband and implored him to let her visit him in Naples, but he refused her. He was on to a good thing and he knew it. Nelson did not deign to return to England until 1800 when Sir William Hamilton was recalled from Naples. The journey of the three is quite legendary. Unable to procure a boat, they instead spent four months travelling through the Hapsburg Empire and then through Germany to Hamburg. Probably the highlight of the trip came at the palace of Eisenstadt near Vienna. It was here that Nelson met Haydn, who had composed a cantata called 'The Battle of the Nile' for Emma to sing to her hero. Nelson also heard Haydn's *Mass in D Minor*, originally titled *Missa in Angustiis* ('Mass for Troubled Times'), but which became best known as the 'Nelson Mass'.

Arriving in Yarmouth on 6 November 1800, the Nelson roadshow headed for London and popular acclaim. When Fanny Nelson finally caught up with her husband she realized how far gone her marriage

---

* In his will Sir William would describe Nelson as: 'my dearest friend ... the most virtuous, loyal and truly brave character I have ever met ... God bless him and shame fall on those who do not say amen.' (www.nelson-society.org.uk).

was. Nelson could barely contain his contempt for her and, when asked to give up his mistress, told Fanny he was separating from her. He signed off half his salary to her in compensation.

In the public eye this was the wrong thing to do. Important men had mistresses, but none had actually left their wife on account of an affair. Many were scandalized by Nelson's actions and doors that were once held open to him were firmly closed.

The only place the three were truly made welcome was at William Beckford's Fonthill estate, where they stayed from 20 to 24 December 1800. Beckford was related to Sir William through his mother. He was an author, well travelled and – oh yes – had been more or less ostracized from 'normal' society for an appalling scandal of his own – the so-called Powderham Scandal of 1784, caused when the 19-year-old Beckford was discovered having a love affair with William, the 13-year-old son of Lord Courtenay. To avoid any more trouble, Beckford's family had sent him off to tour Europe until the business died down.

Well endowed with an enormous inheritance, Beckford had turned Fonthill into a sort of fantasy gothic theme park. When Nelson and the Hamiltons arrived they were received with a rousing rendition of 'Rule, Britannia'. Over the next three nights, Fonthill was the scene of lavish entertainments culminating in a magnificent dinner at Fonthill Abbey, a folly designed by Beckworth complete with a dwarf gatekeeper responsible for opening its massive, 38-foot doors.

In January 1801, Emma Hamilton gave birth to Nelson's daughter, Horatia. Although Nelson was over the moon, the identity of the child was concealed. In September Nelson bought a house in Surrey into which Sir William and Emma moved. The unusual arrangement continued until Sir William died in April 1803. He went to his death in Emma's arms, holding Nelson's hand.

This satire on Sir William Hamilton shows him blindly looking at a collection of objects, which all refer to his wife's relationship with Nelson. (Library of Congress)

At last Nelson and Emma could begin normalizing their relationship and even little Horatia was brought to the house. Alas, it was not to last. When Nelson was shot at Trafalgar he implored that Emma and Horatia were not to be forgotten. Unfortunately the great man's wishes were ignored. Emma was not allowed to attend the state funeral and Fanny received his pension. Emma was ignored and by 1808 was forced to sell the house Nelson had bought for them. In 1812 she was arrested for debt and went to prison with little Horatia. Cast out from prison in 1814 she moved to Calais, where she took solace in the bottle and drank herself to an early grave with liver failure the following January.[27]

CINTRA SHAME

BEFORE he was made a duke, Sir Arthur Wellesley became embroiled in a terrible scandal over an agreement made with the French at the town of Cintra in Portugal. It was bad enough for it to almost sink his military career just at the point when it was becoming interesting.

After the battle of Vimiero on 21 August 1808, the French Army under General Junot* found itself beaten and cut off from its line of retreat into Spain. The hook-nosed Sir Arthur had Junot well and truly over a barrel.

Unfortunately for Sir Arthur command of the army was no longer his – that honour had passed to Sir Harry Burrard, who would not give him permission to pursue the retreating French. The situation became worse with the arrival of the yet more senior Sir Hew Dalrymple, who took command of the army from Burrard. Between them the two were, to put it as kindly as possible, uninterested in ordering anything more strenuous than lunch.

In one of those decisions that was either a brilliant piece of diplomacy, or utter incompetence, Dalrymple's first thought was not to destroy the French, but to do a deal with them. The British

---

* He was the man who had told Napoleon about Josephine's infidelity with Captain Charles. Some speculate that it was this indiscreet disclosure that prevented Junot from being made a Marshal of France.

wanted the French out of Portugal and the French desperately now wanted to leave.

With this in mind Dalrymple met Junot's subordinate, General Kellermann, and organized an armistice, which quickly escalated into a full-blown convention. The terms of their arrangement were that the British would repatriate Junot's army to France, with all its equipment. From being in a position of checkmate after Vimiero, Junot must have laughed all the way back to La Rochelle.

Wellesley had opposed the convention and had walked out of the negotiations, leaving Dalrymple and Kellermann to get on with it. It was a terrible mistake. The wily Kellermann convinced the British commander-in-chief that it would be unfair for him to sign the convention, suggesting that Wellesley should be asked to sign it instead, Kellermann and Sir Arthur being the same rank. Although appearing polite, Kellermann mischievously wanted to link the name of the victor of Vimiero with the convention. Dalrymple obliged and ordered Sir Arthur to sign the document. Wellesley made his second mistake by not reading the document before adding his name to it.

The first he knew about the concessions Kellermann had won was when the details were published in the *London Gazette Extraordinaire* on 16 September. They quickly sparked an outrage.[28] King George III – already well known for his bouts of madness – was furious at the news. He had learned Wellesley's Vimiero despatches off by heart and felt enormously let down by what he read of Cintra. What most offended the British public was that not only were over 20,000 Frenchmen getting away scot-free, but that they were doing so on British ships, which had been provided for their passage.

A caricature of Lord Wellington, 'A Wellington Boot or the Head of the Army'. (Topfoto)

Wellesley returned to London to face the music. He was soon joined by Burrard and Dalrymple, who were recalled from Portugal to face an inquiry. The inquiry was held from 14 November to 27 December 1808. To avoid making the scandal worse in the public eye, all three were cleared of wrong-doing and Wellesley was allowed to return to Portugal with the slate wiped largely clean. Although they were also cleared, the limitations of Burrard and Dalrymple were all too obvious. Neither was given a command again.

As a measure of how bad the scandal was, even the poet Lord Byron was moved to vent his fury. Given his own reputation for sensational and scandalous behaviour, Byron's taking a moral stand on anything is risible, but he said his piece nonetheless.

The original verses in his epic *Childe Harold's Pilgrimage* were quite explicit – for a poet – in their blame:

In golden characters right well design'd,
First on the list appeareth one 'Junot':
Then certain other glorious names we find,
Which rhyme compelleth me to place below:
Dull victors! baffled by a vanquish'd foe,
Wheedled by conynge tongues of laurels due,
Stand worthy of each other, in a row –
Sir Arthur, Harry, and the dizzard Hew
Dalrymple, seely wight, sore dupe of t'other tew.

Convention is the dwarfish demon styled
That foil'd the knights in Marialva's dome:
Of brains (if brains they had) he them beguiled,
And turn'd a nation's shallow joy to gloom.
For well I wot, when first the news did come,

That Vimiera's field by Gaul was lost,
For paragraph ne paper scarce had room,
Such Paeans teemed for our triumphant host,
In courier, Chronicle, and eke in Morning Post:

But when Convention sent his handy-work,
Pens, tongues, feet, hands combined in wild uproar;
Mayor, aldermen, laid down the uplifted fork;
The Bench of Bishops half forgot to snore;
Stern Cobbet, who for one whole week forbore
To question aught, once more with transport leapt,
And bit his devilish quill agen, and swore
With foe such treaty never should be kept,
Then burst the blatant beast, and roar'd and raged, and – slept!

Thus unto Heaven appeal'd the people: Heaven,
Which loves the lieges of our gracious King,
Decreed, that, ere our generals were forgiven,
Inquiry should be held about the thing.
But Mercy cloak'd the babes beneath her wing;
And as we spared our foes, so spared we them;
(Where was the pity of our sires for Byng?)*
Yet knaves, not idiots, should the law condemn;
Then live, ye gallant knights! And bless your judges' phlegm!

However, Byron's friends put pressure on him to remove
these verses and thus the one most famously associated with
Cintra became:

---

* This is a reference to our old friend Admiral John Byng who was executed
by firing squad in 1757.

And ever since that martial synod met,
Britannia sickens, Cintra! at thy name;
And folks in office at the mention fret,
And fain would blush, if blush they could, for shame.
How will posterity the deed proclaim!
Will not our own and fellow-nations sneer,
To view these champions cheated of their fame,
By foes in fight o'erthrown, yet victors here,
Where Scorn her finger points, through many a coming year?[29]

THE GRAND OLD DUKE OF YORK

HOT on the coat tails of Cintra came another, bigger, more disturbing scandal affecting both the British Army and the royal family.

Britain's armed forces were then, as now, nominally under the command of the ruling monarch. At the time of the Napoleonic Wars the monarch in question was George III, who reigned between temporary bouts of madness until 1811, when his fat, morally degenerate, wastrel of a son, George, became regent. The cause of King George's madness was variously attributed to matters as diverse as the loss of America, his failure to take a mistress and the revelation that the Chevalier d'Éon was in fact a man after all. Although the 'madness' was actually caused by a hereditary medical condition, his children's behaviour would have been enough to send any parent round the bend.

For example, Edward Augustus, Duke of Kent, was sent to command Gibraltar, where his tyrannical pursuit of discipline caused the mutiny of the 25th Regiment and the Royal Fusiliers on Christmas Eve 1802. When reports of the mutiny were heard in London, the Duke of Kent was recalled and although he retained the title of Governor of Gibraltar until his death, he was never allowed to return to the rock again.

The most outrageous stories were attached to Ernest Augustus, Duke of Cumberland, Colonel of the 15th Hussars and future King of Hanover. The following allegations were never proven, are of dubious origins and should certainly be taken with a large pinch of salt. Of course, that does not mean they are untrue!

It was said at the time that the duke fathered a child by his sister, Princess Sophie, that he indecently assaulted the wife of Lord Lyndhurst and – most disturbingly – murdered his Piedmontese valet, Joseph Sallis.

In explaining why his valet had been found in bed with his throat cut, the soldier duke came up with an almost supernatural story. He explained that in the middle of the night he was awoken by what he thought was a bat landing on his head. As he came to, the disturbance turned out to be his own sword swishing and slashing down at him from out of the darkness. Parrying the blows with his arms and hands, the duke screamed for help. His valet Neale rushed to the duke's room, where he found the duke's bloodied sabre on the floor. While being attended to by a doctor the duke sent for Sellis, who was found in his room with his throat cut so deeply the head was nearly off.

A quickly convened inquiry found that Sellis had, for some unknown reason, attacked the duke and then, in a fit of remorse, returned to his own room and committed suicide by trying to chop his own head off! This verdict was greeted with as much scepticism then as it would deserve today.

There were several theories that did the rounds of London coffee houses, including the version where Sellis had found the duke in bed with his wife and had been killed to prevent a scandal. Others claimed that Sellis' daughter had committed suicide after being spoiled by the lustful prince – after which Sellis confronted the duke, who had him killed. Lastly was the rumour that Sellis discovered the duke and valet Neale in the throes of an immoral and illegal act for which he was murdered on the duke's authority.

Whichever version you care to believe, it is unlikely that Sellis sawed through his own neck.* However – putting all such rumours behind him – the duke was unaffected by such terrible slanders and went on to marry Princess Frederica of Mecklenburg-Strelitz in 1815, despite the fact that she had a 'loose' reputation and that she was believed to have murdered her previous husband.

Putting all nefarious speculation aside, the worst military scandal to affect the progeny of George III concerned the Duke of York and his mistress Mary Ann Clarke. About this scandal there is no dispute.

The Duke of York was the commander-in-chief of the British Army. This was not just a titular appointment; the duke really did take the role seriously and was, by all accounts, very good at his job. However, as is so often the case, his private life spilled over into the public arena with spectacular results. The duke had married his cousin, Princess Frederica Charlotte of Prussia, in 1791, but the marriage was a disaster and the couple separated, leaving the duke to gain a reputation as a ladies' man. He is thought to have fathered a number of illegitimates, including, it is believed, First Lieutenant John Stillwell, who was killed at Waterloo serving in the 95th Rifles.

In 1802 the duke took the ex-wife of a bankrupt stonemason as a mistress and set her up with a generous annuity of £1,000. Mrs Clarke turned out to have extravagant tastes and blew £16,000 of the duke's money in their four-year relationship. In addition to her annuity Mrs Clarke used her position to illegally sell commissions and promotions. In return for payment, she would lobby the duke on her petitioners' behalf.

---

* Sellis' ghost is said to haunt St James's Palace to this day – if you believe in that sort of thing.

In 1806 the duke ditched his expensive mistress and offered her an annuity of £400 if she behaved herself and did not speak publicly about their relationship. The termination of the relationship was a disaster for Mrs Clarke, who had run up serious debts on the back of her royal connections. With the end of the gravy train her creditors called in their debts. By 1808 Mary Ann Clarke saw no option but to blackmail the duke into restoring her full annuity and paying off her debts. The Duke of York took a principled stand and refused her.

Mrs Clarke was as cunning as she was charming. Rather than make accusations on her own, she went to a place where the duke could really be hurt: Parliament. What she needed was a sympathetic Member of Parliament who had a grudge of his own against the duke. She found such a person in 'Colonel' Gwyllym Lloyd Wardle, MP for Okehampton. Wardle had been colonel in the Ancient British Fencibles, a militia unit which had been disbanded by the duke's reforms in 1802. Wardle had been unable to secure a commission in the regular army and so had turned his attentions to Parliament, where he had a reputation as a radical.

On 20 January 1809 Wardle stood up in the House of Commons and moved for an inquiry into the Duke of York's conduct as head of the army.[30] In the course of the inquiry Mrs Clarke was called as a witness and appeared before a group of goggle-eyed MPs, literally bursting out of an exquisitely cut blue silk gown. Her evidence was compelling and the committee of inquiry established that bribes had indeed been paid to Mrs Clarke.

But how much did the Duke of York know? Mrs Clarke stated that he knew everything and produced a letter proving so written in the duke's hand. Oddly enough, this evidence was not allowed as it was proved that Mrs Clarke was an accomplished and expert forger, perfectly able to mimic the duke's handwriting.

The duke was acquitted, but the scandal had damaged public opinion to the point that effigies of him were being burnt in the streets. Even Parliament, which had to a certain degree protected him from the worst of the accusations, called into question his taking a mistress. Feeling he had no option, on 17 March the Duke of York resigned as commander-in-chief. In addition, Mrs Clarke was paid £7,000 and granted a pension of £400 per annum, provided she destroyed all copies of love letters from the duke.

Mary Ann Clarke is said to have had a love affair with Colonel Wardle. She was later imprisoned for nine months after trying to blackmail the Chancellor of the Exchequer for Ireland. She quit Britain after her release and went to France. The Duke of York meanwhile resumed his command of the army in 1811 once memories of the affair had died down.

'The Modern Circe or A Sequel to the Petticoat', an 1809 caricature on the scandal of the Duke of York's mistress selling army commissions. (akg-images)

THE PETERLOO MASSACRE

WHILE France underwent a political revolution in the late 18th century, Britain experienced an industrial one. The prolonged period of war between Britain and France saw an increase in industrial production, notably in the manufacture of cotton for uniforms. However, when peace was established in 1815 and army cutbacks came into force, the result was an economic slump and high unemployment.

For industrialists this slump was exacerbated by the introduction of the so-called Corn Laws – a measure introduced in 1815 to artificially inflate the price of imported corn. This was nothing but a means of protecting the privileged land-owning class, who benefited enormously by the playing field being made uneven in their favour.

In addition to the depression, there was the question of universal male suffrage and a desire to end the corrupt voting system. It was scandalous that a backwater like Old Sarum, with three houses and 11 voters, returned two MPs to Parliament, while Manchester – one of the biggest industrial centres in the world, with 200,000 inhabitants – had absolutely no representation in Parliament at all.

This, then, was the backdrop to a rise in political radicalism, which quite frankly terrified the ruling elite. Ever since the American and French revolutions, the British establishment had been concerned that revolution might one day blow up in England.

On 16 August 1819 a public meeting was called by the radical 'Patriotic Union Society' in Manchester to discuss some of the issues of the day. A crowd estimated at up to 80,000 strong gathered at St Peter's Field to hear a number of radical orators. The event was good natured enough. There were the obligatory flags and banners calling for an end to the Corn Laws and for universal suffrage, but certainly nothing to merit what happened next.

A group of local magistrates had been convened to watch the meeting and ensure it did not get out of hand. With no regular police force then in existence, the leader of the magistrates, William Hulton, had mobilized a sizeable detachment of regular troops and yeomanry, including the 15th Hussars, who had fought at Waterloo.

Once the speakers got onto the podium and began addressing the crowd, Hulton panicked. Deciding he had heard enough from this seditious rabble he ordered the Deputy Constable of Manchester, Captain Joseph Nadin, to arrest the speakers and the ring leaders behind the meeting.

It was a ridiculous request. Nadin took one look at the size of the crowd and said that he would need assistance if he was going to have any chance of getting to the podium, let alone making any arrests. Instead of useful assistance he was sent three score of cavalry troopers from the Manchester and Salford Yeomanry to back him up.

When the horsemen came into view and formed a line at first the crowd seemed undaunted. The speakers called for the crowd to stand firm and not to be intimidated by such a shabby show of force.

The yeomen were a fairly recently formed militia unit of middle-class shopkeepers and tradesmen. Hearing excited shouts coming from the crowd, they gave a shout of their own, drew swords and charged like a pack of drunken hooligans into them. Their target was the speakers' platform, but such was the density of the crowd that the yeomen were not able to pass through. At this point they began striking down at the heads and outstretched arms of the crowd with their sabres. Once the mass realized that the people nearest the horses were being attacked, they began to break up and panic set in. Eventually the yeomen reached the platform and began arresting the speakers and a number of journalists who were covering the event. With their blood up the yeomen then began going after and pulling down the flags and banners that had been erected by the crowd.

Watching the yeomen in action, William Hulton mistakenly believed they were in trouble and were being assaulted by the crowd. Hulton therefore excitedly ordered the 15th Hussars onto the field to save the yeomen. The hussars were no undisciplined mob; when they charged onto the field there was only one outcome.

Ten minutes after Hulton had given the fateful command St Peter's Field was clear except for discarded clothes and some tattered flags, not to mention the dead, dying and injured.

In the wake of the cavalry charge 11 people lay dead, among them a woman and child. Hundreds more were wounded from sword cuts or being trampled by horses. People had received sword cuts to the arms and hands. One man had his nose severed by the downward swipe of a cavalry sabre. To offer some defence to the regular hussars, much of their effort was spent trying to restrain the hooligan yeomen who went into action before them.

The radical press had a field day reporting the event. James Wroe of the *Manchester Observer*, in reference to Waterloo, described the action that day as the 'Peterloo Massacre'. In return for reporting the story he was arrested! By any measure, the action taken by Hulton was disproportionate. However, as a sign of the times, he was not chastized, but applauded. Radical meetings and publications were heavily suppressed.

So much for Britain's so-called heritage of freedom of speech.

ACT II

*'MANIFEST
INFAMY'*

MISRULE, BRITANNIA

T HE century between Waterloo and the First World War (1815–1914) is often referred to as the *Pax Britannica*. Aping the *Pax Romana* ('Roman Peace') the dominant British Empire was thought to have brought stability to much of the world, whether its help was wanted or not.

All over the world countries somehow found themselves being governed by over-dressed, polite, reasonable gentlemen from a small, damp, overcast island somewhere halfway round the globe on the north-eastern edge of the Atlantic.* Even now people are wondering how the British got away with it for so long.

During this supposed period of peace, not a year passed by without British soldiers being engaged in conflict somewhere on the planet. Naturally, with so many soldiers busy painting the planet red, scandals were aplenty.

Of course, one of the great cornerstones of the British Empire and its army was tea. Through deserts, jungles, mountains, and on the high seas, the British endured all with a calming 'cuppa'. Even today, faced with competition from exotic herbal infusions, lattés and espressos, tea still enjoys a lofty position

---

* As the CIA's online *World Factbook* helpfully points out, in Britain 'more than one-half of the days are overcast'. See: www.cia.gov/cia/publications/factbook/index.html.

among hot beverages, with 62 billion cups drunk in Britain every single year.*

The chief importer of tea up to the Victorian era was the British East India Company. It was probably the most successful commercial enterprise in the history of trade and, contrary to British notions of fair play, totally unscrupulous when it felt the urge. Since 1600 the East India Company had enjoyed a virtual monopoly on trade with the East and in particular the import of tea. Until the Great Indian Mutiny of 1857, it also ruled large swathes of India, having its own military bases and, thanks to Charles II, a mandate to start wars in order to secure and protect its deals.

Although the East India Company was dominant in India, most of the world's tea came from China. To avoid running up a trade deficit with China, the East India Company funded the purchase of tea by selling opium back to the Chinese. The opium was grown on East India Company land in India and shipped by the boat load into China. To use modern parlance, the East India Company literally flooded the market with the drug and, before long, drug use along the coastal areas was endemic, with an estimated 3 million Chinese using opium.[31]

Faced with this terrible scourge, in 1836 the Chinese authorities began to take on what amounted to probably the biggest narcotics cartel in the history of the world. The Chinese criminalized the abuse of opium and clamped down on opium dens where the drug was smoked. As a deterrent, anyone caught with opium or found using it would suffer the death penalty, as would traffickers bringing opium into the country.

---

* Statistic from the UK Tea Council, February 2006. See www.tea.co.uk for more unexpectedly interesting facts.

Despite the illegality of the opium trade, the British scandalously continued to pump it in, bribing Chinese officials to turn a blind eye to their actions. Aware the trade was still flourishing, in 1839 a Chinese government official, Lin Tse-hsu, got tough, confiscated and destroyed 20,183 chests of British opium. Lin then wrote a letter to the British monarch, Queen Victoria, in which he quite reasonably asked for her intervention against the illegal traffic in drugs. He bemoaned the 'barbarian merchants' smuggling opium into China for the pursuit of profit and asked Victoria if she would eradicate the opium fields in British-controlled India.

Fighting between Britain and China broke out again in 1856. In this cartoon of 1858, Britannia is threatening China, holding a gun-shaped teapot, asking, 'A little more gunpowder, Mr. China?' (a play on words as gunpowder is also a kind of tea). (HIP / Topfoto)

Britain's response was to attack China and thus began the First Chinese War of 1839–42. This was better known as the Opium War, and in it the Chinese were no match for the modern British Army and suffered a succession of defeats. The war resulted in the Treaty of Nanking (1842), under which China ceded Hong Kong to Britain and paid the British £2 million – a strange case of paying compensation for being attacked. Britain was granted most-favoured nation status and, among other things, allowed to continue the sale of opium as never before.

MUTINY!

THE British Empire didn't always have things its own way. In a worrying precedent for modern times, the hard-fought First Afghan War (1839–42) was the worst disaster to befall a British army in the East until the capture of Singapore by the Japanese in 1942.

The wiping out of a column of British troops by Afghan tribesmen dented the prestige of the East India Company to the extent that it needed a quick victory elsewhere to restore its reputation. The conquest of Scinde (Sindh – now a province of Pakistan) was accomplished by Major-General Sir Charles Napier, who admitted to his journal: 'We have no right to seize Scinde; yet we shall do so, and a very advantageous, useful, humane piece of rascality it would be.'[32]

This blatantly illegal war caused a torrent of public criticism back home in Britain. The newly established British satirical magazine, *Punch*, published a cartoon of Napier with the caption: 'Peccavi – I have sinned'. This Latin pun on the place-name Scinde showed the public's displeasure clearly enough.

There was further fallout from the Afghan War with the loss of caste suffered by surviving sepoys who had broken a religious taboo by serving beyond the frontiers of India. There was an underlying feeling that the British were surreptitiously attempting to convert the native troops to Christianity by making them outcasts from their own religions. This suspicion among the sepoys appeared to receive confirmation in 1857 with the introduction of the 1853 pattern Lee-Enfield rifle into the subcontinent.

Although an advance on the muskets that had shot Napoleon's columns to pieces at Waterloo, the 1853 pattern rifle shared one key design feature with the old Brown Bess. When loading, the soldier had to bite open the cartridge containing the gunpowder charge and ball, before pouring them into the barrel. To protect the charge, the cartridges for the new rifle were coated in grease. It was rumoured that this coating was made from a mixture of cow and pig fat, which caused enormous offence to Hindu and Muslim soldiers alike.

Realizing this might be a problem, the British offered to let the sepoys make their own cartridges using beeswax or vegetable oils. When this failed to stop the rumours, a new drill was introduced so that the cartridge was torn by the hand rather than in the mouth. This too failed to placate the sepoys, who argued that they might well forget to do this in the heat of the battle and go back to tearing cartridges with their mouths.*

On 29 March 1857 a sepoy in the 34th Bengal Native Infantry (BNI) named Mangal Pandey shot at his sergeant-major on the parade ground at Barrackpore, near Calcutta. During his court martial the British believed that Pandey was under the influence of 'bhang' – a derivative of the cannabis plant – but others claimed that Pandey was protesting about the cartridges. Pandey was hanged

---

* There is a modern sequel to this affair. In 2001 a Hindu group attacked a McDonald's restaurant in Mumbai after reports in the United States accusing McDonald's of using beef fat in the preparation of French fries. In the face of continued protests, McDonald's issued a statement claiming that all cooking oil used in its India restaurants was 100% vegetarian.

and, as a further punishment, the 34th BNI was disbanded. On 9 May, 85 troopers of the 3rd Light Cavalry in Meerut refused to handle the new cartridges. The troopers were paraded before the assembled garrison and publicly humiliated, having their uniforms torn off before being shackled and sent off to serve hard labour. This time the sepoy garrison rose up and released the prisoners. The mutineers broke into an armoury and massacred whichever Europeans they could find. From there the rebellion erupted across the subcontinent but, fortunately for the British, there was little unity in the uprising and it was put down.[33]

The British backlash was fierce and became known as 'The Devil's Wind'. Through the winter of 1857–58, the British retook everything they had lost. Atrocities committed by the mutineers left the British soldiers in no mood for clemency. According to one correspondent in *Blackwood's Edinburgh Magazine* of 1857, the sepoy 55th Regiment was singled out to set an example to other regiments. The punishment was so shockingly harsh it was decided that only a third of the condemned men would suffer it for fear of provoking a public outcry in Britain. The correspondent describes the scene in language typical of the era:

> It was an awfully imposing scene! All the troops, European and native, armed and disarmed, loyal and disaffected, were drawn up on parade, forming three sides of a square ... Forming the fourth side of the square were the guns (9-pounders), ten in number, which were to be used for the execution ... The first ten were picked out – their eyes were bandaged, and they were bound to the guns, their backs leaning against the muzzles, and their arms fastened to the wheels. The port-fires were lighted, and at a signal from the Artillery-Major, the guns were fired. It was a horrid sight that met the eye: a regular shower of human

fragments of heads, of arms, of legs, appeared in the air through the smoke, and when that cleared away, these fragments lying on the ground – fragments of Hindoos, and fragments of Mussulmans, all mixed together, were all that remained of those ten mutineers. Three times more was this scene repeated, but so great is the disgust we all feel for the atrocities committed by the rebels, that we had no room in our hearts for any feeling of pity; perfect callousness was reflected on every European's face ... But far different was the effect on the native portion of the spectators; their black faces grew ghastly pale as they gazed breathlessly at the awful spectacle. You must know that this is nearly the only form in which death has any terrors for a native. If he is hung, or

THE NEW YEAR'S GIFT.

PAM (TO SIR COLIN). "WELL—UPON MY WORD—EH!—I'M REALLY EXTREMELY OBLIGED TO YOU—BUT—EH!—HOW ABOUT KEEPING THE BRUTE!"

Cartoon from Punch, *2 January 1858, showing Sir Colin Campbell, Commander-in-Chief in India, presenting the leashed tiger of India to Palmerston, the prime minister, who shelters nervously behind a chair, reluctant to accept this barely tamed 'gift'. (HIP/TopFoto)*

shot by musketry, he knows that his friends or relatives will be allowed to claim his body, and will give him the funeral rights required by his religion: if a Hindoo, that his body will be burned with all due ceremonies; and if a Mussulman, that his remains will be decently interred, as directed in the Koran. But if sentenced to death in this form, he knows that his body will be blown into a thousand pieces, and that it will be altogether impossible for his relatives, however devoted to him, to be sure of picking up all the fragments of his own particular body; and the thought that perhaps a limb of some one of a different religion to himself might possibly be burned or buried with the remainder of his own body, is agony to him.[34]

CRIMEAN SHAME

PERHAPS the biggest outcry against the military during the Victorian era came in the Crimean War (1853–56). The British government's mismanagement of the war went far beyond being a scandal – it was a complete disgrace. The accusations were many but, above all, it was the unsanitary conditions in which the troops lived that caused most concern.

The diaries of the medical officers in the Crimean army list a catalogue of complaints. 'Some of the camps were very injudiciously chosen,' complained one. Another noted that the men were so weakened they were 'unable to undergo any fatigue, [even] to carry their knapsacks'.[35]

Unfortunately for the poor soldiers forced to live in them, camps were then chosen because of their strategic value or convenience, with little concern for the prevalence of disease. Although the study of hygiene was still in comparative infancy, people knew that when an army camped by a swamp, the men got sick.

The Inspector-General of Hospitals, Sir John Hall, complained: 'At Balaklava, they built their huts on a very unhealthy site. I protested against it, in the strongest way I could, but without effect; and the consequence was that shortly after the men had spotted fever.'

Another medical officer, Dr Hanbury, highlighted the problems faced by the army in his log: 'November, 1854. Health of the army rapidly deteriorated from defective diet, harassing duties, hardships, privations, and exposures to the inclement season ... Cholera increased; cold, wet, innutritious and irritating diet produced dysentery, congestion and disorganization of the mucous membrane of the bowels, and scurvy.'

The diaries of regimental surgeons in the Crimea paint an equally stark picture of the suffering. To offer but a few examples:

1st Regiment, December 1854: 'Scarcely a soldier in perfect health, from sleeping on damp ground, in wet clothing, and no change of dress; cooking the worst; field-hospital over-crowded.' January 1855: 'Type of disease becoming more unequivocally the result of bad feeding, exposure, and other hardships.'

20th Regiment: 'The impoverished condition of the blood, dependent on long use of improper diet, exposure to wet and cold, and want of sufficient clothing and rest, had become evident ... Scurvy, diarrhoea, frost-bite, and ulceration of the feet followed.'

30th Regiment: 'Duties and employments extremely severe; exposure protracted; no means of personal cleanliness; clothing infested with vermin; since Nov. 14, short allowance of meat, and, on some days, of biscuit, sometimes no sugar, once no rice; food sometimes spoiled in cooking; tents leaked; floors and bedding wet; sanitary efficiency deteriorated in a decided manner.'

33rd Regiment, December 1854: 'Cold and wet weather, coupled with insufficient food, fuel, and clothing, and severe and arduous duties, all combined to keep up the sickness; 48.8 percent admitted to the hospital in this month.'

34th Regiment, November, 1854: 'Cholera broke out. It rained constantly. Troops had no other protection from the damp ground than a single wet blanket ... Without warm clothing, on short allowance of provisions, in want of fuel. The sanitary condition of the regiment deteriorated rapidly: 56 percent of the men admitted to the hospital.'

41st Regiment, November and December 1854: 'No respite from severe duties; weather cold and wet; clothing ill-adapted for such climate and service; disease rapidly increased; 70 percent of the men in the hospital in two months.'[36]

What was very different about the Crimean War was the invention of the electric telegraph, which allowed journalists to report the truth of what was going on quickly enough for public opinion to have an effect on the conduct of the war. The most famous journalist

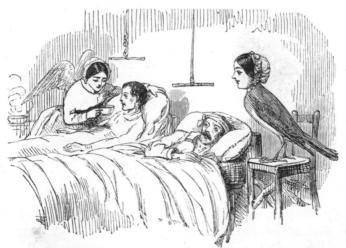

A drawing of Florence Nightingale watching a nurse at work in 1854 from Punch. *(Oxford Science/HIP/Topfoto)*

present was William Russell of *The Times*. Despatched as a war correspondent, Russell's reports were widely read and included very strong criticisms of the incompetent military leaders and the suffering of the troops. Russell's reports became so important that they are credited with helping to bring about the fall of the Prime Minister, Lord Aberdeen, in January 1855.

The pressure had mounted on the government after *The Times* put out an appeal for donations to provide welfare for the troops. In its leading article of 12 October 1854, *The Times* opened with the line: 'Every man of common modesty must feel, not exactly ashamed of himself, but somehow rather smaller than usual, when he reads the strange and terrible news of the war.' It continued with a description of the conditions at the Scutari hospital, where at least 4,000 patients were suffering from wounds, cholera and fever. The surgeons were swamped by the appeals for aid and there were no British nurses. It continued:

> But what is almost incredible, but nevertheless true, there is not even linen and lint to bind wounds. It certainly reflects great disgrace somewhere or other, that a material as necessary to the cure of wounds as a hospital itself should have been forgotten, and that, while the Turkish Government has provided a palace for the reception of the wounded, the British Government has not even found linen to bandage their wounds.[37]

The appeal for public help went exceedingly well. In addition to financial aid, on 21 October 1854 Florence Nightingale and a staff of 38 women volunteer nurses set off for the Crimea, arriving at Scutari in early November. In 1855 Aberdeen's successor, Lord Palmerston, sent a commission led by Dr John Sutherland out to the Crimea to investigate and report on the problems and their causes.

During this visit Sutherland met Florence Nightingale at Scutari and witnessed the abuse and negligence for himself. 'The hospitals at Scutari were magnificent buildings, apparently admirably adapted to their purpose; but, when carefully examined, they were found to be little better than pest-houses,' he wrote.[38]

He visited the camps and commented on how '[the] damp, unventilated, and undrained huts, in some parts of the camp, produced consequences similar to those in cellar-dwellings at home'. He also bemoaned how the once 'beautiful village of Balaclava was allowed to become a hot-bed of pestilence, so that fever, dysentery, and cholera, in it and its vicinity and on the ships in the harbour, were abundant ... Filth, manure, offal, dead carcasses, had been allowed to accumulate to such an extent, that we found, on our arrival, in March, 1855, it would have required the labour of three hundred men to remove the local causes of disease before the warm weather set in.'

Disgusting.

THE FAIRFAX RAID

O FF now to America for an unhappy quartet of falls from grace, corruption charges, and riotous behaviour.

Despite the country being in a state of civil war, life was tolerably good for General Edwin Henry Stoughton. Being a general certainly had its advantages. He had men at his command, a comfy bed and champagne aplenty. In hushed tones it was even said that Stoughton had made his mistress, Annie Jones, an honorary major and had awarded her with her own tent.

On the evening of 8 March 1863, Stoughton hosted a party at his headquarters in Fairfax for his mother and sister, who had come down from Vermont to see him. The last of the revellers left in their carriages before 1am and Stoughton, quite drunk and worn out from the evening, collapsed onto his mattress and fell into a deep sleep. He certainly had no idea of the embarrassment about to befall him...

Out in the darkness of that March night was John Mosby, a Confederate guerrilla fighter known as the 'Gray Ghost'. Mosby had well earned that soubriquet, conducting lightning raids well into Union-controlled territory. For this he was described by Union officer Colonel Wyndham as a 'horse thief', a slight Mosby decided he would avenge by capturing the said colonel in his headquarters at Fairfax.

The date set for the raid was the same night that Stoughton was entertaining his family guests. Under the cover of a miserable, rainy night, Mosby and his men rode through the Union lines into

Fairfax and began seizing prisoners and horses. Fortunately for Wyndham, he had decided to visit the capital and was not in his quarters that evening.

Instead of going after Wyndham, Mosby rode over to Stoughton's headquarters in the Episcopal rectory. The Confederate raider and five others knocked loudly on the door to the building. Eventually a window was opened and someone asked who was there. 'Fifth New York Cavalry,' replied Mosby, 'with a despatch for General Stoughton.' The door opened and Mosby took hold of the startled staff officer by his nightshirt. At gun point he whispered his name in the lieutenant's ear and asked to be taken to Stoughton.

A light was struck and Mosby was shown up to the general's bedroom from which loud snoring could be heard. Mosby entered the room and, when the general showed no signs of stirring at the intrusion, Mosby pulled off the bed clothes, lifted the general's nightshirt and gave him a good slap across the backside. Stoughton was startled into consciousness. He registered that his room was full of people, and that a man was telling him he was now a prisoner of war. Still intoxicated, he indignantly demanded to know what was going on.

Mosby asked him 'Have you ever heard of Mosby?' Stoughton replied he had.

'I am Mosby,' the confederate revealed. 'Stuart's cavalry has possession of the Court House; be quick and dress.'

It took some time to get Stoughton dressed. He was a stickler for proper attire and stood in front of a full-length mirror preening himself as if getting ready for a parade. Mosby was quite concerned at the time he was taking – he was surrounded by hostile troops in the middle of Union-controlled territory after all. To speed proceedings up Mosby had two of his men assist the general. One even picked up and returned his pocket watch to him when the half-dazed general left it on the bureau.

While getting dressed Stoughton asked Mosby if the Confederate general Fitzhugh Lee was with him. Stoughton had gone through West Point with Lee and so wanted to meet him – no doubt hoping to extricate himself from this predicament. Mosby lied that Lee was with him and that he would take Stoughton directly to him ... but first they had to go for a little ride. Horse riding is not an activity recommended for those with a hangover and Stoughton must have hated every moment of his unexpected trip.

As the Confederates were about to set off there was a moment of pure comedy. A window opened and a voice bellowed out asking what cavalry was doing on the street. The voice belonged to Colonel Johnstone, who was in temporary command of a cavalry brigade. It was greeted by laughter, at which point Johnstone realized the riders were enemy troops.

Unlike Stoughton, Johnstone managed to escape, largely because his wife held up Mosby's troopers in the hallway while her husband climbed out the back window in his underwear – some joked that this was the only resistance offered to Mosby's men all night. Johnstone ran off into the garden and hid in an 'outhouse' – in other words the outside privy. Johnstone's unusual escape became a subject of mirth for the rest of his life and earned him the nickname 'outhouse' Johnstone. He resigned soon after the raid.

Stoughton was equally embarrassed by the nature of his abduction. About his loss Abraham Lincoln appeared unconcerned. Learning that Stoughton had been captured along with 30 men and 58 horses he is believed to have said, 'Well, I am sorry for that. Generals I can make, horses I cannot afford to lose.'[39]

THE NEW YORK DRAFT RIOTS

With the American Civil War in its third year and with no sight in end, on 3 March 1863 the United States Congress passed a conscription act to raise 300,000 recruits for the army. All able-bodied males between the ages of 20 and 35, plus all unmarried men between 35 and 45, would be entered into a lottery from which the candidates would be drawn. Although the draft was universal, it provoked outrage because of provisions whereby men could buy their way out of service, or pay for a replacement to take their place.

In New York, a city heavily populated by recently arrived immigrants, the exemption fee of $300 was way above the means of most. The conscription act was the last in a series of class and racial issues that had been simmering in the city since well before the war. Rather than finding a land of opportunity, the majority of immigrants arriving in the city had found themselves condemned to a life of iniquity and exploitation by unscrupulous capitalists. The $300 exemption fee was interpreted as yet another injust and blatant means of favouring the rich at the expense of the poor.

In the month leading up to the first conscription lottery in New York, the Democratic Party stirred up discontent among the white working classes, in particular poor Irish immigrants. The Democrats denounced the draft law as a scandalous violation of civil liberties and predicted a mass influx of ex-slaves from the South to northern industrial cities. Using well-versed, negative racial stereotypes, it was claimed these freed slaves would not only rob the good, honest, god-fearing, white folk of their jobs, but carry off their daughters into wedlock as well. From the point of view of the average Irish immigrant, he was being drafted to fight a war on behalf of the very people who would soon put him out of work. Nor was it lost upon on him that black males were exempt from the draft because they were not considered full citizens.

As the day of the first draft drew closer, news from the bloodbath at Gettysburg (1–4 July) began arriving in New York. The combination of political stirring and news of heavy casualties at the front was enough to spark one of the biggest riots in American history.

The draft began on Saturday 11 July 1863 and passed off reasonably quietly. After the names were posted the following day, talk of resistance began to mount. On the Monday morning protestors began flooding out of the Five Points slum area. Armed with clubs and cudgels they set fire to the assistant provost marshal's office before heading into the richer end of town where properties were attacked and looted. As the buildings were engulfed by flames, the fire brigade did nothing but watch them burn. Unfortunately for the authorities the New York firemen were furious that they were not exempted from the draft so were in no mood to help.

As the rioting spread, anger turned from the rich to New York's black community. Several thousand rioters arrived outside the 'Colored Orphan Asylum' on Fifth Avenue in the early evening of 13 July. The 233 children inside the building were saved, but the mob burned the four-storey building down, despite the efforts of chief engineer John Decker of the New York Fire Department. Three times he put out fires kindled by the rioters and then attempted to calm the crowd. His entreaties fell on deaf ears and he was seized by the mob. Decker was only saved by the intervention of a few burly firemen who waded into the throng to rescue him. An hour and a half later the asylum was a heap of smouldering rubble.[40]

Desperate times called for desperate measures. A warship was sent to cover the business district in Wall Street with its guns. Employees prepared homemade bombs, while workers at the Bank Note Company prepared vats of sulphuric acid to pour over the rioters. When the *New York Times* building was threatened, its owner Henry Raymond and editor Leonard Jerome   the maternal grandfather of Winston Churchill – protected themselves and the building by positioning Gatling guns at the windows!

The abolitionist *New York Tribune* offices fared somewhat worse and were on the verge of being overrun when police from the 26th Precinct launched a furious baton charge on the rioters. Clubbing them mercilessly, the policemen cleared a mob estimated at 5,000, leaving behind them a trail of dead, disfigured and broken-limbed rioters.

Wednesday 15 July saw the arrival of Federal troops rushed back from Gettysburg to put down the revolt. As many as 6,000 soldiers began patrolling the streets, returning fire against rioters as they came into contact. By Friday morning the riot had been put down and some degree of normality returned to the city. Amid the smouldering ruins at least a hundred people had been killed and several million dollars' worth of damage had been caused. The city's black community was left in a state of terror and many quit the city in fear of their lives.

Although the rioting was quelled, the rioters had achieved a degree of success. The rioting had highlighted some fundamental social ills in American society and Abraham Lincoln realized he had gone too far with his conscription targets. To take the heat out of the city, he lowered the draft quota for New York by more than a half.

THE BELKNAP SCANDAL

THE presidency of Ulysses S. Grant was marked with a number of stinging corruption scandals that ultimately tarnished the reputation of this Civil War hero. The chief among these scandals took place in 1876 and involved the Secretary of War and former Civil War major-general William Belknap.

To understand the scandal, we need to know less about Belknap and more about his wife. During the Civil War, Belknap had met two Kentucky girls, Carrie and Amanda Tomlinson. Belknap married Carrie, and when Amanda was widowed she moved in with the Belknaps. In 1870 Carrie became sick and died. Belknap became engaged to Amanda who – although by no means unique in her love of the latest Paris fashions – was fortunate enough to visit the French capital and indulge her passions, stocking up her wardrobe before getting married.

On her return from Paris, Amanda Belknap put Washington high society under siege. The Belknaps became famous for hosting extravagant parties, which led many to wonder how they managed it on Belknap's relatively modest $8,000 government salary. The War Secretary explained that they received dividends on investments Amanda inherited from her first husband. When this explanation was not believed, the couple claimed that Belknap had made some clever speculations before taking up his position as Secretary of War. It all smelled too fishy.

 108

There was a lot of corruption out West. In 1872 there had been allegations of bribery by merchants to get their hands on the lucrative Indian trading posts, which were administered by the War Department under Belknap. The speculation that something rotten was afoot grew after the Democrats gained control of the House of Representatives following the 1874 elections.

Hiester Clymer, the new chairman of the subcommittee for War Department expenditures, reopened the investigations into corruption in the army and Indian post traderships and uncovered a trail of evidence going back to 1870, when Mrs Belknap had her husband give a childhood friend's husband, Caleb P. Marsh, the rights to maintain a trading post at Fort Sill in the Indian territories. Marsh then subcontracted the position of post trader at Fort Sill to a John Evans in return for an annual payment of $12,000. On 10 October 1870, Belknap endorsed the arrangement and allowed Evans to maintain the trading post. In return for this, Marsh paid Belknap a back-hander amounting to $1,500 a quarter – which was equal to three-quarters of Belknap's government salary.

Marsh was called before the House Committee on Expenditures in the War Department on 29 February 1876. He explained the full depth of the corruption, and that, from October 1870 to December 1875, Belknap received half of every payment Evans made to Marsh. Summing up, the committee declared that Belknap was 'basely prostituting his high office to his lust for private gain' and resolved to impeach him.

With Marsh's damning testimony, Belknap realized the game was up. He rushed to the White House to submit his resignation to the President. By now Belknap was in tears. The President, who was an old friend of Belknap's, did not realize the extent of the allegations and probably believed that Belknap had been deceived by his wife, who was responsible for the deal. Thinking Belknap was doing the honourable thing to protect his wife, Grant accepted Belknap's resignation at once.

That afternoon there was fury in the House of Representatives when they learned that Grant had allowed Belknap to resign and had thus thwarted their plans to impeach the Secretary of War. In fact, they were so angry they decided to impeach Belknap anyway – just for the hell of it. It was morally wrong that Belknap could wash his hands and walk away scot-free.

Belknap went on trial but was eventually found not guilty on 1 August – not because anyone thought he was actually innocent, but because most believed they had no jurisdiction over Belknap, whose resignation had made him a private citizen.

The fallout from the impeachment attempt did not end there. The scandal severely damaged Grant's re-election chances. It also threw a number of fashion and jewellery stores in New York into crisis – Mrs Belknap had run up seriously large debts before the bubble burst.

An important part of the Belknap scandal was the involvement of George Armstrong Custer – old 'Long Hair' of 7th Cavalry fame. It is highly probable that Custer's involvement played some part in the recklessness that led to his death at the battle of the Little Big Horn.

There is some speculation that the whole Belknap scandal was sparked by Custer. Towards the end of the summer in 1875 Belknap had travelled to Fort Abraham Lincoln, which was then commanded by Custer, a former general who had been forced to take the lower rank of lieutenant-colonel after post-Civil War military cut backs. Prior to this visit Custer had been investigating the inflated prices at the trading post – inflated prices he and his men were obliged to pay. He was shocked to learn that the fort's trader kept only $2,000 out of the $15,000 profit his post earned – the rest disappeared in illegal pay-offs. Custer privately accused Belknap of being behind this corruption and so had only the briefest dealings with him during the visit.

Custer's snub became common knowledge and the talk of the frontier. It is believed that Custer told his friends in the Democratic Party about Belknap's corruption, also accusing the President's brother, Orvil Grant, of making a fortune out of an Indian trading post while the local Indians were starving.

When Belknap's impeachment trial began on 17 April, Custer was called to Washington to testify. This was bad news for Custer – not because he feared naming names, but because a major military expedition was being planned into Indian Territory and he did not want to miss it.

Custer's testimony was explosive. In it he described how the contractor at Fort Sill turned up with a consignment of grain for the cavalry which Custer suspected had been stolen. He refused to receive it. When he made his suspicions known to the military governor of Dakota, Major-General Alfred Terry, Custer received an order to accept the consignment. Custer told the committee that he thought this order had come from Belknap, although his evidence was only based on hearsay. Despite this it fitted the general pattern which was emerging about Belknap.

Custer's testimony outraged Grant. Custer tried to see President Grant on numerous occasions, but was rebuffed. Desperate to return to his command, Custer asked for permission to leave Washington, but was denied. He left anyway and took the train to Chicago on 2 May.

When Custer stepped off the train the next day, he was arrested on the President's orders. Grant also rubbed salt into the wound by announcing that General Terry would take command of Custer's

111

forthcoming expedition. Custer was crestfallen, but he was saved by the Democratic press, which accused Grant of acting like a latter-day Caesar. Custer was allowed to resume his journey west, but was still considered under arrest.

Custer pleaded with Terry to intercede on his behalf with the President and a compromise was finally agreed. Terry would command the column and Custer would command his regiment in the field. On 17 May 1876 the 7th Cavalry left Fort Abraham Lincoln and rode out onto the pages of history.

There is some speculation that Custer harboured ambitions of becoming president, with some postulating that the Democrats had offered him the job in return for the information against Belknap. All Custer needed was a quick victory to send him off on a wave of popularity.

Is that what made him so eager to take risks in the campaign ahead?[41]

SURVIVING CUSTER

O N 25 June 1876, Lieutenant-Colonel Custer rode into immortality at the battle of the Little Big Horn. With 655 men, he attacked an encampment of Sioux and Cheyenne Indians. Without appreciating the size of the forces ranged against him – or with complete disdain for the enemy – Custer broke Napoleon's golden rule about concentrating in the face of the enemy and split his small command into three groups.

One of the three groups had been entrusted to Major Marcus Reno, with orders to attack the native encampment from the north. Unfortunately for the already exhausted cavalrymen, when Reno's detachment arrived in the agreed position it was attacked by overwhelming numbers and forced away from supporting Custer, who found himself attacked by large numbers.

Custer tried to make it to higher ground to form a defensive position but his command was butchered to a man in minutes.*

---

* Custer's body was found naked and with two bullet wounds. It was widely reported at the time that Custer was not scalped or mutilated like the rest of his men, either out of respect, or because he was not recognized. In contrast, there are other reports that Custer was quite badly hacked up and that the stories of his body being preserved intact were only put out for the benefit of his wife Elizabeth. For the various accounts of Custer's last moments see Stephen Ambrose, *Crazy Horse and Custer* (Garden City, NY: Doubleday, 1975) and Dee Brown, *Bury My Heart at Wounded Knee* (New York: Holt, Rinehart and Winston, 1970).

Meanwhile, Reno and his detachment fought a desperate action until relieved by additional forces under General Terry. In view of the extremely perilous position Custer had placed him in, Reno did well to survive with just 32 killed.

Alas, as in the case of Aristodemus at Thermopylae, survivors somewhat muddy the heroism of famous last stands. Almost immediately people began to accuse Reno of cowardice for not falling with Custer, and the pressure of these accusations soon began to take its toll. A year on from the battle, while Reno was in command of the military post at Fort Abercrombie, Dakota, he faced a court martial on charges of 'conduct unbecoming an officer and a gentleman'.

On 8 March 1877 the court martial heard how Reno had became embroiled in a scandal involving the wife of a subordinate officer, Captain James M. Bell. According to the charges, on 18 December, while Captain Bell was absent from Fort Abercrombie, Reno had seized Bell's wife, 'taking both her hands in his own, and attempting to draw her person close up to his own'. His advances repulsed, Reno made a second attempt on 21 December, placing his arm around Mrs Bell's waist.

No doubt considering Reno a pest, Mrs Bell failed to invite the garrison commander to a social gathering that Christmas to which all the other officers were invited. Learning of this snub, Reno became enraged and told the Fort's post trader, John Haselhurst: 'This means war! Mrs. Bell has thrown down the gauntlet, and I will take it up. Perhaps these people do not know the power of a commanding officer. I will make it hot for her, I will drive her out of the regiment.'

At the time, a certain Reverend Wainwright was staying with Mrs Bell as a guest of her husband. Reno wrote to Wainwright on December and asked him to refrain from holding services. When Wainwright enquired why, Reno told him that post trader Haselhurst had objected to Wainwright preaching after several officers in the garrison clubroom had questioned his relationship with Mrs Bell. According to Reno, Haselhurst had heard an officer say: 'That Mr. Wainwright would have his goose as well as another man, and he could have it with Mrs. Bell.' Reno urged Wainwright to leave Captain Bell's quarters saying to him: 'Mrs. Bell's reputation is like a spoiled egg – you cannot hurt it. She is notorious in the regiment as a loose character.' He claimed that several officers had asked for her to be expelled from the regiment – all of which was a pack of lies. Reno then smugly told one of his lieutenants: 'Mrs Bell ought to know better than to make a fight with me; her character is too vulnerable' – implying she had some guilty secret to hide.

On New Year's Eve Reno delivered his final humiliation. It had been arranged for Mrs Bell to play the organ at the garrison church

The retreat of the US 7th Cavalry under Major Reno at the battle of the Little Big Horn, as depicted by a native participant in the battle. (Art Media/HIP/TopFoto)

service. While everyone was preparing to attend the service, Reno sent out a message that Mrs Bell would not be permitted to play the organ and that, if she did so, Reno would put a stop to the services. At the court martial an additional charge was levelled against Reno, namely that he had attempted to bribe Eliza Galloway, a servant employed by assistant surgeon Dr Davies, to testify falsely at the hearing.

Reno pleaded 'Not Guilty' to the charges but was found guilty on six out of seven counts. He was dismissed from the service but then reprieved on the direct intervention of President Rutherford Hayes, who, in light of Reno's 20 years' good service, modified the sentence 'to suspension from rank and pay for two years from the 1st of May 1877'.

While he was suspended, the taunts of cowardice at the Little Big Horn continued, leading Reno to request an official inquiry into these charges. The inquiry exonerated Reno of all charges of cowardice, concluding on 11 March 1879: 'the conduct of the officers throughout was excellent, and while subordinates, in some instances, did more for the safety of the command by brilliant displays of courage than did Major Reno, there was nothing in his conduct which requires animadversion from this Court.'

Despite this verdict, Reno just could not hold it together. On 28 November 1879 he was called before a court martial at Fort Meade, Dakota, again on charges of 'conduct unbecoming an officer and gentleman'. This time Reno was accused of creating a brawl on 25 October 1879 in a public billiard saloon and violently assaulting a subordinate – Second Lieutenant Nicholson – with a billiards cue. It was only when an infantry officer threatened Reno with arrest that he calmed down.

It turned out that this had not been the first such incident in the billiard saloon. On 8 August he was drunk and disorderly and 'did several times, wantonly and in a riotous manner, knock money out of the hands of the saloon keeper Mr. Joseph Smythe, scattering said money over the floor, and did, in a wanton and riotous manner, smash in with chains the glass of one or more of the windows of said billiard saloon'. The court martial also heard how Reno had been in a 'disgusting condition of intoxication' at the residence of Mr W. S. Fanshawe, post trader, on 3 August.

Lastly, the presiding officer heard how on 10 November 1879, Reno did 'in the darkness and at a late hour in the evening, surreptitiously enter the side grounds adjoining the private residence or quarters of his commanding officer, Col. S. D. Sturgis, Seventh Cavalry and did peer into a side ... window of the family sitting-room ... approaching so near and so stealthily as to very seriously affright and alarm that portion of the family ... which had not yet retired for the night'.

Again Reno pleaded 'Not Guilty' but this time was dismissed from military service. Reno died in disgrace from cancer in 1889. It was not until the 1960s that Reno won a posthumous reprieve and he is now buried at the Custer memorial.[42]

THE SHAMBLES IN AFRICA

To a degree mirroring events in North America, on 22 January 1879 a British contingent was massacred by a native army at Isandlwana in southern Africa. A force under the British commander-in-chief, Lord Chelmsford, had crossed into Zululand on 11 January. He set up camp at Isandlwana, split his forces in two, and went off in search of the Zulu army. Having defeated other African tribes, Chelmsford was scared of only one eventuality – that the Zulus would turn and run before he had a chance to catch them. He would have done well to consider the fate of Custer just three years before.

Unknown to the British, large numbers of Zulu warriors were in the vicinity of the British camp. Although the Zulus were not expecting to fight that day, they encountered a British patrol and fighting developed. The British soldiers left in the camp must have felt quite a lump in their throats when over 20,000 Zulu warriors came rushing into view. A message was sent to recall Chelmsford, but he ignored it and decided to continue with his own plan to hunt Zulus. It was inconceivable to him that British soldiers could be beaten by spear-wielding savages. How wrong he was. By the end of the afternoon almost 1,200 of Chelmsford's men were dead.

News of Isandlwana reached Britain on 11 February and was greeted with horror and public outcry. A scapegoat was required and as the commander in the field, after a disaster of this magnitude, Chelmsford knew it would most likely be him. Prime Minister

Disraeli reported to Queen Victoria that his cabinet wanted to bow to public pressure to recall Chelmsford, but he gave no such order. Chelmsford enjoyed the favour of Queen Victoria and so Disraeli felt obliged to protect him. However, when the public clamour looked like turning on Disraeli, the politician dropped Chelmsford like a hot potato, and told the Queen he would have to be recalled.

In his defence, Chelmsford thrashed around looking for someone else to blame. He played up a myth that a shortage of ammunition was the cause of the defeat at Isandlwana. He also unjustly blamed a subordinate who had been slain in the battle. His biggest saving grace was a simultaneous action against Zulus at Rorke's Drift, which, by any measure, was an amazing feat of heroism in the face of overwhelming odds. The bravery of the defenders at Rorke's Drift quickly eclipsed the disaster at Isandlwana – with six Victoria Crosses initially awarded to the defenders.

Even this was a cause for raised eyebrows. The two commanding officers at the station, lieutenants Chard and Bromhead, were not on the original list of recipients, but were secretly added later by Chelmsford without any consultation.[43] Most of their fellow officers had a very poor opinion of the two and it was quickly pointed out the real brains behind the defence were those of Acting Assistant Commissary James Dalton. While Chard and Bromhead were all for abandoning the post, it was Dalton who urged them to turn it into a defensive position. Dalton was finally awarded the Victoria Cross after a press campaign.

Shaken by the defeat, a year after Isandlwana Disraeli's government fell and he was replaced by Gladstone, a fierce critic of the Zulu War. Unfortunately for Gladstone, he too would fall foul of military disaster. The siege of Khartoum (13 March 1884 – 26 January 1885) by the forces of the self-proclaimed Mahdi, Mohammad Ahmed, caused a storm of protest in Britain. The British commander at Khartoum, General Charles Gordon, refused to follow government advice and evacuate the city, leaving it in the Mahdi's hands. Equally stubborn, Gladstone's government refused to send a force for his relief.

It was only after Queen Victoria's intervention that Gladstone agreed to send a relief force, but this only set off in November. It arrived in Khartoum on 28 January, only to find that the city had fallen two days before and that Gordon's severed head had been presented to the Mahdi by his victorious soldiers. When the story broke at home, public outrage outstripped that which had greeted news of Isandlwana. This time there was only one villain – Gladstone himself. Even the Queen criticized him bitterly. Formerly known by the initials G.O.M. ('Grand Old Man'), after the failure to relieve Khartoum Gladstone became the M.O.G. 'Murderer of Gordon'.[44]

After both Isandlwana and Khartoum, the loss of face caused the British to send punitive expeditions, which meant victories against Victoria's Empire were almost always short-lived. After Gordon's death, Lord Kitchener was sent to defeat the dervish rebellion, something he finally achieved at the battle of Omdurman in 1898.

Kitchener saw himself as a sort of imperial superhero. He was certainly no stranger to controversy. The battle of Omdurman was a bloodbath where the dervish army was all but slaughtered by all manner of modern weapons – including exploding shells, machine guns and dumdum bullets. At the battle was Winston Churchill. He wrote to his mother on 26 January 1899: 'I shall merely say that the victory at Omdurman was disgraced by the inhuman slaughter of the wounded and that Lord Kitchener was responsible for this.'[45]

After the battle, when Kitchener came across the Mahdi's tomb he had the Royal Engineers blow it up. The tomb had already been used for target practice by British gunners, but Kitchener's demolition order caused uproar in Britain and led to questions in Parliament about the desecration of a holy site. Worse was to follow. Under Kitchener's command, the Mahdi's embalmed corpse was taken out of its resting place and thrown into the Nile – except the head. In revenge for Gordon's beheading, Kitchener is said to have kept the Mahdi's skull in an old kerosene tin while pondering what to do with it. When this was leaked to the press it caused more outrage in Britain, with the editor of the *Manchester Guardian* comparing Kitchener's conduct to the Huns and Vandals. Even Queen Victoria felt moved to write to Kitchener and urge him to temper his actions.[46]

'A Lesson', a comment on the British defeat in the Zulu War, in Punch, 1879.
(Mary Evans Picture Library)

SCANDAL AT TRANBY CROFT

Q UEEN Victoria's eldest son, the future Edward VII, or 'Bertie'
as he was known, was a man who liked his pleasures and who,
with his mother the longest-serving British monarch in history, had
little to do but indulge himself. He was well known for his mistresses
and his love of Paris, which was then in its belle époque. It was
perhaps Bertie's Francophilia that edged Britain away from its blood
ties with Germany into forming an alliance with France.*

But enough about Bertie's good points. He was a notorious
gambler to boot, with a predilection for the game of baccarat, which
was inconveniently illegal at the time. It was illegal because it was
purely a game of chance, with no skill attached to being victorious.
In that sense it was immoral and – apart from the Opium Wars and
all the other scandalous episodes we have thus far uncovered – one
thing Queen Victoria would not tolerate was immorality. 'We are
not amused,' as she is often quoted as having said.

On 8 September 1890 the Prince of Wales and some friends were
guests at Tranby Croft, the home of Sir Arthur Wilson, a
distinguished shipbuilder. They were there to attend the races at
nearby Doncaster and in the evening their attentions turned to

---

* A piece of royal trivia for those not in the know: the Prince of Wales' last
'official' mistress, Alice Keppel, was the great grandmother of Camilla
Parker Bowles, who became the mistress of Bertie's great grandson,
Charles, Prince of Wales.

other forms of sport. The prince suggested that the guests play baccarat and produced his own personalized baccarat playing set.

Among the players was the soldier Sir William Gordon-Cumming, a lieutenant-colonel of the Guards and a brave, distinguished veteran of the Zulu War considered destined for greater things. During the play, the son of the host, Arthur Wilson, noticed that Sir William was cheating. He saw that through sleight of hand Sir William was altering the value of his stake depending on whether or not he had won or lost the hand.

A second game was arranged for the following evening and a different baccarat table produced. Again, it was believed that Sir William was cheating in the same manner as the night before – by altering his stake at the crucial moment.

On Wednesday 10 September five of the players confronted Sir William with the evidence. The Prince of Wales was informed what had occurred and although Sir William utterly denied the claim he offered a solution to the business. The prince was eager to avoid being caught up in a gambling scandal. He proposed that Sir William would sign a declaration that he 'would never touch a card again' and, in return, the matter would remain secret among those gathered before him. Everyone agreed. And that would have been the end of the matter except...

There is no firm evidence as to how the story found its way into print but most accounts point the finger of blame at Bertie's mistress, Daisy. The wife of Lord Brooke, Earl of Warwick, the notoriously indiscreet Daisy was better known to acquaintances as 'Babbling Brooke'. In January 1891 details of the baccarat cheat began appearing in the foreign press and before long the matter was well known in England. With the news, Sir William's military career and social life were effectively at an end.

Faced with ostracism from his clubs, his friends and his colleagues, Sir William had few options. In a similar situation many would have taken the honourable route out and shot themselves. But Sir William considered himself the injured party. He had upheld his end of the bargain – it was others who had failed to keep theirs. Remember, it had been the prince's idea to play the illegal card game in the first place and Sir William had only signed the letter to end the matter and prevent the scandal from becoming public. He was, in fact, totally innocent of the charges. At least that is what he told the jury when the matter went to court on 2 June 1891.[47]

The trial lasted seven days and was notable for the presence of Bertie throughout, sitting on a special chair that had been constructed next to the Lord Chief Justice. Sir William, the plaintiff, accused his five accusers of slander.* During the trial, the Prince of Wales was called by Sir William as a witness and was examined and cross-examined about his role in the card game. This was enormously embarrassing for the royal family and led to much criticism of Bertie's errant ways in the press.† One suspects that is exactly what Sir William planned when making the charges.

At the end of the trial on 9 June the jury quickly found in favour of the defendants and what was left of Sir William's reputation was ruined, forcing him to leave the army. As the leader in *The Times* declared: 'A man who defrauds the friends whom he meets at the card table has forfeited his honour. He has committed a mortal offence; society can know him no more.'

---

*   For the record they were Mrs Arthur Wilson, Mr A. S. Wilson, Mr and Mrs Lycett Green and Mr Berkley Levett. *The Illustrated London News* (Saturday 20 June 1891) p.587.

†   In 2002 Princess Anne became the next member of the royal family to appear in court, this time for offences under the Dangerous Dogs Act.

DREYFUS

ALONG with the Vichy government and the scum of its Milice,* perhaps the biggest stain on French history, certainly in terms of a military scandal, was the Dreyfus Affair. The century which began with the triumph of Marengo ended with the acrimonious imprisonment of an innocent man by bigoted anti-Semites.

On 15 October 1894, Captain Alfred Dreyfus reported as ordered to the General Staff Headquarters in Paris. Also following orders, he was in civilian dress, which did not puzzle him unduly. When he arrived he was escorted to the office of the chief of staff, where he was met by the director of the Sûreté Cochefort and the staff major the Marquis du Paty de Clam. The latter spoke and told Dreyfus that the chief of staff, General Boisdeffre, would shortly be with them; in the meantime, he asked, would Dreyfus mind writing a letter for him as he had a bad finger. By now Dreyfus was starting to get suspicious. The room was filled with clerks; why ask him to write?

It was a cold autumn day and Dreyfus had been inside only a few minutes. When he picked up a pen his hand was shaking a little. 'Why, what is the matter with you?' asked du Paty de Clam. 'You're trembling!' Dreyfus explained his fingers were cold. When he

---

* The Milice was a fascist French paramilitary police set up during the Vichy era of 1940–44, when France was under Nazi occupation. Recruited from Frenchmen, the Milice (lit. militia) was probably more feared by the Resistance than the Gestapo.

resumed, his hand was steadier. A moment later du Paty de Clam stood up and boomed out: 'Captain Dreyfus. I arrest you in the name of the law. You are charged with high treason.' The Frenchman was dumbstruck. What did they mean?[48]

Dreyfus was suspected of being the author of an unsigned, handwritten list (*bordereau*) addressed to the German military attaché, Maximilian von Schwartzkoppen. The list, which betrayed secret information on French artillery, had been intercepted the previous month at the German embassy by a Frenchwoman employed as a cleaner in von Schwartzkoppen's office. On 11 October 1894, General Mercier, Minister of War, informed President Casimir-Perier that the guilty party had been found and that an arrest would follow. The trap set for the suspected man – i.e. Dreyfus – was to get him to unwittingly provide a handwriting sample that could be compared to the handwriting on the bordereau. That is why du Paty de Clam had made Dreyfus write the letter and why he had delighted in seeing Dreyfus shaking – a clear indication of guilt if ever there could be.

With Dreyfus safely locked up in the prison of Cherche-Midi, a case was now constructed to prove his guilt. Dreyfus was a native of Alsace. In 1872 when Alsace was ceded to the German Empire, the Dreyfus family moved to France, with the exception of his eldest brother Jacques, who remained behind in Mulhausen to run the family business. Alfred Dreyfus joined the École Polytechnique at the age of 19 and was commissioned into an artillery regiment in 1882. He was a brilliant officer and became the first Jewish officer promoted onto the Army General Staff in 1893 as a probationer. Rather than being a cause for celebration, it was these merits that marked Dreyfus for trouble: family ties to the German Empire with specialist artillery knowledge and access to sensitive staff information. Dreyfus was one of a handful of potential suspects to whom these credentials could apply – but Dreyfus was the only one who was Jewish and that is why the others were ignored.

If they had cared to look a little further they might easily have discovered the real villain of the piece, the intelligence officer Major Walsin-Esterhazy. Having got into debt, Esterhazy had resorted to treason and sold documents to von Schwartzkoppen. Key to the evidence was the special, distinctly thin paper on which the bordereau was written. It was not available in Paris, but Esterhazy used an identical type. His colleague Major Henry knew this, but kept quiet about it.

When the court martial began on 19 December 1894, the president, Colonel Maurel, announced that the debates would be held *in camera*, which led to protestations by Monsieur Demange, Dreyfus' counsel. However, there were still telling pieces of evidence that could have proved Dreyfus innocent. The fact that the author of the bordereau had mentioned going on manoeuvres when Dreyfus had been excused that year's manoeuvres was overlooked as an inconvenient irrelevance. The Bank of France and General Staff's own handwriting expert, Gobier, looked at Dreyfus' dictated letter and the bordereau, and in his assessment the handwriting did not match. However, Gobier was dismissed and replaced in the investigation by Alphonse Bertillon of the Sûreté. Bertillon gave technical reasons which revealed how Dreyfus had cleverly disguised his handwriting, which further confirmed his guilt! Even the prison director, Forzinetti, who had spent time with Dreyfus since his arrest concluded when asked: 'Dreyfus is as innocent as I am.' He was ignored.[49]

The killer blow in the trial was delivered by Henry who, without being asked to give any evidence or proof of his statement, revealed that someone had informed the service there had been a traitor among the officers since February. He theatrically declared: 'I assert that the traitor is there!' and pointed at Dreyfus.

When the judges retired to consider their verdict, there was a further irregularity when General Mercier passed to them several secret documents and a covering letter, none of which the defence were allowed to see. Unsurprisingly, on 22 December 1894 Alfred Dreyfus was found guilty of high treason. He was sentenced to deportation to a fortified prison and made to suffer the ignominy of being stripped of his rank before the Paris garrison. He arrived in South America on 12 March 1895 and was transferred to the prison on Devil's Island on 13 April. Sharing his cell with insects and poisonous spider crabs, Dreyfus must have realized very quickly how the penal colony earned its nickname: the Dry Guillotine.

J'ACCUSE!

FROM wrongful arrest to scandalous cover up, the second part of *l'Affaire Dreyfus* is equally shocking. On 1 July 1895 George Picquart became head of French intelligence. Through the usual means, he came into possession of a note, which had the usual secret call sign for von Schwartzkoppen and was addressed to Major Esterhazy. At first Picquart believed he had uncovered another case of treason, but slowly it dawned on him that Esterhazy was the author of the bordereau. Interestingly, every attempt he made to raise the Dreyfus case was met with a tidal wave of invective. He knew something was very badly wrong.

At the same time, Dreyfus' brother Mathieu kept his brother's flame burning in the public eye. Through the evidence of the handwriting on the infamous bordereau, Mathieu Dreyfus also came to the conclusion that Esterhazy was the guilty party. As a private citizen he could cut through certain formalities which were blocking Picquart's investigation. On 15 November 1897, Mathieu Dreyfus published an open letter to the Minister of War naming Esterhazy as the author of the bordereau.

Esterhazy demanded a court martial and was tried on 10–11 January 1898. Of course, he would not have done so if he did not think he would be protected and the trial was a sham. Esterhazy was exonerated of all charges. The only victim in the trial was Picquart. The intelligence chief had been asked to testify on

Esterhazy's behalf, but had refused to do so – he was after all convinced of Esterhazy's guilt. For refusing to aid his brother officer against the godless conspiracy of the Jewish Dreyfusards, Piquart was sent to North Africa for his sins.

On the same day that Picquart received this sentence, 13 January, the scandal went up a gear in intensity. The novelist Émile Zola published an open letter in *L'Aurore* to the French President, Félix Faure. Under the headline 'I ACCUSE!' the article laid the duplicity and bigotry of Dreyfus' accusers bare for all to see. It concluded with a series of condemnations – naming du Paty de Clam as the unconscious 'diabolical creator of this miscarriage of justice'. It also blamed the handwriting experts for making fraudulent reports, with the caveat 'unless a medical examination declares them to be suffering from a disease that impairs their eyesight and judgement'.[50] It really was explosive stuff.

On 14 January the affair really kicked off into full swing. France became divided into two camps: Dreyfusards and anti-Dreyfusards. In the face of a torrent of criticism, the antis came out fighting. On 23 February Zola was sentenced to a year in prison and fined 3,000 francs; the next day Picquart was dismissed from the army for 'grave faults'. Zola fled to England and Picquart, despite having been sacked, found himself under arrest on 13 July for illegally communicating official documents.

Although it seemed the anti-Dreyfusards had maintained the upper hand, the enormous scrutiny forced them into making a fatal mistake. If the bordereau was not considered strong enough evidence, they would fabricate some more. Picquart's successor, Hubert Henry, forged a note purporting to be from the Italian attaché to von Schwartzkoppen discussing Dreyfus. On 13 August this forgery was exposed and Henry was summoned to explain himself. He was arrested and killed himself. On 4 September Esterhazy fled to Belgium and from there went to England. And there – you would think – was the end of it. How wrong.

On 9 June 1899, Dreyfus was recalled from Devil's Island, for a retrial. The second trial began on 7 August. A pale-looking Dreyfus was put into a new uniform and sent once more into the lion's den. From the start it was clear that his innocence was by no means a foregone conclusion. As a mark of how unpopular Dreyfus was in many quarters, seven days into the trial someone 'unknown' shot and severely wounded his defence council, Fernand Labori, on his way to the court-room in Rennes.

On 9 September 1899 Dreyfus was found guilty by a vote of five to two. He was condemned to ten years' deportation.

Fortunately common sense prevailed: the French President pardoned Dreyfus on 19 September. Although a free man, he was still burdened with dishonour and spent the next six years trying to reclaim his position in the army. In 1906 he was reinstated with full honours and awarded the *Légion d'honneur* as a mark of respect. Also in 1906 Picquart was made Minister of War in recognition of his moral courage and integrity.

Zola's letter to the press, J'Accuse. (Topham Picturepoint)

MISERY IN THE CAMPS

A FTER his campaign in the Sudan, Kitchener was instrumental in one of the most unsavoury actions of the Pax Britannica period. The Anglo-Boer War had broken out in 1899 and had by 1901 descended into a guerrilla war. Lord Kitchener advocated a scorched earth policy to prevent Boer guerrillas receiving subsistence from their farms – in effect he wanted to starve them out. In addition to burning 30,000 farmhouses, the British removed or butchered livestock and destroyed crops. Most controversially, from the beginning of 1901 they began rounding up somewhere in the region of 120,000 Boers – mostly women and children – who were put into concentration camps dotted along the main railway lines.

The British concentration camps are infamous. They were overcrowded and rations were either insufficient or unsuitable for the many children in custody. Those families who had men fighting with the Boers were refused meat in their rations and the otherwise poor diet led to diseases like measles, typhoid and dysentery among the children.

The plight of the concentration camp victims was highlighted by Emily Hobhouse, a delegate of the South African Women and Children's Distress Fund. She circulated a report on the conditions to MPs, as a result of which the Fawcett Commission was sent to South Africa between August and December 1901. This commission visited most of the camps and found that those in the Orange Free

State and Transvaal were appalling. The mortality rates in the camps were high in the extreme. Although the deaths were caused more out of incompetence and neglect than deliberate extermination, over 26,000 Boers died in them – around 80 per cent of them children.

A French perspective of the war in L'Assiette au Beurre *in 1901, commenting on the silence surrounding the concentration camps in the Transvaal.*
(Mary Evans Picture Library)

Not that this appeared to cause Kitchener to lose much sleep. He actually had Hobhouse arrested as a security risk on her second trip to South Africa in December 1901.

Of apparently less concern at the time, but scandalous nonetheless, there were also concentration camps for native Africans. Between the Orange Free State and the Transvaal there were over 50,000 Africans in British camps – about 6 per cent of the African population. In the African camps at least another 14,000 perished through want and neglect.[51]

Putting both figures together, the British had interned 170,000 people, about one in four of whom died in less than two years. No wonder the European press accused Britain of waging a war of extermination.[52]

As if the camps were not bad enough, Kitchener caused complete outrage in the Boer community not only by recruiting large numbers of native Africans into the British Army, but by giving them weapons. For the Boers, this was too much. They thought the war should remain one between white people. When black soldiers were captured they were shot out of hand. After the end of the war in 1902 it was said the arming of black soldiers was one of the causes of friction that eventually led to the apartheid system in the country. Not that this would have caused Kitchener to lose much sleep either.

Kitchener returned to Britain a conquering hero and was awarded £50,000 by a grateful country. In South Africa, more than a century on, he is remembered for the evil of his camps. Among the outrages committed, it is said that he ordered powdered glass to be sprinkled into the sugar given to inmates and that he had fish hooks hidden in the tins of bully beef. True or not, they help explain the widely held belief that Kitchener's management of the war is one of the darkest stains on British colonial history.

COMPROMISED POSITIONS

HAVING fought with Kitchener at Omdurman and in the South African War, General Hector 'Fighting Mac' Macdonald was ordered to Ceylon (Sri Lanka) in 1902 as commander of the forces there. Shortly after his arrival a Ceylon newspaper printed an anonymous letter which insinuated that Macdonald was a practising homosexual and had relationships with local boys. More accusations followed and, amid angry protests, the Governor of Ceylon, Sir J. West Ridgeway, confronted Macdonald with the accusations and warned him he faced a court martial if he remained in Ceylon. Macdonald left Ceylon and went to consult with King Edward VII.

Unfortunately for Macdonald, true or not, the stigma attached to the charges was devastatingly bad. To put the scandal into some sort of context, the playwright Oscar Wilde had only recently finished serving his prison sentence for 'gross indecency' – a euphemism for homosexual acts. The Wilde case was the most high-profile of its kind since the trial of Captain Jones in 1772.

Unimpressed with Macdonald's petition, the king sent the soldier back to Ceylon to face the music. While travelling back to his post and an inevitable court martial, he stopped in Paris and checked into the aptly named Hotel Regina. One morning, coming down to breakfast Macdonald saw a headline in the *New York Times*: 'GRAVE CHARGE LIES ON SIR H. MACDONALD'. Realizing that the scandal had reached the international press, the soldier went up to his room and shot himself in the head with a revolver.*

Around the same time in Germany there were an unprecedented number of embarrassing scandals involving the 'outing' of figures associated with the military. The first of these high-profile scalps was the arms manufacturer Friedrich Krupp. Reputedly the richest man in Germany at the beginning of the 20th century, the industrialist spent much of his time at Capri, where he is supposed to have engaged in homosexual acts with local 'mandolinists and street Arabs'.[53] There were lurid tales of orgies with young boys in fantastically decorated grottos pandering to every deviancy. Stupidly, there was also a photographer whose wares found their way into the hands of the local police force.

Rumours were one thing, but photographic evidence had to be acted on. Krupp was told to leave the island and the story was reported in Italian newspapers. On 8 November the conservative Catholic *Augsburger Postzeitung* newspaper was the first to run the story in Germany. Shortly afterwards, Krupp's wife Margarethe received anonymous letters referring to the breaking scandal. Understandably upset by the revelations, she went to speak with Kaiser Wilhelm II about the matter. When Krupp returned from Capri he had his wife sent to a mental hospital in Jena to keep her out of the way until things blew over.

Instead the scandal blew up into a storm. On 15 November 1902 the Social Democrat newspaper *Vorwärts* took up the story and ran an article entitled 'Krupp auf Capri' which focused on his illicit activities. Because of the political affiliations of the newspaper, the

---

* It is thought that the story was a slander set up by Ridgeway to rid himself of Macdonald and that it was the governor who leaked the story to the *New York Times*.

article was met with a wave of public indignation. The newspaper was sued and all available copies of the article were seized.

On 21 November the physicians 'looking after' Margarethe went to consult with her husband at the Krupp family residence near Essen. From this point on things become muddled, except to say that the following morning Krupp was found dead. The attending physicians recorded that he had suffered a fatal stroke, but no autopsy took place, which immediately led to rumours of suicide. In the fallout the Kaiser was quick to close ranks; he attended the funeral and the action against *Vorwärts* was withdrawn. Margarethe was suddenly found restored to sanity by her husband's demise and was released, with the family business passing onto his daughter Bertha.*

Unknown to the public at the time, Krupp had not confined his activities to Capri. His name had appeared on a secret dossier held by the Berlin criminal police of known homosexual blackmail cases among prominent Berlin residents. It seems that Krupp had procured work for a number of lads from Capri who worked as waiters in the Hotel Bristol, where he resided when in Berlin. Police investigating the extent of Berlin's underground homosexual scene took in a footman from the hotel for questioning. When they asked him where he got such an expensive diamond ring, the footman revealed it had been given to him by Krupp because 'Fritz was my friend'.[54]

Elsewhere in 1902, few eyebrows were raised by the resignation of Imperial Germany's ambassador to Austria-Hungary. Prince

---

* In 1906 Bertha married Gustav von Bohlen und Halbach, who took control of the company and asked the Kaiser's permission to take his wife's name – becoming Gustav Krupp. It is popularly believed the legendary 'Dicke Bertha' (Big Bertha) howitzer was named after Bertha Krupp. From surviving photographs of Mrs Krupp it would appear that any physical comparisons between her and the 43-ton monster siege gun are entirely unwarranted.

Eulenberg had become one of the Kaiser's closest confidents and was a calming influence on his sometimes unpredictable, stormy nature. It was Eulenberg who had convinced the Kaiser to assume personal rule and not to be troubled by the pronouncements of the Reichstag. Eulenberg also ran a hunting club at his family estate which Wilhelm II was known to attend once a year. The members of this close coterie became known by its opponents as the 'Table Circle'. Eulenberg's closest associate in the clique was Count Kuno von Moltke – the military commander of Berlin. Von Moltke was suspected of being homosexual after not contesting his wife's evidence when she divorced him.

In 1900, Eulenberg's brother had been exposed as a homosexual and there were those who sought to tar Eulenberg with the same brush. Chief among these was the newspaper editor, Maximilian Harden. In 1892 Harden had created the *Die Zukunft* ('The Future') weekly paper. Harden was never one to shy from speaking his mind, and articles published in *Die Zukunft* twice put him in prison. Such notoriety only served to increase his newspaper's circulation and make Harden an extremely popular read.

Much of Harden's information seems to have been provided by the old Iron Chancellor, Bismarck, who had fallen out of favour with the Kaiser and been obliged to offer his resignation in 1890. Bismarck was understandably upset and revenged himself on the Kaiser's new advisors. Asking Harden to visit him in 1892, Bismarck hinted that some of the closest advisors round the throne were secret homosexuals – chief among them Eulenburg.[55] When the Krupp scandal broke in 1902, Eulenberg must have feared being exposed and so resigned as ambassador citing exhaustion. Some suspect that Eulenberg had been blackmailed by Harden into resigning.

Eulenberg came back into the political picture in 1906, just at the moment when a number of high-profile outings were about to take place. Count Fritz Hohenau of the diplomatic service was blackmailed by a jockey with whom he had been intimate. Desperate, the count went to Commissioner Hans von Tresckow

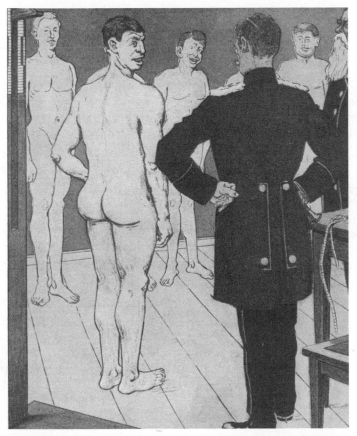

'Attention', a caricature commenting on the alleged homosexuality in the Prussian Garde du Corps, from around 1907, Wahr Jacob. (akg-images)

of the Kriminalpolizei in Berlin and, because the police kept photographs of suspected homosexual blackmailers on record, he was able to identify the jockey and have him arrested. Unfortunately the story found its way into the press and the count was forced to resign from the diplomatic service and retire to Italy.

The count's brother was an aide-de-camp to the Kaiser and commander of the Cuirassier Guards. According to von Tresckow, Hohenau's brother had similar tastes but was even more imprudent in his liaisons, taking advantage of his position to coerce subordinates into improper relationships.

Apparently homosexuality was rife in the regiments posted in Berlin and Potsdam, particularly in the beautifully turned-out cavalry regiments. Von Tresckow complained in his diary that the commanders of the Berlin and Potsdam Guard Regiments came almost daily to seek his advice about the prevalent pederasty among the soldiers. He in turn complained to the military authorities that the conduct of soldiers in some quarters, including the Tiergarten, amounted to their behaving like prostitutes for the pleasure of the cultured classes. When the Minister of the Interior was propositioned by a soldier, von Tresckow sent plain clothes policemen to patrol the districts for soldiers behaving improperly. The agents' reports on the soldiers were so outrageous that von Tresckow had to raise the subject with General von Kessel.[56]

Scenting blood, Max Harden ran a story in November 1906 with codenames for the principal characters, including 'the Harpist' (Eulenberg), 'Sweetie' (von Moltke) and 'Darling' (the Kaiser). His biggest beef was a homophobic assumption that Wilhelm II was pursuing a tame approach to international politics as a result of homosexual advice. A few months later in February 1907 Harden was more explicit and linked the names of von

Moltke and 'Phili' (Eulenberg) with the disgraced Hohenau. By associating Eulenberg and von Moltke with Hohenau, Harden was clearly 'outing' them. Von Moltke offered Harden out for a duel – but the journalist declined.

Instead von Moltke brought a libel suit against Harden, who called von Moltke's ex-wife as a witness. This proved a trump card for Harden as the former Frau von Moltke testified that her former husband and Eulenberg had engaged in an amorous relationship.[57] Harden was found innocent of libel, which established that von Moltke was in fact homosexual. However, through a technicality, there was a retrial in which Harden's witnesses were discredited. In December 1907, Harden was found guilty and given a four-month sentence.

In June 1908 Eulenberg went to court and was embarrassed when ten witnesses described watching through a keyhole as Eulenberg performed indecent acts. The trial was quickly halted as Eulenberg fell ill and was confined to a hospital bed. It never resumed.

The Kaiser distanced himself from the so-called Table Circle and took new advisors, who were a little more bull-headed and who ultimately talked him into fighting the First World War.* But if there were any lingering doubts about the prevalence of homosexuality in his army these were dispelled during a trip to Bavaria in 1908. One evening, the head of the military secretariat, Dietrich Graf von Hülsen-Haeseler, appeared before the assembled personages dressed as a ballerina, started dancing and then dropped dead in front of the Kaiser. Unfortunately the exact details do not appear to have been recorded and that was one scandal that remained very definitely hushed up.[58]

---

* Harden's victory in breaking up the Table Circle is cited by some as one of the causes of the First World War. Had Eulenberg and co. prevailed with their more diplomatic approach perhaps war would have been averted. By the time Harden realized his mistake millions were dead.

THE PASSION OF COLONEL REDL

THINGS were certainly very bad for the Kaiser, but spare a thought also to the poor Austrian emperor who suffered similar problems of his own. On 24 May 1913 Colonel Alfred Redl – until recently the head of Austrian army intelligence – undressed and stood naked before the mirror in his quarters, put a pistol to his head and fired. He left behind a note to his brother which read:

> Levity and passion have destroyed me.
> Pray for me.
> I pay with my life for my sins.
> Alfred. 1:15 A.M.
>
> I will die now. Please do not permit a post-mortem examination.
> Pray for me.

To understand this cryptic note one should understand that Redl had been blackmailed into spying for the Russian secret police after they had discovered his homosexuality. Clearly it was not an ideal situation for Austria's intelligence chief to be in – but what could he do? The Russians expertly pandered to Redl's exotic tastes and were rewarded with copies of Austria's military plans on the eve of the war. He also reported to the Russians the conversations he had with Walter Nicolai, his opposite number in Germany.

His undoing came after he was promoted in 1912 to chief of staff to General Giesl in Prague. Redl was replaced by Captain

Maximilian Ronge, who quickly introduced a new form of secret postal censorship with a special focus on mail coming from the frontiers. On 2 March 1913 two packages were opened filled to the brim with cash. Ronge was very eager to meet the person who came to collect the money, never in a million years expecting it to be Redl.

Ronge and three officers went to Redl's room in the Hotel Klomser and confronted the former secret service chief. Ronge asked Redl how far his betrayal had gone – Redl replied that everything would be found in his Prague home. Redl then asked for a revolver.

Ronge allowed the traitor a soldier's way out. He put a revolver down on his desk and left him to his own devices. The four men went for a coffee, sending a detective every half hour to check on him. It was not until 5am that the detective found Redl's naked body in front of the mirror. Next morning the full extent of Redl's activities became clear. His Prague residence was searched, revealing large amounts of cash, expensive champagne and secret correspondence with his Russian handlers.

Initially the scandal was kept under wraps for the sake of Emperor Franz Joseph, but a porter at the Hotel Klomser and the locksmith who helped break into Redl's residence both spoke to the press. When the news of the scandal broke, there was an understandable amount of anger, not just at Redl's treachery, but the manner of his death. By giving him a pistol Ronge had allowed him to take the easy way out and denied the authorities a chance properly to interrogate him.[59]

THE ZABERN AFFAIR

ALTHOUGH Alsace-Lorraine had been annexed by Imperial Germany in 1871, on the eve of the First World War the majority of the population still had family and patriotic ties to France. It would probably be exaggerating to say that Germany tiptoed round the sensibilities of the population, but it was careful not to provoke anger directly – at least not until the Zabern Affair of late 1913.

Serving in the 99th Infantry Regiment in garrison at Zabern (Saverne in French) was a certain Lieutenant Günter von Forstner. One day, this Prussian-born officer was instructing local recruits in what to do in case of civil unrest. During the session he commented on how a Prussian soldier had been imprisoned for two months for striking an Alsatian. He apparently told his recruits: 'Ach! I would not have punished you for doing this. On the contrary, for every one of these dirty *Wackes* whom you strike, I will give you 10 marks.'[60]

Not only was this statement provocative – it was against Prussian army regulations to offer a cash incentive for assaulting civilians – it was directed at young, native Alsatian recruits who were also highly insulted by the use of the derogatory term *Wackes*. According to the serving American ambassador to Germany, James Gerard, *Wackes* was a term used among the people of Alsace which translated to something like 'square-head', though it is given by some French sources to mean *voyou* – lout or rascal. Regardless of the nuance, to hear it come from the lips of a Prussian was extremely insulting.[61]

On 6 November the story was carried by two local Alsatian newspapers and caused quite a scandal. The day after it was published a mob appeared outside the window of von Forstner's ground-floor apartment shouting, among other things – 'dirty Prussian!' Over the next 24 hours the unrest spread and von Forstner's colonel found himself confronted with an angry crowd outside a tavern. Making reference to his small grey moustache and large ears they shouted 'grey haired rabbit! – we're not *Wackes*!' On the 9th, the garrison barracks were under a state of virtual siege as a crowd of up to a thousand again went to von Forstner's apartment. The local fire brigade was called out and ordered to turn its hoses on the crowd, which did little to dampen the excitement. In fact the arrival of the local *pompiers* was said to have added a sense of carnival around the place and caused much hilarity.

By now the Zabern Affair was beginning to attract the attentions of journalists from Paris, Berlin and London. What had begun as a local grievance quickly escalated into an international debate about the Alsace-Lorraine issue. More urgently it became the subject of debate in the German Reichstag. There had been many instances in Germany of harsh treatment of civilians by officers, which caused antagonism against the whole Prussian military system. The Zabern Affair caused a great outcry against militarism, even in quarters where no socialist tendencies existed.

A week after the affair had sparked into life, von Forstner was at it again. On 15 November one of the local newspapers reported that the young Prussian officer had been overheard telling his men: 'For my part, I authorize you to shit on the French flag.' More unrest followed, until the evening of 28 November when the Germans decided to take control. Colonel von Reuter ordered Lieutenant Schad to set up machine guns and seize protestors. Unfortunately, among those snatched were the President, two judges and the State Attorney of the Zabern Supreme Court, all of whom had got mixed up in the mob after leaving the court building. Their arrest added to the perceived incompetence of the garrison and its commander.

Von Reuter and Schad were themselves arrested and faced a court martial for ordering troops to move against the civilian population. They were subsequently acquitted on the ground that they had acted under the provisions of an 1820 law which allowed garrison commanders to take control in the event of civil unrest. The use of the word *Wackes* was forbidden in military areas, and was not to be used by German troops to describe Alsatians in any circumstance.

One might have thought von Forstner – the man who started the affair – had learned a lesson from all this. Quite the opposite in fact, the real scandal was yet to occur.

While conducting field manoeuvres outside Zabern, von Forstner got into an argument with a lame shoemaker and struck the man with his sword. This act of brutality put the Prussian before a court martial. He was initially sentenced to a year in prison, but was let off on appeal, pleading he had acted in self defence!

Three centre-left political parties raised the issue of this occurrence at Zabern in a debate in the Reichstag, from 4 to 6 December 1913. They were outraged when the War Minister, von Falkenhayn, barked at them that von Forstner was the kind of courageous young officer the country needed and that the military was not about to take notice of irresponsible murmurings by members of the press and other 'hysterical individuals'. In response a motion of censure against the government was debated – for the first time in the history of the German Empire.

The following day the German Chancellor announced that the Kaiser had removed the 99th regiment from Zabern.[62]

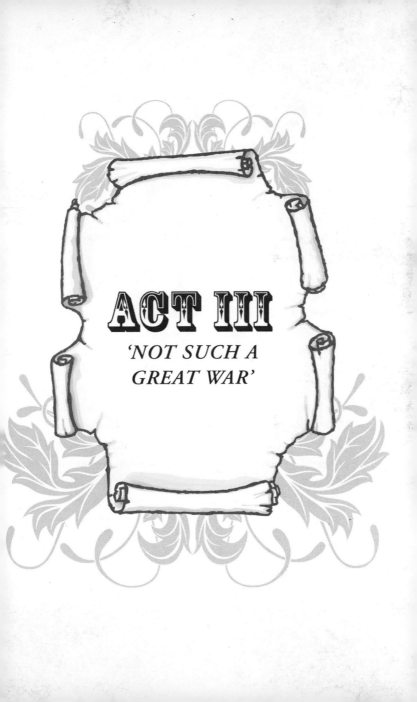

ACT III

'NOT SUCH A GREAT WAR'

THE WRONG TROUSERS

THROUGHOUT history, uniforms have served a double purpose. As well as identifying legitimate combatants, uniforms have been a mark of prestige, empowering the individual with greater height, broader shoulders and an ego to match.

Until the age of smokeless gunpowder and the proliferation of rifled weapons, it did not matter a hoot what garish combinations were worn onto a battlefield. The chance of an individual being deliberately hit by an aimed shot at anything more than a hundred yards was remote in the extreme. Even when fighting at close quarters, within a few volleys the battlefield would be engulfed in so much gunpowder smoke that combatants were lucky if they could see more than a few yards in any direction.

During the 19th century technology began to quickly outpace attitudes to warfare and fighting. As Confederate soldiers at Gettysburg learned to their cost, Napoleonic-style massed infantry assaults were a thing of the past. Even the conservative British read the writing on the wall and had ditched their famous red coats for a khaki service dress by 1900. This neutral shade made them much less conspicuous on the battlefield. In 1910 Prussian Blue gave way to feldgrau in the Kaiser's army, a shift echoed by the armies of Russia, Austria-Hungary, Turkey, Serbia, Bulgaria and Japan, all of whom adopted more neutral colours and reserved brightly coloured cloth for peacetime parades.

Noting these changes, in 1911 the French Minister of War, Adolphe Messimy, announced France would follow suit with a modern, neutral-coloured uniform. There was total uproar. Since 1829 the French Army had worn blue coats and brilliant red trousers. The new uniforms Messimy proposed looked, to put it bluntly, too German, and the French were not going to tolerate this – the proposal was an affront to everything they believed in.

This might seem preposterous now, but at the time the former Minister of War, Eugène Étienne, publicly announced: 'Abolish red trousers? Never. France is red trousers!'

French uniforms were a product of their military doctrine: Frenchmen attacked. They did not hold on, or defend; they took the offensive and were irresistible when doing so. Although the French Army had been divided over Dreyfus, the recovery of Alsace-Lorraine and revenge for defeat by Prussia in 1870 took on a sort of religious fervour. A strategy of assault took shape, culminating in Plan XVII – a French drive through the Ardennes into the heart of Germany and on

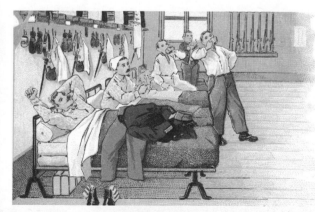

A pre-First World War postcard shows French soldiers in the barrack-room. (Roger-Viollet/Topfoto)

to Berlin.* This attack would be irresistible, because the French nation had willed it so – it was as if a mass hypnosis had occurred. In 1913 a new field regulation went as far as to state: 'The French Army, returning to its traditions, henceforth admits no law but the offensive.'[63] The mania was so ingrained that the army even rejected the adoption of heavy artillery as a defensive, and therefore defeatist, measure.

This was the same insanity that wanted to arm soldiers in the French Revolution with pikes rather than muskets. In the hundred years since Waterloo, the myth had grown that French soldiers under Napoleon had conquered Europe at the point of the bayonet. In reality, the lesson of the Napoleonic Wars had been completely missed: fire power delivered by steady troops would blow the head off an advancing body of troops, no matter how patriotic they were. If the French had failed to break through the British muskets at Waterloo, what chance would they have breaking through German barbed-wire entanglements and machine-gun nests a century later?† The answer was of course a foregone conclusion and Messimy's worst fears were realized in August 1914 when thousands of red-trousered Frenchmen and white-gloved officers in full dress and plumes were martyred by German machine guns. Only then was a new uniform introduced.

---

* Plan XVII predicted that the Germans would respect Belgian neutrality and thus assumed that the French could concentrate the bulk of their forces for offensive operations. Incredibly, almost the same thing happened in the Second World War, when the construction of the infamous Maginot Line stopped at the Belgian border, rather than contining to the coast.

† In all fairness, the British commander, Sir John French, went to war convinced that cavalry would play a decisive role in the conflict and that they should be armed principally with swords rather than firearms. See Robin Neilland, *The Great War Generals on the Western Front* (London: Robinson, 1999), p.59.

THE SHELL SCANDAL

O N 10 March 1915 the British began their first major offensive of the Great War at Neuve Chapelle. After initial success the attack was halted on 13 March. Despite an enormous artillery bombardment, the advancing soldiers had found that German barbed wire had not been cut sufficiently for them to break through. Perhaps more crucially there had been difficulties with communication as German shells cut the wires of British field telephones.

On the other hand, the British commander, Sir John French, confided to the *Times* war correspondent, Charles Repington, that the failure of the offensive was entirely due to a lack of artillery shells provided by the government. If only he had been given enough high-explosive shells the offensive would have been a success.

Sniffing a scandal in the making, Repington reported French's remarks back to London and, on 14 May 1915, *The Times* ran with this story, which laid the blame squarely at the door of Prime Minister Asquith's Liberal government.* The ensuing crisis became known as the 'Shell Scandal' and brought down Asquith's government nine days later.

Probably the biggest casualty of the whole affair was our old friend Lord Kitchener, who was then Minister for War. The Liberal

---

* Repington knew all about scandals. He had been an officer in the British Army but had been forced to resign after it was revealed at a divorce hearing that he had been having an affair.

MP David Lloyd George thought that Kitchener was incapable of overhauling the production of the munitions industry and so encouraged Lord Northcliffe, owner of *The Times* and the *Daily Mail*, to blame the old soldier for the mess. The stunt nearly backfired on Lloyd George because public opinion was behind Kitchener, who was extremely popular in the country at large. Circulation of Northcliffe's papers plummeted.

In fairness, Kitchener had already identified the munitions shortage and complained that Britain went into the war entirely unfit for a major European conflict. In comparison with the armies of France and Germany the British Expeditionary Force was tiny and went to war with just 200 rifle rounds per man.

The problem was that the autocratic Kitchener was ill suited for cabinet politics, where matters had to be discussed, and had little idea of collective cabinet responsibility. He was used to giving commands and seeing them obeyed. This put him at odds with his civilian counterparts.*

Under the new coalition government, Asquith remained Prime Minister and Kitchener Minister for War. However a new post was created for Lloyd George as Minister of Munitions and all production was taken out of Kitchener's hands.

---

* The Duke of Wellington had a similar problem when Prime Minister. He said of his first cabinet meeting: 'An extraordinary affair. I gave them their orders and they wanted to stay and discuss them.' From 10 Downing Street website: www.pm.gov.uk.

THE *LUSITANIA* MEDAL

PERHAPS the most infamous event of the First World War was the 1915 torpedoing of the Blue Riband-winning liner, *Lusitania*. Its sinking provoked a wave of anti-Hun hysteria in Britain and America and was the first of three events which had a bearing on drawing the United States into the war. It also provoked some interesting counterclaims from inside Germany, which accused the British of foul play and cover up.

The *Lusitania* set out from New York on 1 May 1915, carrying 1,257 passengers. At the time Germany had a policy of unrestricted warfare against shipping destined for Britain – even those flying a neutral flag – and a warning not to travel on the liner was issued by the German embassy:

NOTICE!

TRAVELLERS intending to embark on the Atlantic voyage are reminded that a state of war exists between Germany and her allies and Great Britain and her allies; that the zone of war includes the waters adjacent to the British Isles; that, in accordance with formal notice given by the Imperial German Government, vessels flying the flag of Great Britain or any of her allies, are liable to destruction in those waters and that travellers sailing in the war zone on ships of Great Britain or her allies do so at their own risk.

IMPERIAL GERMAN EMBASSY
WASHINGTON DC APRIL 22 1915

Unfortunately for all concerned, this notice was kept out of the newspapers and not posted until the day of departure, by which time most either did not see it, or had already paid for their tickets.

On Friday 7 May, the *Lusitania* was spotted off the Irish coast by a German submarine. Without issuing any warning, the commander of the U20, Walther Schwieger, ordered a single torpedo to be fired at the liner, which struck beneath the bridge of the ship.

In itself, this torpedo was probably not enough to send the vessel to the bottom as precautions had been taken, including the sealing of bulkhead doors. But a moment after the first strike the passengers and crew felt a second, bigger explosion rip a hole in the starboard side of the liner, which began to list heavily. Just 18 minutes later, the *Lusitania* was gone, taking 1,198 souls to the bottom, 128 neutral American citizens among them.

Naturally enough there was outrage at the sinking of the passenger ship and in particular the deaths of the American citizens. Britain thought America should go to war with Germany over the affair, but President Wilson did not want to be dragged into the European conflict and felt that a formal protest was sufficient. The Germans put out a claim that the second explosion on the *Lusitania* was caused by the first torpedo striking war munitions secretly and illegally stowed on board. They even insinuated that the British had sunk the ship themselves in order to drag America into the war.

The sense of outrage was accentuated in August 1915 by the production of the *Lusitania* medallion by Karl Goetz, a Munich medal producer. Goetz blamed the British government and Cunard for allowing the *Lusitania* to sail despite the warnings of the German embassy. Unfortunately, Goetz made a mistake with the medal, putting the date of the sinking as 5 May rather than the 7th. British intelligence seized on this and claimed that it implied advanced planning of the attack – that the fate of the *Lusitania* had been planned before its departure from New York. The Director of Naval Intelligence, Sir Reginald 'Blinker' Hall, ordered 300,000 copies of the medal to be produced in Britain, which were then distributed far and wide to neutral countries, showing how the Germans were 'celebrating' the death of so many innocents. At a time when the Kaiser was keen not to drag America into the conflict, it was a public relations disaster for Germany.

A cartoon showing the announcement of the departure of the Lusitania, *and the warning issued by the Imperial German Embassy. (Topham Picturepoint)*

A MARTYRED NURSE

ABOUT the same time that Karl Goetz was tinkering with his tools in Munich, the second in our trilogy of German outrages was playing itself out in occupied Belgium. The Kaiser's armies had already done enough for them to be demonized as a barbarian horde, but, coming as it did in the wake of the *Lusitania*, the following outrage really did seem to set the Germans apart as the true descendants of Attila.*

Edith Cavell was a British nurse who had worked in Brussels since 1907. When Belgium was overrun by the German Army in 1914, Cavell stayed behind and in addition to her work caring for wounded soldiers, became the head of an escape network, which smuggled Allied soldiers into neutral Holland. Recuperated British, French and Belgian soldiers were provided with papers and false passports which allowed them to elude capture.

In addition to this, though strenuously denied at the time, Cavell was also working for British intelligence, supplying data on German forces. It was through the arrest of two sub-agents that the Germans learned of Cavell's secret activities and arrested her in August 1915.

Despite the intervention of neutral American and Vatican diplomats, Cavell was put on trial on 7 October charged with having

---

* Factually speaking the true descendants of Attila are the Hungarians. However, the spiked German *Pickelhaube* was said to resemble the spiked helmets of the Huns, hence the derogatory British usage.

assisted in the escape of Allied troops. She pleaded guilty to the charge, freely admitting that she knew she had done wrong, but that she was proud to have served her country. On 11 October she was sentenced to death by firing squad. A British padre visited her on the eve of her execution and heard her deliver the immortal lines: 'Standing, as I do, in the view of God and eternity, I realize that patriotism is not enough. I must have no hatred or bitterness towards anyone.'

In the early hours of the morning after she received her verdict, soldiers arrived and took her to the place of execution. She was

Raemaekers cartoon on the death of Edith Cavell. (TopFoto)

loosely bound and blindfolded and given the services of a clergyman. The German soldiers had been given special instructions not to aim wide because their target was a woman and were reassured that the 49-year-old Cavell was not a mother. The eight men discharged their rifles from six paces and all found the mark. A witness examining her body declared that death had been instantaneous as the exit wounds were the size of fists and one bullet had struck her on the forehead. This did not prevent rumours that the soldiers had refused to fire and that an officer had been forced to finish the job with a pistol. It is also rumoured that one soldier was shot dead alongside her for throwing down his rifle.

The death of this patriotic woman was used for maximum propaganda value around the world. A statue of her was put up near Trafalgar Square. Miss Cavell was portrayed as an innocent nurse shot on trumped-up charges of espionage.

Again the Germans were quick to justify their actions, although they must have realized that they had committed a serious mistake. The German Secretary for Foreign Affairs, Artur Zimmermann, agreed that it was a terrible thing for a woman to be executed, but argued that a state in wartime could not be expected to allow crimes to go unpunished just because the perpetrator was female. He complained that the British and American press were guilty of sensationalism. He pointed out that the Germans had taken a number of female soldiers in Russian uniform prisoner – if they had been killed in combat, would the world have accused the Germans of barbarity against women? Edith Cavell knowingly exposed herself to the dangers and was therefore a legitimate casualty of war. It may have been a well-reasoned defence, but it certainly did the German cause no favours and served as a rallying cry for Allied recruiters.[64]

THE MEXICAN CONNECTION

THE last in this mini-series of self-inflicted Teutonic disasters is the notorious Zimmermann Telegram. Fresh from justifying the execution of Edith Cavell, Foreign Minister Zimmermann hatched his latest brainchild on an unsuspecting world. It was brilliant. To prevent America from entering the war on the side of the Allies he would ensure they were kept busy elsewhere by asking Mexico to invade the United States!

On 16 January 1917 he sent a coded telegram to the German ambassador in Mexico, Heinrich von Ecklardt, with the terms of a deal: Germany was about to restart unrestricted submarine warfare – it had previously stopped this tactic in the wake of the *Lusitania* episode. If America declared war, Germany offered Mexico a military alliance with generous financial support and the understanding that Mexico would regain its lost territories of Texas, New Mexico and Arizona.[65]

At the time the telegram was composed, Germany and America were actually in the middle of peace discussions. Because of this, President Wilson invited the Germans to use the American diplomatic cable for communications between Berlin and the German embassy in Washington. Zimmermann took advantage of this to send his telegram to Mexico via Washington. It was duplicitous, but he was not alone in such shenanigans. Unknown to Zimmermann and the Americans, the dastardly but hugely effective British secret services were secretly monitoring the American diplomatic cable. When they broke the German cipher the contents of the Zimmermann Telegram were explosive enough to at last shake Wilson off the fence and into joining the war.

The only trouble the British had was in proving the authenticity of the document. They could hardly turn round and admit spying on their potential ally – such a breach of trust would be disastrous. Instead they targeted the method used by the German embassy in Washington to retransmit the telegram to Mexico. British intelligence guessed that the German embassy would use a commercial telegraph company to retransmit the message.

They were correct – the telegram had been sent through Western Union. Better still, a copy of the telegram was kept by Western Union and this was obtained by a British agent in Mexico. The British could now go to the Americans and explain that one of their agents had found this incriminating telegram in Mexico without revealing the true means of obtaining it.

On 23 February the British Foreign Minister delivered a decoded version of the telegram to the US embassy in London. Two days later it was on the desk of President Woodrow Wilson. After some deliberation, Wilson gave the telegram to the press on 1 March. The result was quite unexpected.

At the time Mexico was about as popular in the United States as it had been in Davy Crockett's time. The revolutionary general Pancho Villa had raided New Mexico the previous year and provoked a US punitive expedition under General Pershing, which had only been withdrawn in January 1917. Nor were the Germans flavour of the month, with the *Lusitania* sinking still fresh in the memory. But, inexplicably, so strong was the average American's aversion to fighting a war in the Old World, that the Zimmermann

Telegram was believed to be a hoax – a set-up job by the perfidious Brits, which, in some respects, was true.

However, lady luck was with the British Empire again. Just as the impact of the telegram was in danger of fizzling out, its author made an extraordinary intervention. Artur Zimmermann came out and told the world that the telegram was real. As he had done with the shooting of Edith Cavell, Zimmermann then tried to defend the indefensible. He attempted to justify his tactics by saying they were only to be carried out *if* America declared war on Germany first. In plain terms, he dug a hole for himself and, although the hole began to fill with water, he did not stop digging.

Wilson reacted by asking Congress to arm American merchant shipping; then, on 2 April 1917, he asked Congress to declare war on Germany. It did so on 6 April. Zimmermann held on to his position until that August when he resigned.

As a postscript to the affair, it was Zimmermann's idea to allow Lenin to travel back to Russia in 1917 to bring about a coup which would take Russia out of the war. To this end Zimmermann's plans were all too effective and thus began almost eight decades of totalitarian Soviet repression.

WITH 'SNOW' ON THEIR BOOTS

O NE of those foolish wartime rumours circulated around England in 1914, that Russian soldiers had landed in Scotland 'with snow on their boots' and were heading south to join the British in the field against the Huns. In keeping with this well-known Great War bedtime story, we present this tale of foreign soldiers arriving in Britain – but with a very different white powdery substance ... cocaine.

Anyone thinking that drug abuse among soldiers started during the Vietnam War should think again – the soldiers of the First World War had their own stories about 'Charlie' too.*

It is commonly believed the recreational use of cocaine was introduced to Britain by Canadian soldiers arriving during the First World War. Canadian soldiers were said to have picked up the habit from visiting the United States, in particular New York, where the use of the drug was already well established. Although the drug was available in Britain the habit does appear to have been restricted mainly to prostitutes, introduced to it by overseas servicemen.

When word about the drug started to circulate, there was a terrible sense of shock in the British press. *The Times* ran the headline: 'THE COCAINE HABIT – A SOLDIER'S TEMPTATION'. According to the article, the drug had come from India and was smuggled to

---

* There is strong evidence that Napoleon's soldiers first introduced the habit of hashish abuse to the West following his 1798 Egyptian Expedition. See the author's *French Soldier in Egypt* (Oxford: Osprey Publishing, 2003).

Britain by enemy Austrian ships. 'Cocainomaniacs', *The Times* revealed, were rendered so paranoid by the drug that they carried pistols to protect them from imaginary foes.

Giving credence to the drug panic were two court cases involving members of the Canadian Army. One unit based in Folkestone, Kent, was said to have as many as 40 habitual cocaine users. The commander sent a corporal to find out where his men were buying the drug. The corporal managed to buy some 'snow' in a pub from a small-time crook named Horace Kingsley and also from Rose Edwards, a London prostitute. The two dealers were arrested, but as cocaine was not then a controlled substance, there were few grounds to charge them on. Whereas Edwards claimed to have bought the powder from a man in a London pub, Kingsley reported that he simply bought the stuff in a pharmacy in Dover. He claimed that he gave the powder to soldiers he had befriended in order to make them 'keener' while going about their duties. After some head-scratching the army finally concocted the charge of 'selling powder to members of His Majesty's Forces, with intent to make them less capable of performing their duties'. Both were convicted by a magistrate and sentenced to six months' hard labour. More serious was the charge levelled at Lieutenant George Codere, who was accused of murdering a canteen sergeant in a camp in Surrey. One witness reported that Codere had acted as if he was on drugs, which led the press to report that Codere was a cocaine user.[66]

By July 1916, the government and public were so worried about the cocaine threat that its use was prohibited by the Defence of the Realm Act, Regulation 48B.*

---

* The same act earlier introduced Britain's infamous licensing laws, which governed pub opening times. According to the politician David Lloyd George, drink was a bigger enemy to Britain than the Germans or Austrians!

HOW TO WIN IMPORTANT FRIENDS
AND INFLUENCE PEOPLE

IN 1923 Tutenkhamen's tomb was opened by Howard Carter and his backer, Lord Carnarvon, who went on to die two months later of the so-called 'Mummy's Curse'. A few months later his widow, Almina, the Dowager Countess Carnarvon, married a divorcee, Lieutenant Colonel Ian Onslow Dennistoun.

It's bad enough when your first husband dies of a 3,000-year-old Egyptian curse, but the Lady Carnarvon really picked a stinker in Dennistoun – for he had a very guilty secret that the world was about to share.

Dennistoun had divorced his wife Dorothy in Paris in May 1921 and had made an arrangement that he would support her when he was in a financial position to do so, providing she did not go to court to secure payments. However, by the time of his remarriage Dennistoun had not only neglected to pay anything to his ex-wife, he had actually borrowed money from her amounting to £952. While he enjoyed the high life, living it up in a luxurious apartment, Dorothy had yet to receive a penny. Such was her allegation when she took the matter to court in March 1925.[67]

Lieutenant Colonel Dennistoun would have done well to make arrangements for his former wife, because she had an unbelievable story to tell, which she did while giving evidence. From before the war, perhaps since 1912, Dennistoun had come up with an unusual arrangement with his wife. In order for him to gain promotions and favour, Dennistoun effectively sold his wife to Sir John Stephen Cowans, Quartermaster General of the British Army. In return for his wife's favours, Dennistoun received a nice appointment as secretary to the Governor of Jamaica and then, during the war, choice appointments in Gibraltar, plus his promotion from captain to lieutenant colonel and his appointment as Cowans' deputy at Versailles. In court Dennison denied that he gave consent for his wife to be Cowans' mistress, but evidence was produced (including letters) which showed that the allegation was true.

It might seem inconceivable that such a respected figure as Cowans could be so base. The general was thought of as a genius, often referred to as 'the best quartermaster since Moses'.[68] However, in addition to his irregular arrangement with Mrs Dennistoun, it seems that Cowans had an involvement with a certain Mary Cornwallis West, the estranged wife of the Duke of Westminster and mistress to the Prince of Wales. 'Patsy', as she was best known, was eager to promote the cause of her lover Patrick Barrett, a sergeant in the Royal Welch Fusiliers, and procured for him a commission. When this scandal broke in December 1916 Cowans was administered little more than a rap over the knuckles and allowed to continue in his post.

The Dennistoun trial lasted three mud-raking weeks and was headline news throughout. The jury awarded Dorothy Dennistoun a considerable sum against her former husband, reported at $30,000 by the American magazine *Time*. More importantly, changes to the law were introduced in Parliament to limit the reporting on divorce cases in an attempt to avoid the sort of obscene details exposed in the case of Dennistoun v. Dennistoun.[69]

RED LETTER DAY

THE Zinoviev Letter of 1924 forms one of the great conspiracies of modern British history. Did 'Old Establishment' members of the British secret service really conspire to ensure the defeat of the socialist Labour Party in the 1924 election, or was the whole business a case of red herring?

On 9 October 1924 the British Foreign Office was sent a copy of a letter dated 15 September 1924 from Grigori Zinoviev, the head of Comintern – the organization set up by Moscow to control communist activity abroad – to the Central Committee of the Communist Party of Great Britain. The letter appeared to be preparing the way for a Soviet-style revolution in Great Britain. The letter was leaked to the press on 25 October 1924. The headline in the *Daily Mail* was sensational: 'CIVIL WAR PLOT BY SOCIALISTS' MASTERS; MOSCOW ORDERS TO OUR REDS; GREAT PLOT DISCLOSED'. This caused much embarrassment to Britain's first socialist Prime Minister, Ramsay MacDonald, who had recently done a trade deal with the Soviet Union and gone some way towards normalizing diplomatic relations with the regime.

Of particular alarm were instructions relating to the infiltration of the armed forces prior to the planned revolution. The text included the following instructions:

From your last report it is evident that agitation-propaganda work in the Army is weak, in the Navy a very little better. Your explanation that the quality of the members attracted justifies the quantity is right in principle, nevertheless it would be desirable to have cells in all the units of the troops, particularly among those quartered in the large centres of the country, and also among factories working on munitions and at military store depots. We request that the most particular attention be paid to these latter.

In the event of danger of war, with the aid of the latter and in contact with the transport workers, it is possible to paralyse all the military preparations of the bourgeoisie and to make a start in turning an imperialist war into a class war ...

The Military Section of the British Communist Party, so far as we are aware, further suffers from a lack of specialists, the future directors of the British Red Army.

It is time you thought of forming such a group, which, together with the leaders, might be, in the event of an outbreak of active strife, the brain of the military organization of the Party.

Go attentively through the lists of the military 'cells', detailing from them the more energetic and capable men, turn attention to the more talented military specialists who have for one reason or another left the Service and hold socialist views. Attract them into the ranks of the Communist Party if they desire honestly to serve the proletariat and desire in the future to direct not the blind mechanical forces in the service of the bourgeoisie, but a national army.

Form a directing operative head of the Military Section.

Do not put this off to a future moment, which may be pregnant with events and catch you unprepared.

Desiring you all success, both in organization and in your struggle,

With Communist Greetings,

...ZINOVIEV

The remarks were inflammatory and if true would have been an enormous cause for concern. However, there was an element of mischief-making in the timing of their publication – just four days before a general election, which the Labour Party lost.

Although it is true that the socialist government would probably have lost the election without the sudden appearance of the Zinoviev Letter, the timing of the release led many to believe that the British secret services had fabricated the letter to topple the government. There could not be a more serious charge in a democratic country. After decades of claims and counterclaims, a Foreign Office investigation into the Zinoviev Letter in 1999 led to a fairly satisfactory account of the scandal.[70]

As claimed by the Soviet government at the time, the letter appears to have been forged – probably by anti-Bolshevik dissidents in Latvia unhappy with MacDonald's policy towards the Soviet Union. The secret services do not get off the hook entirely. The report concluded that secret service officers did leak the letter to the Conservative Party, the main suspect being Major Desmond Morton, who later went on to become Churchill's personal assistant during the Second World War.

M'LADY'S A TRAMP

THE case of Lady Howard of Effingham bears many similarities to the infamous Mata Hari case of the First World War. Mata Hari was a well-known exotic dancer and courtesan who was shot for espionage in 1915. To this day no one is actually sure whether Mata Hari really was a spy or not, but her behaviour was so suspicious, and the people she had affairs with so well connected, that the French authorities had to assume the worst. The same was true of Lady Howard, but in her case she was protected by her marriage to an English lord and so security services' suspicions were kept well under wraps and did not come to light until her dossier was released in 2006 revealing her outrageous tale.

Lady Howard was born Malwina Gertler in Budapest, 1908. 'Manci' was raised in Poland from where she travelled to Britain in 1935 and came to the notice of the intelligence services for a failure to register her alien status. Despite arriving penniless, Manci soon gained a reputation as a party-goer in exalted circles. Attending the cocktail parties of the rich and famous, Manci was colourfully described by the socialite Lord Cottenham as: 'a not unattractive gypsy gamin type, highly sexed, I should say, [who] possesses considerable facility for copying the Mayfair chatter with an accent more foreign than it need be, but does not always simultaneously smile with her eyes, which are those of a thoroughly intelligent monkey'. Sir Robert Vansittart, Permanent Under Secretary at the Foreign Office, was less kind. He described her as a 'tart'.

In 1938 the Secret Intelligence Service (later MI6) discovered that Manci was the mistress of a wealthy Polish arms dealer well known for running guns into Spain, which was then in a state of civil war. In addition to gun-running, Eduard Weisblatt was also suspected of being an agent for the OGPU (Soviet military intelligence) and/or the Nazis. The French security services suspected he worked as a double agent for both.

Around this time, in November 1938, Manci became engaged to Lord Howard of Effingham, the son and heir of the Earl of Effingham. When he met Manci, Lord Howard was an undisclosed bankrupt fond of his drink and it appears the marriage was purely a business arrangement: he needed money and she needed a British passport. Weisblatt bankrolled the deal and continued his love affair without interruption – even during her honeymoon with Lord Howard in Paris.

After the fall of France in 1940, Weisblatt found himself in the French capital without any means of travelling to England to meet Manci. Likewise, she could not get an exit visa to visit him in Paris. Instead she began securing contacts by offering sex to soldiers, airmen and Royal Navy officers, not to mention a number of high-profile diplomats, including the ambassadors of Russia, Turkey, Egypt and Iraq. She had a contact in the War Office and was even close to Anthony Eden, who was soon to be appointed as Secretary of State for War.

The security service MI5 suspected she was using her contacts for espionage, but they could not get proof. The security service was unable to intercept her mail to Paris because she used her favours to have the mail sent in secure diplomatic bags. Perhaps hers were innocent love notes – but some members of MI5 were convinced otherwise. Persuading the politicians in charge of internment was another matter altogether.

It was only when Manci added to her circle a Hungarian cook in the household of the Prime Minister's son, Randolph Churchill, that the necessity to prevent a scandal got Manci interned. She was arrested in February 1941 and sent to Holloway prison. She was interviewed by the security services who were at pains to find any evidence of wrong doing.

In fact her interviewer at Holloway, Joan Miller of MI5, thought her colleagues had overreacted. She described Manci as being in a terrible state, 'distraught to the point of incoherence' and blamed her incarceration on a 'rotten taste in men'. As for her gun-running boyfriend, Miller believed it was entirely his fault she was under suspicion. Miller described Weisblatt as: 'Fat subversive and boring in bed.' She also overheard a rumour doing the rounds in society coffee shops that Manci had a habit of 'reading the *Daily Mirror* while he made love to her'.[71]

A few months later she was released on the orders of the Attorney General because of 'a fairly complete absence of evidence' – a verdict backed up by MI5's head of counter espionage, Guy Liddell, who admitted that the case against her was 'very thin'.[72]

So was she a spy or not? Everything pointed to it, but even in wartime the law must be obeyed and there was no proof of Lady Howard having done wrong. She divorced Lord Howard in 1945 and eventually settled in Australia.[73]

THE MIDWAY LEAK

IT was the biggest secret of the Second World War. Britain and the United States were frequently able to break the machine ciphers used by Germany and Japan with devastating results. Secrecy was paramount; for if either of the Axis partners realized their security had been breached, they would have been able to make changes and set Allied code breakers back years, lengthening the war and perhaps even throwing its eventual outcome into doubt.

Although a high degree of secrecy was generally maintained there was one security breach following the battle of Midway, 4–7 June 1942 that caused angry spasms in high places. Before Midway, American code breakers had been able to intercept Japanese signals, allowing American Admiral Chester Nimitz to ignore a Japanese feint and instead concentrate his carriers at Midway, and inflict a heavy defeat.

Despite the fact that the US Navy warned its servicemen not to divulge information about the battle to the press, on 7 June 1942 the *Chicago Tribune* ran the headline 'NAVY HAD WORD OF JAP PLAN TO STRIKE AT SEA'. Although no correspondents had been at Midway, a reporter had been on the carrier *Lexington* during the earlier battle of the Coral Sea. Stanley Johnston was an Australian veteran of the First World War and a reporter on the *Chicago Tribune*.

The *Lexington* had been hit at Coral Sea, and, along with many other survivors of that ship, Johnston was transferred to the USS *Barnett*, en route to San Diego. On the way back, Johnston shared

172

a cabin with the executive officer from the *Lexington*, Commander Morton Seligman. While Johnston was writing up his report on the Coral Sea, he saw several classified papers, including one which gave the US Navy's final appreciation of the Japanese order of battle for the battle of Midway. It is unclear if Seligman showed these papers to the reporter, or if he carelessly left them lying around in the cabin.

The reporter copied the list and filed it along with his report when he returned to the *Chicago Tribune* on the night of 6 June. Managing Editor 'Pat' Maloney was more interested in the battle account, and put the order of battle in as a sidebar. However, when looking for a suitably punchy front-page headline to put with the piece, Maloney came up with the one above.

It was a good headline, but apart from the list of ships there was nothing in Johnston's Coral Sea report to back this up. Maloney instead attributed the story to a nameless reliable source in 'naval intelligence' from Washington. When the story appeared next day the navy was appalled.

The story also found its way into a number of other papers – the *Washington Times Herald* ran the sensational headline 'U.S. KNEW ALL ABOUT JAP FLEET. GUESSED THERE WOULD BE A FEINT AT ONE BASE, REAL ATTACK AT ANOTHER.'

Navy chiefs feared that if the Japanese got wind of this story they might guess their codes had been broken and change them. After private meetings between the navy and Johnston on 8 June, the navy sought indictments of the principal employees of the *Chicago Tribune* on 9 June, claiming that newspaper reporters were sworn to secrecy and that Johnston had betrayed the trust placed in him.

An added complication was the fact that the owner of the *Tribune*, Colonel Robert R. McCormick, was a longtime opponent of President Roosevelt. It might be perceived that Roosevelt was using this story as a stick with which to beat McCormick unfairly.

Also, as with the Herbert Yardley 'Black Chamber' affair of 1928, if the government pressed ahead with the prosecution, it would be admitting there was a grain of truth in the evidence. When his code-breaking department was shut down due to government cutbacks in 1929, Yardley revealed that the US had broken Japanese codes and gained an unfair advantage in the negotiations during the Washington Naval Conference of 1921–22. His book became a best seller in Japan, but no action could be taken. Equally, in the run up to Pearl Harbor, US code breakers had agonized over certain information they obtained because to use the contents of the messages to prosecute individuals, the government would first have to reveal the extent of its code-breaking capabilities.

Finally, the British Admiralty delegation in Washington were concerned that a trial would further compromise the Allies' special intelligence methods. They argued that preservation of the secret outweighed 'almost any other consideration'.

Taking all this into account, on 14 July, the special prosecutor, William D. Mitchell, presented his findings to Attorney General Francis Biddle and Secretary of the Navy Frank Knox. After lengthy investigation he suggested that the national interest would be best served by dropping the matter completely. Everyone agreed and quietly hoped that perhaps the Japanese had missed the rumpus.

Within a matter of weeks the Japanese did make serious changes to their cipher practice and on 15 August they altered the Japanese Fleet General-Purpose System, which had only been in service for two months. Whether this was the result of the leaks is a mystery.

In all such stories there is always a fall guy. In this case it was Seligman. With the President's approval, Seligman was barred from all future promotions. He was allowed to retire from the service in 1944.[74]

THE SLAPPING INCIDENT

I N 1943 General George S. Patton Jr was at the cusp of his powers.
He was a dynamic, hard-driving, foul-mouthed monster of a
general, who was in his element leading the charge across German-
occupied Sicily.

While commander of the Seventh Army, General Patton made
frequent visits to the hospitals to see that the wounded were being
properly cared for. On 2 August he had a particularly emotional day
when he gave Purple Hearts to 40 wounded soldiers including one
mortally wounded soldier in an oxygen mask. The following day he
visited another hospital in Sicily. Again the sight of more brave,
wounded men moved him deeply.

Entering the last ward on his visit Patton came across Private
Charles H. Kuhl. The soldier did not appear wounded, so Patton
asked him what the matter was. Kuhl simply replied, 'I guess I
can't take it.' Patton flew into a rage. He started swearing at the
soldier, then slapped him across the face with his gloves. He
grabbed him by the scruff of the neck and physically kicked him
out of the tent. There was no place in Patton's vocabulary for the
term *battle-fatigue*.

Two days after the event Patton issued an order to Seventh Army
commanders warning them not to let men shirk their duty by
allowing them to claim they were nervously 'incapable of combat'.
In future all such men should not be sent to hospitals, but charged

with cowardice in the face of the enemy if they refused to rejoin their units.

On 10 August, while on his way to meet General Bradley, Patton paid a surprise visit to an evacuation hospital. After meeting a few wounded men, Patton came across Private Paul G. Bennett, who was sitting huddled up and shivering. Patton asked the sobbing soldier what the trouble was.

'It's my nerves.'

'What did you say?'

'It's my nerves, I can't stand the shelling anymore.'

'Your nerves, hell; you are just a goddamned coward, you yellow son of a bitch.'

In a fit of temper Patton slapped the man, saying, 'Shut up that goddamned crying. I won't have these brave men here who have been shot at seeing a yellow bastard sitting here crying.'

Patton then struck Bennett a second time and sent his helmet liner flying off. Turning to the admitting officer he yelled, 'Don't admit this yellow bastard; there's nothing the matter with him. I won't have the hospitals cluttered up with these sons of bitches who haven't got the guts to fight.'

Returning his attention to Bennett, Patton continued menacingly: 'You're going back to the front lines and you may get shot and killed, but you're going to fight. If you don't, I'll stand you up against a wall and have a firing squad kill you on purpose.' Patton then reached for his pistol. 'In fact, I ought to shoot you myself, you goddamned whimpering coward.'

By now Patton's shouting had attracted the attention of all the nurses and patients in neighbouring tents, many of whom witnessed the general's explosive rage. The hospital commander, Colonel Currier, put himself between Patton and Bennett. Patton shouted at

Currier, 'I want you to get that man out of here right away. I won't have these brave boys seeing such a bastard babied.'

Patton left the tent and continued the tour, but kept referring back to Bennett. He told Currier, 'I can't help it, but it makes my blood boil to think of a yellow bastard being babied.' As he was leaving the base he again addressed the hospital commander. 'I meant what I said about getting that coward out of here. I won't have those cowardly bastards hanging around our hospitals. We'll probably have to shoot them some time anyway, or we'll raise a breed of morons.'[75]

Patton sped off leaving a shocked hospital in his wake. Later he explained to Bradley what had happened at the hospital: 'There were a couple of malingerers there. I slapped one of them to make him mad and put some fight back into him.'

Bradley was horrified by Patton's attitude. The next day he received a report from the hospital about Patton's actions. The report pointed out that when Private Kuhl was later examined he was found to be suffering from chronic dysentery and malaria. Kuhl had not been able to sleep. He was sent back from the artillery battery he was serving on to a rear aid station and had been given some medicine to make him drowsy. Private Bennett, meanwhile, far from being a coward, had been in the regular army for four years. He had served well until a friend had been wounded on 6 August. When he was ordered to be evacuated Bennett had pleaded not to be sent away from his unit. Then Patton had turned up.

Bradley did not pass the report on to Patton, who was his superior; nor did he go over Patton's head and pass the report on to headquarters. Instead, Bradley locked the report in his safe in a sealed envelope.

While Bradley would not deal with the situation, the surgeon Colonel Arnest sent a copy of the report to Brigadier General

Frederick A. Blessé, Eisenhower's chief surgeon. When Eisenhower read the report he was in a dilemma. On the one hand Patton should be severely punished for striking an enlisted man in a hospital. On the other, Eisenhower felt that as a battlefield commander Patton was indispensable to the war effort. He decided to write to Patton in the strongest possible terms warning him that such conduct would not be tolerated in future. Furthermore, he ordered Patton to apologize to all the individuals concerned.

But that was far from the end of it. The story found its way into the hands of war correspondents attached to Patton's Seventh Army. Three of them confronted Eisenhower and tried to force him into sacking Patton. Although Patton was hard on his men, generally speaking he was very popular. With the press it was a different matter – they hated him. However, Eisenhower was able to impress on them the importance of retaining Patton for future campaigns in Europe and assured the reporters he had dealt with Patton severely. After hearing the letter Eisenhower had sent Patton, the reporters agreed to drop the story for the benefit of the war effort.

On 21 August Bennett was unexpectedly summoned to meet Patton. Fearing the worst, Bennett went off to Palermo only to be met by Patton who offered his handshake by way of an apology. Likewise Private Kuhl was sought out and Patton offered him an explanation of his actions along with an outstretched hand. Kuhl is said to have accepted Patton's offer with a broad grin. Explanations for his conduct – but not quite apologies – were then given to the hospital staff and to every division in Patton's army. But that still was not the end of it.

In November 1943 the story found its way to the journalist and broadcaster Drew Pearson. When the story was told in the United States there was an almighty uproar. To 'play fair' with the embedded journalists who had kept their silence on the matter, Eisenhower's chief of staff, General Bedell Smith, held an informal press conference. Eisenhower instructed Smith to hold nothing back and tell the full truth. Unfortunately, Smith got his facts wrong.

When asked what action Patton had faced, Smith said that no reprimand had been administered. Ten minutes later, this news was in Washington and causing an even bigger stink. Eisenhower was forced to order a correction, but by then all the damage had been done.[76]

The clamour against Patton was led by a number of senators and congressmen who called for his dismissal. There were even cartoons that made Patton out to be a Hitler-like figure. Again this led to Eisenhower having to justify why Patton had to be retained. But although Eisenhower protected Patton, his trust in his temperament was severely dented. The slapping incident robbed Patton of the overall command of the American ground troops on D-Day. That honour went to Patton's former subordinate, General Bradley.

To close this tale, almost every commentator on the affair has reached the same conclusion. Ironically, Patton was most probably suffering from battle-fatigue himself and the incidents were a form of breakdown from the stress he had been under. Interestingly, when news of the incident reached the Germans, they surmised that the whole thing was a stunt engineered to deceive them over Patton's future role, which allowed the Allied invasion planners to use Patton in a variety of deception stunts.[77]

THE DEATH MATCH

THE history of the Ukraine during the Second World War is a grim chapter of human experience. In contrast to the countless atrocities that came to light after the liberation of Kiev by Soviet forces in November 1943, fantastic propaganda stories began to emerge about the bravery of a group of football players who had taken on the might of the Nazi war machine.

A tale emerged that a football match had been played between a team of Ukrainian bakery workers and a team representing the Nazi armed forces. From the various surviving accounts Stalin's propagandists put together an electrifying story of heroism and resistance to the fascist invaders. It was known as the 'Death Match'.

The most popular version of events was that a group of footballers from the illustrious Dynamo Kiev team had been trapped inside Kiev while it was fighting the German onslaught in 1941. Unable to escape the German encirclement, the 11 players were put to work in a bread-making factory where, to alleviate the hardships of their fellow workers, they played football exhibitions to sustain morale.

As time went by the Germans heard of this team and, eager to prove the superiority of the Aryan race, arranged a game against the Ukrainians. Under the name FC Start the ex-Dynamo players lined up against Flakelf ('anti-aircraft eleven') who were, according to legend, the best players from the German Luftwaffe. In front of a large crowd FC Start hammered the German team, easily winning.

Outraged at this setback, the Germans demanded a rematch. This time any pretence of sporting behaviour went out of the window. Before the game kicked off, the Ukrainian players were visited in the dressing room by the German referee – an SS officer. He told the FC Start players that they were expected to give the Nazi salute at the beginning of the match. Conscious that the eyes of Kiev were upon them, the Ukrainians instead gave a traditional Soviet-style sporting salute at the beginning of the game with both arms raised in the air. Out of necessity, but also very symbolically, the team were dressed in red – the colour of the Soviet flag.

In the first half of the match the half-starved Ukrainian players were literally kicked off the park by the Germans. Despite the constant fouling and the biased SS referee, FC Start scored and went into the interval leading the game. During the break, a second SS officer entered the Ukrainians' dressing room and threatened them. He left them in no doubt that they would be shot if they did not lose the match in the second half. As the two teams kicked off, armed German troops with vicious, snarling dogs encircled the pitch. According to some accounts, shots were fired by German soldiers in the crowd.

Caught in an impossible situation the Ukrainians played to win and won the tie. After the match had finished, so the official account went, the FC Start team was arrested, put onto a truck and sent to a death camp at Babi Yar where they were gunned down still wearing their football kit.

It is an incredible story, and really caught the imagination. The only trouble was – it was not strictly true. As the Germans were pushed back out of the Soviet Union, members of FC Start team who had been reported shot began to turn up – and they had a rather different take on the story.

The FC Start players were arrested, but some time after the match. One of them was indeed executed, having been accused of belonging to Stalin's secret police – the NKVD. Another player disappeared, but he was thought to have been a Nazi informer.

The remaining players were taken to a forced labour camp at Babi Yar, but not immediately after the match. Babi Yar did have a reputation for working inmates to death and during their time there four more of the FC Start players were executed. However, they were not shot because of their role in the football match. They were among many others randomly selected for execution as part of a wide-ranging reprisal against partisan attacks.

The surviving FC Start players became somewhat of an embarrassment to the authorities. As was often the case in the Soviet Union, yesterday's hero became today's traitor. Rather than being fêted as the heroes they had been made out to be, the surviving players were hauled in for questioning by the Soviet authorities under the very serious charge of collaborating with the Nazis.

It turned out 'Death Match' had in fact been only one of a number of games played by FC Start against Axis and local opposition. It raised a difficult question. Were the team playing to rally the spirit of Kiev, or were they traitors – at best misguided individuals who played football with the enemy while their comrades were giving up their lives?

In the paranoid dark age of Stalin's reign, it could certainly appear so. The outlook appeared desperately bleak for the surviving players, but at last fortune smiled on them. The Soviet authorities decided it was best for everyone's interests to ignore the truth and continued to promote the 'Death Match' legend. When Stalin died in 1953 the surviving FC Start players gained the recognition they deserved – as patriotic sportsmen who did their bit resisting the German Army.[78]

THE D-DAY WITCH TRIAL

O N 23 March 1944 a sensational trial opened in the Old Bailey. Victoria Helen Duncan (AKA 'Hellish Nell') was charged and found guilty of conspiracy to contravene the Witchcraft Act, 1735. The seven-day trial caused a sensation when it was widely reported by the tabloid press of the day. With the Allied invasion of France expected in the spring of 1944, the exact landing grounds were one of the most important, closely guarded secrets in the world. It was said that Hellish Nell had been locked up in Holloway prison at His Majesty's pleasure to prevent her from accurately foreseeing and revealing to the world that Normandy was the target.

Helen Duncan was a Scottish medium who had been holding séances since well before the start of the war. It is well known that there was an upsurge in Spiritualism and interest in the paranormal following the trauma of the First World War. Many grieving people turned to mediums in a bid to make contact with their lost loved ones and find what we today would describe as 'closure'.

Alas, this less than scientific field has long been a breeding ground for charlatanism and it would appear that Mrs Duncan was widely suspected of being a fraud. By all accounts, her séances saw her passing into a trance-like state. When in this state, 'ectoplasm' – the paranormal goo in which the spiritual manifestation would reveal itself – would emanate from Mrs Duncan's mouth. It would appear that instead of emitting genuine, bona fide, supernatural ectoplasm,

Mrs Duncan had been caught out using cheesecloth. She had been denounced by the London Spiritual Alliance in 1931 and at a séance in Edinburgh three years later had been caught out when a sitter made a grab at the 'ectoplasm' and found it to be an undergarment!

Despite this, she remained popular and moved to the naval town of Portsmouth where she found ample custom for her services among the families and loved ones of sailors. Wartime only increased her appeal and in late 1941 she apparently came up trumps by telling of the loss of HMS *Barham* at a séance.

The description of this séance may have been embellished but, to give Mrs Duncan the benefit of the doubt, it is claimed that she summoned the spirit of a sailor with the name HMS *Barham* clearly visible on his hatband. The apparition hovered over a woman and said: 'Sorry, Sweetheart, my ship sank in the Mediterranean. I've crossed over to the Other Side.'[79] Spookily the woman's husband was on board the *Barham*, but no one had told her it had sunk.

It is unclear whether the woman contacted the Admiralty or whether it was the editor of *Psychic News*, but the effect was the same. The battleship *Barham* had indeed been lost after it was struck by three German torpedoes on 25 November 1941. Instead of announcing the loss, the Admiralty decided to keep the news secret, in order to deceive the Nazis over the strength of the Royal Navy in the Mediterranean. Not even the next of kin had been informed.

When the Admiralty heard about Hellish Nell's manifestation, they were understandably concerned. If this news got out it would cause an uproar among the relatives, not to mention giving Goebbels an easy propaganda victory. They decided there was no option but to go public with the story, which they did on 27 January 1942.

Following this incident Duncan was monitored by the authorities. When she was finally arrested in 1944 it is commonly supposed it was because she was on the south coast where the Allied build-up for D-Day was taking place. If she was arrested because she was a security threat, the authorities may have suspected Duncan had a more earthly source of information that had allowed her to pull off the *Barham* stunt. If she did have informants passing her restricted information, then perhaps she would try to grab the headlines by predicting the D-Day landing sites.

Well ... that is the conspiracy theory at least. If one looks at the arrest, the truth might appear more mundane. On 19 January 1944 Duncan held a séance in which 'ectoplasm' appeared to be coming from her mouth. Among the paying audience was the navy's Lieutenant Stan Worth, who had purchased two tickets: one for himself and one for a plainclothes police officer. At a given moment there was the sharp report of a whistle being blown and the policeman made an unsuccessful grab for the ectoplasm, which he believed was a white sheet. Duncan and three members of the audience were arrested and taken in on charges of vagrancy.

The act under which Duncan was eventually charged – the Witchcraft Act, 1735 – had been introduced in the reign of George II. The act covered people who fraudulently claimed to have contact with the spirit world in order to make money. Anyone found guilty of this charge was to be treated in the same way as a vagrant, which may be where the vagrancy charge came from. When prosecuting Mrs Duncan the authorities claimed she was a 'pest' and accused her of making money by fraudulently claiming she was in a position to bring about the appearance of spirits of the deceased.

Several notable people were called by the defence, who also announced that Duncan was prepared to demonstrate her abilities by conducting a séance in the courtroom. This offer was rejected. However, a number of people did give evidence that appeared to back

Duncan. Among these were Vincent Woodcock, who claimed to have seen his dead wife at a séance and Alfred Dodd, a well-respected author, who claimed he was a regular guest at Duncan's séances and had witnessed the materialization of his late grandfather at one of them.

After a seven-day trial, the jury found Duncan guilty. She was sentenced to nine months' imprisonment and was released on 22 September 1944 – well after the Normandy invasion took place.

On 3 April 1944 news of the business reached the ears of Prime Minister Winston Churchill. In fact, because of the press coverage he could hardly have avoided the trial: even the normally sensible broadsheet *The Times* ran the headline 'WITCHCRAFT ACT OFFENCES'.

At such a critical time, on the verge of the greatest invasion in military history, Churchill was livid that the public had been so engrossed in the trial. He made his feelings known in a memo to the Home Secretary:

> Let me have a report on why the Witchcraft Act, 1735, was used in a modern Court of Justice.
>
> What was the cost of this trial to the State, observing that witnesses were brought from Portsmouth and maintained here in this crowded London for a fortnight, and the Recorder kept busy with all this obsolete tomfoolery, to the detriment of necessary work in the Courts.[80]

But wait a moment ... Churchill has a point here. Helen Duncan was arrested in Portsmouth. Why was she brought to London and tried in the Old Bailey and imprisoned in Holloway? Surely she could have been dealt with in Portsmouth if all she was considered to be was a devious old crone? Perhaps the security services really were scared she might have had supernatural powers after all!

ACT IV

*'COLD WAR
FALLOUT'*

THE ATOMIC SPIES

IN an address in 1946, former British Prime Minister Winston Churchill made a speech about how an 'Iron Curtain' had descended across Europe. This remark is seen by many as the proper opening of what we now know as the Cold War.

In fact, Churchill had missed the boat. If the truth is told, the Cold War began in 1941 when Hitler's armies invaded the Soviet Union and drove almost right up to the gates of Moscow. Many communist supporters and socialists around the world had previously been appalled at Stalin for the Nazi–Soviet pact of 1939, but saw it as a patriotic duty to ensure that the Soviet Union was given everything it needed to survive Hitler's armies: including the secrets of the atomic bomb.

While the British and Americans strove to eliminate Nazi espionage on their shores, their Soviet allies spied on them at every level. When the Soviets detonated their first nuclear weapon in 1949 it came as a massive shock to America and precipitated a wave of anti-communist hysteria, better known as McCarthyism – a topic we will return to shortly.

In the summer of 1949, the FBI learned that Klaus Fuchs, a German-born British scientist, had been passing secrets relating to the atomic bomb to the Soviet Union. Fuchs was arrested by British authorities on 2 February 1950. He admitted his involvement in Soviet espionage but gave only the sparest details of his Soviet contact in America. After painstaking investigation by the FBI, the contact was identified as Harry Gold, a Philadelphia chemist. On May 22, 1950, Gold confessed his espionage activity to the FBI. Through investigating Gold the FBI were led to David Greenglass, a US soldier working on the secret atom bomb 'Manhattan Project' at Los Alamos, New Mexico, in 1944 and 1945.

Harry Gold stated that he acted as a courier between Greenglass and his Soviet contact, who was known only as John, but who was later identified as Anatoli Yakovlev, the former Soviet vice-consul in New York City. Further interrogation of Greenglass and his wife Ruth implicated Greenglass' sister Ethel and her husband, Julius Rosenberg, as instigators of the plot. At the same time a naval ordnance engineer disclosed that radar engineer Morton Sobell – a former classmate of Rosenberg – was also involved in espionage activities.

With Greenglass pleading guilty to charges of espionage conspiracy, the Rosenbergs and Morton Sobell were arrested and put on trial. All three pleaded not guilty to the charges and went to court on 6 March 1951. They were all found guilty and on 5 April, sentences were passed. Sobell was imprisoned for a term of 30 years, without parole. The Rosenbergs, who continued to protest their innocence, were both sentenced to death by electric chair.

Before passing sentence Judge Kaufman let the Rosenbergs know exactly what he thought of them. He said that their crime was worse than murder as it had put the atomic bomb in the hands of the Russians years before Soviet scientists would have been able to perfect the technology themselves. Most startling was his accusation that their treachery had directly caused the Korean War and that millions of innocent people would suffer because of them.

Amid mass protests in Washington DC and New York City – all of which the FBI blamed on communist agitators – and an appeal by the Pope, the sentence was carried out on 19 June 1953. At 8pm, 35-year-old Julius Rosenberg was led to the execution chamber in New York's notorious Sing Sing prison. Visibly pale, he was strapped into the electric chair without a word and killed. Fifteen minutes later his wife was led into the chamber. Just before Ethel Rosenberg, 37, was placed in the electric chair, she drew the prison matron towards her, and kissed her. Visibly affected, the matron quickly turned and left the execution chamber. Outside the chamber in the corridor a rabbi could be heard intoning a psalm. Ethel was electrocuted, but required a second electric shock before she died. The couple were survived by two young sons.

The execution of the Rosenbergs was one of the most miserable episodes of the Cold War era. It was later proved through the release of decoded Soviet transmissions that Julius Rosenberg was indeed guilty of espionage. To what extent he handed the Soviets an atomic bomb is still a matter of debate. What proved most controversial was the severity of the sentence. Klaus Fuchs, the German-born British scientist, received just 12 years in prison – and it is almost universally agreed that he played a much more significant role in passing atomic secrets to the USSR. Some have said that it was the Rosenbergs' refusal to admit their treachery that led them to the electric chair.

What most now agree on is that Ethel Rosenberg was sentenced to death without any firm evidence that she was a spy. Later in his life, her brother, David Greenglass, said that he implicated Ethel on the advice of the authorities in order to save his life and protect his own family. Greenglass later admitted that he lied when he claimed that Ethel used to type his espionage reports before they were handed to the Soviets. It was the belief that Ethel typed the notes that sent her to her death. Even if Ethel had known what her husband was doing, surely that was not a cause for killing her?

UN-AMERICAN ACTIVITIES

B ORN out of the troubled, turbulent and violent half century preceding them, the 1950s have become a sort of Golden Age of Hollywood glamour and rock n' roll. But in the United States, posing as a shield against un-American ways of life, a cancer was eating away at the very democratic core of the country. More of an enemy to America than even Joe Stalin, we have the witch-finder general himself, Senator Joe McCarthy.

In the 1950s Senator McCarthy whipped up a storm of hostility against anything remotely radical, left wing or communist. People in government positions and in the public spotlight found themselves being denounced and subject to aggressive investigations and trials. Many people had their careers irretrievably damaged because they did not fit in with McCarthy's 'Brand America'.

In most cases to deny the charges of un-Americanism was only to make one appear more tainted, more deviously unpatriotic. However, one man was able to fight back and regain his reputation with the support of sympathetic journalists. His name was Milo Radulovich.

Radulovich was a reserve US Air Force weather officer based in Dexter, Michigan. In 1953, with McCarthyism in full flow and with the Rosenbergs on death row, Radulovich was told he would be discharged from the Air Force because his father and sister had been accused of being communist sympathizers.

His father, a Serbian-speaking Yugoslavian immigrant, subscribed to newspapers from his home country, one of which had links to the American Slav Congress, which had been designated a communist organization by the US Attorney General. His sister's crime was that she was labelled as a civil-rights activist.

To Lieutenant Radulovich's eternal credit, he refused to take this decision lying down. He demanded an official hearing and went about procuring legal assistance. To represent the lieutenant was a bold step for a lawyer to take. The chances were that by representing Radulovich the lawyer would end up being denounced as a communist himself – this is partly how the whole McCarthy witch-hunt succeeded.

Fortunately he found Charles Lockwood, a semi-retired lawyer. Lockwood decided that this case needed public exposure and contacted Russell Harris of the *Detroit News*. Through Harris, the attorney Ken Sanborn joined in the defence team. Although conservative himself, Sanborn was also a lieutenant in the Air Force Reserve and was a former classmate of Radulovich. Both Sanborn and Lockwood agreed to defend Radulovich without a fee.

Despite this noble defence, the outcome of Radulovich's hearing was never in doubt. When Radulovich saw he had made the front page of the *Detroit News* he was terrified and rightly so. His hearing was held by three colonels who had read the newspaper coverage. They told Radulovich, 'Well everything would have been OK, if you had just kept your mouth shut.' They then tried to do a deal with him: 'I'll tell you what,' said one of the colonels. 'You denounce your sister and everything's going to be fine. That's all you have to do. Denounce her. And your father.' Radulovich declined to do this and was stripped of his commission.[81]

The *Detroit News* followed up its report on the story with the outcome of the hearing. The article came to the attention of Ed Murrow, the presenter of a popular TV show called *See It Now*.

Murrow and his partner Fred Friendly had been kicking around for months looking for a story that would expose McCarthyism for all it was. The show sent a reporter who spent two days interviewing Radulovich, his wife, father, sister, brothers, their neighbours and other people throughout the town. The interviews were broadcast on 20 October 1953 along with an invitation by Murrow which gave the US Air Force or anyone else an equal amount of time to refute the facts presented in their half-hour show. No one was forthcoming. Instead, amid a wave of popular support for the sacked lieutenant, the Air Force reinstated Radulovich a month after the broadcast.

This marked a turning point and gave people a new confidence against McCarthy. A few months later, on 9 March 1954, *See It Now* turned its guns directly on McCarthy. Their show consisted of film clips of McCarthy put together in such a way as to highlight his tyrannical manner. When McCarthy appeared on the show on 6 April and was given a chance to refute the portrayal of him, he did nothing but further damage his public reputation.

A cartoon of 1954 commenting on McCarthy's investigation of all elements of American life. (Leslie Illingworth, the Daily Mail, 12 March 1954, National Library of Wales, © Solo Syndication/Associated Newspapers)

At the same time McCarthy was being discredited by Murrow, he tried to pick a fight with the US Army. McCarthy accused Brigadier General Ralph Zwicker of promoting an army dentist suspected of communist leanings to the rank of major. In reply the army accused McCarthy of trying to obtain preferential treatment for G. David Schine, a friend of the anti-communist lawyer Roy Cohn. On 22 April 1954 a special committee was formed to adjudicate over these conflicting charges, the hearings of which were televised.

One of the most memorable moments of this televised hearing came on the afternoon of 9 June. The army had hired Joseph N. Welch of the Boston law firm of Hale & Dorr as its special counsel. When Welsh pressed McCarthy's council to hand over their supposed list with the names of people suspected of communism in defence plants, McCarthy replied that one of Welch's young colleagues at Hale & Dorr was a member of an organization with communist sympathies and accused Welch of unwittingly aiding communists. Welch hit back at the Senator with the ever memorable line: 'Have you no sense of decency, sir, at long last? Have you left no sense of decency?'

Like Robespierre in the French Revolution, McCarthy did not survive his own reign of terror. Ironically enough, he came under investigation himself, this time by the US Senate. On 2 December 1954 McCarthy was censured by a vote of 67 to 22 and his evil rule of fear at last came to an end.

THE POISONED APPLE

ALAN Turing is widely recognized by scientists as being among the founding fathers of the computer age. He was a genius, hopelessly eccentric and, in the secret world of code breaking, one of the brightest brains of the Second World War.

Working at the British code-breaking establishment at Bletchley Park, Turing's mathematical genius helped to develop the machines that broke the German Enigma cipher. Rather than try to work out the code, which had something like 150,000,000,000,000,000,000 possible variations, Turing's solution was to build a machine that would eliminate all the things the code could not be. By this process of elimination, the code would be broken.

In 1945 Turing was awarded the OBE for his services in wartime. While quietly continuing to work in the field of code breaking, he was employed by Manchester University in the field of computing. Unfortunately, like many we have encountered thus far, Turing was a homosexual at a time when practising homosexuality was a crime. Around Christmas 1951 Turing met a 19-year-old unemployed man, Arnold Murray, with whom he had a relationship.

Having invited him to his home on several occasions, Turing later accused Murray of stealing money from him and asked him to leave. Soon after this incident, Turing's home was broken into. He suspected that Murray was behind this and so went to the police. In the course of the police investigation, Turing admitted that he and

Murray had been having a relationship. Turing was arrested and on 31 March 1952 was convicted under the same 'gross indecency' charge levelled against Oscar Wilde.

Instead of a prison sentence, Turing consented to a hormonal treatment that would 'cure' him of his homosexuality. This hormone treatment has been described as a form of chemical castration. It also had the side effect of temporary breast enlargement.

The treatment lasted for a year, during and after which Turing continued to work at the university as normal. However, because of his conviction, Turing's security clearances were all revoked. For someone who had worked so closely on, and had such knowledge of, the biggest secret of the Second World War, this repudiation by the Establishment must have hurt badly. Indeed, although he showed little outward sign of depression, the rejection, coupled with the humiliation of the hormone treatment, must have pushed Turing too far to the edge.

On 8 June 1954 Turing's housekeeper found him dead in bed. There was a white froth around the corners of his mouth and a half-eaten apple beside his bed. An inquest later heard that Turing, who was just a few weeks from his 42nd birthday, had committed suicide by eating an apple laced with cyanide.*

Although most believe that Turing killed himself, many have wondered about the possibility of assassination, because of Turing's involvement in the secret service and the potential for him to become a security risk. There is, of course, absolutely no proof that this was the case. The biggest scandal here is perhaps not that Turing broke the rules but rather the attempts to 'cure' this wartime hero of something which 13 years later was no longer considered a crime.

---

* The use of the apple is thought to have been in homage to the Disney film *Snow White*.

FOOLS' GOLD

As plans go, Operation *Gold* was brilliant. To prevent an enemy eavesdropping on their wireless traffic, armies try to send their communications through secure land lines. So in August 1954, the CIA and British secret service started to dig a tunnel into Soviet-controlled East Berlin to tap into the underground cables used by the Soviet military to communicate from its Eastern Bloc bases to Moscow.

The tunnel was an amazing feat of ingenuity. It ran for 1,476 feet, was about 12 feet below the surface, and 6½ feet in diameter. More than 3,000 tons of earth were excavated during its construction, all of which had to be disposed of secretly. The actual taps were another major achievement. The Soviet cables were pressurized with nitrogen to protect the wires from moisture. When the taps were inserted there was a danger the nitrogen would leak out and register a loss of pressure that could be detected by the Soviets. Therefore, placing the 295 individual taps had to be performed extremely quickly without the slightest room for error. Amplifiers were then placed inside the tunnel to boost the signal enough for it to reach the end of the tunnel. The messages were recorded on 600 tape recorders using 800 reels of tape per day. As a final touch the tunnel was packed with enough plastic explosives to collapse it if the Soviets found out.

There was so much activity underground that when Berlin received a light dusting of winter snow, the heat rose up through the ground and melted the snow above the tunnel. Embarrassed spy chiefs quickly installed air conditioning inside the tunnel to reduce the ambient temperature to avoid such mistakes in future. Seemingly they had thought of everything ... the only trouble with the plan was that the Russians knew all about it from the start.

To understand why Operation *Gold* was fatally flawed we must first cast ourselves back into the Second World War. George Blake was born with the surname Behar in Holland to a Dutch mother and a Jewish father from Constantinople; he then became a naturalized British subject. With his dual nationality, during the Second World War Blake was recruited by the secret British sabotage organization Special Operations Executive, or SOE. He then joined the Secret Intelligence Service and after the war went on to serve in Korea, where he was captured.

At some time during his three years of captivity at the hands of the North Koreans, Blake was recruited as a Soviet spy. Why he switched sides has long remained a mystery. Blake claimed that it was a genuine conversion to the ideals of communism. Many others believe that he was brainwashed.

Brainwashing was a Chinese-inspired technique. By inflicting physical and psychological stress through incarceration, isolation and sleep-deprivation, the captive would slowly have his views and beliefs washed away by a steady stream of communist propaganda, lectures and debates. The process was slow and succeeded because the dog-tired victim finally persuaded himself that he had made the conversion to communism himself. If Blake was subjected to such a regime he would have been convinced that his conversion to communism was entirely his choice.

When Blake was released from North Korean captivity in 1953, he continued to work with MI6. When the subject of Operation

Gold came up, he took the minutes of the meeting and passed all the details over to his Soviet handlers before a shovel was raised.

Although the Soviets knew what they were looking for it took them months of painstaking searches using heat-seeking equipment to discover the exact location of the tunnel. All the time it is believed they ran a deception operation, pumping countless hours' worth of mostly useless information into the 440,000 telephone calls that were recorded during the 11 months the tunnel was active.

The Soviets' prime concern was not to expose Blake's treachery. They therefore waited until the night of 22 April 1956, when a party of KGB intelligence officers posing as telecom workers 'accidentally' discovered the tunnel. In order to avoid an even bigger scene, the Americans chose not to detonate the explosives and the tunnel was exposed to the world. It then became a tourist attraction to curious East Berliners.

George Blake was eventually exposed as a spy by a Polish defector in 1959 and was sentenced to 42 years in prison. Strangely enough he managed to break out of jail five years later and escape to the Soviet Union.

THE U-2 SCANDAL

ON 1 May 1960 Soviet air defences picked up a target heading northwards, flying at 68,000 feet. The appearance of this unidentified craft was a mite embarrassing for the Soviets, who were just about to put on their annual display of military prowess in a Red Square May Day parade. What was most galling is that there was very little the Soviets could do about the intruder. Since 1956 the Americans had been flying photo-reconnaissance missions over their airspace using the high-altitude U-2 spy-plane with impunity.

The aircraft continued to be tracked while Head of Air Defence Biryuzov was being berated by Nikita Khrushchev over the telephone for his inability to shoot the intruder down. The Soviet premier was furious that the Americans were conducting an operation on a national holiday and only two weeks before a scheduled peace summit between the two nations in Paris. So desperate did the calls for a shooting down become that a Soviet fighter was sent from the field at Sverdlovsk and told to ram the U-2. Luckily for the pilot he could not find the intruder.[82]

However, as the U-2 reached Sverdlovsk a SAM missile battalion launched its missiles at the spy-plane. One of the 14 missiles fired exploded behind the U-2 aircraft and was close enough to send pieces of shrapnel tearing through the tail section and wings.

Inside the aircraft CIA-hired pilot Francis Gary Powers heard a hollow thud and saw an orange flash behind him. He quickly started to lose control of the machine. His first thought was to set off the self-destruct sequence to leave no wreckage for the Soviets to examine, but there was a problem. After the explosion, Powers had been jolted forwards in his chair. If he ejected, both his legs would be amputated. From activation there would be just 70 seconds for Powers to get clear from the aircraft – without the eject system this would be highly difficult. He removed the canopy and, because the plane was spinning, was propelled out of the cockpit too quickly for him to reach the destruct button. As he fell to safety a second missile struck the doomed aircraft and scattered fragments of it over several miles.

Within hours, investigators were eagerly recovering aircraft parts, in particular the film from the U-2's spy cameras. The film

Soviet cartoon called 'The Art of Camouflage' commenting on Eisenhower's dedication to the cause of peace during the U-2 crisis. (Topfoto)

was discovered intact, allowing the Soviets to develop it and see exactly what the Americans had been looking at. They also found pilot Powers alive and took him to the KGB's infamous Lubyanka prison in Moscow. Not that they admitted as much to the Americans.

On 3 May, the US government announced the loss of a scientific aircraft over Turkish airspace. The report said that the aircraft was believed to have crashed in a lake in eastern Turkey after the pilot reported an oxygen equipment malfunction. Two days later more announcements were made; this time the State Department and NASA issued statements to reinforce the peaceful role of the mission.

On 7 May the Soviets announced that Powers was still alive. This came as a shock to the US government, who had assumed that Powers had either died in the crash, or had the good sense to use the cyanide needle the CIA helpfully provided so that the pilot would be spared the horrors of torture. This disclosure forced the US to admit they had flown over Soviet territory and had been doing so for a number of years. Khrushchev kept his powder dry and waited for the most opportune moment to make US President Eisenhower look as bad as possible. He did not have to wait long.

Khrushchev, Eisenhower and British Prime Minister Harold Macmillan had been invited to Paris by French President Charles de Gaulle for a peace summit scheduled for 16 May. Instead of peace discussions taking place, the summit was torpedoed by Khrushchev, who brought along photographs recovered from the shot-down U-2. Eisenhower refused to apologize for the incident, throwing in the line that it was his duty to protect America from another Pearl Harbor. Khrushchev stormed out and Eisenhower was left with a large splodge of egg on his face.

In August 1960 Powers was subjected to a show trial in Moscow. It lasted three days, at the end of which Powers was sentenced to ten years' imprisonment. He actually returned home early in 1962 along with an American student, Frederic Pryor, in exchange for the Soviet spy Rudolph Abel, who was held by the United States.

Powers' return to the United States was by no means the end of the matter. Questions were immediately asked as to how on earth he had been shot down in the first place. The known ceiling of the Soviet SAM missile was 63,000 feet, and Powers should have been nearer to 70,000 feet – so what had gone wrong?

The truth is, we still do not know. A Senate Committee on Armed Services cleared Powers of any blame, although some in the CIA wondered if Powers had fallen asleep during the long tedious flight.[83]

Francis Gary Powers later became a helicopter pilot for KNBC-TV in Los Angeles. On 1 August 1977 his Bell 206 Jetranger helicopter crashed on the way back from covering a brush fire. Powers and his cameraman, George Spears, were both killed. The crash was later blamed on fuel starvation: Powers had run out of gas.

THE PROFUMO AFFAIR

Coming as it did in the middle of the Cold War, after a succession of scandals rocking the British establishment and armed forces, the Profumo Affair ranks almost as highly as the one that consumed Alfred Dreyfus.

John Dennis Profumo was a high-flying British politician and Secretary of State for War in the Conservative government of Harold Macmillan. Entering the House at the age of 25, he was the youngest Member of Parliament and he also had a fabulous war record, being mentioned in despatches during the North Africa campaign and landing in Normandy on D-Day with an armoured brigade. Married to the actress Valerie Hobson in 1954, fortunes were rising for Jack Profumo as the 1960s began. Many tipped him to reach the highest positions in government.

On 8 July 1961 Profumo and his wife were attending a party thrown by Lord Astor at his Cliveden estate, which was attended by the President of Pakistan as guest of honour. As the guests were finishing off their dinner, two characters were outside frolicking by the pool.

Lord Astor rented a cottage on the estate to Dr Stephen Ward, a high-profile osteopath, occasional artist and full-time party animal. Ward was very well connected in society circles and had an amazing knack of attracting the most beautiful women. With him that night was a stunning 20-year-old, named Christine

Keeler, whom he had met working as a show girl at Murray's Cabaret Club in London's Soho district.

As part of the horseplay around the pool, Keeler had taken off an ill-fitting swimming costume she was wearing and was naked when Lord Astor and Profumo came out to see what all the laughter was about. It was then that Profumo was introduced, by Ward, to Keeler. Leaving the pool and putting a towel over herself, Keeler was also introduced to Profumo's wife, who offered to lend Keeler one of her swimming costumes. A few days after the event, Profumo called Astor and a meeting with Keeler was set up. The affair was consummated soon after.

Also at the estate that weekend was Captain Yevgeny 'Eugene' Ivanov, the assistant Soviet naval attaché in London, a known GRU military intelligence officer. At the same time as Keeler was seeing Profumo she pursued her own interests in Ivanov. This was a highly complicated arrangement. What if Ivanov was having an affair with Keeler in order to use her to blackmail Profumo for secrets?

MI5 picked up on Profumo's liaison with Keeler very quickly. In fact, they were informed about it by Stephen Ward, who had liaisons with the secret services. Realizing the obvious implications for national security, MI5 contacted the Cabinet Secretary, Norman Brook, and warned him about the risk Profumo was taking. Brook spoke to Profumo about the matter. Profumo wrote to Keeler on 9 August to say that he could not see her and also advised Brook to warn another member of the cabinet about seeing Keeler. The identity of this politician has never been revealed.

Profumo did see Keeler a few times more, but the affair came to an end in December 1961. The first inkling of its becoming a public scandal appeared only on 31 July 1962, when a few lines were published in *Queen* magazine. In a regular column entitled *Sentences I'd Like to Hear the End Of* journalist Robin Douglas-Home, nephew of the Foreign Secretary, wrote:

> ... called in MI5 because every time the chauffeur driven Zil drew up out her front door, out of the back door into a chauffeur driven Humber slipped ...

From the makes of cars involved, it was clear that there was a link connecting a woman, someone from the Soviet embassy (which used Zil limousines), someone in the British government, and the security service MI5. Despite these cryptic clues no one was yet in a position to push the matter any further.

All this changed in a bizarre totally unrelated event. Keeler began a turbulent relationship with Aloysius 'Lucky' Gordon, a West Indian man from whom she had bought marijuana. After numerous bouts of violence, Keeler moved in with another West Indian man named Johnny Edgecombe. On 27 October 1962 Edgecombe attacked Gordon with a knife, leaving him with a slash across his face requiring 17 stitches. Keeler realized she was mixing with a dangerous crowd and tried to distance herself from both men. On 14 December Edgecombe arrived at Stephen Ward's apartment looking for Keeler, who happened to be there, visiting her friend Mandy Rice-Davis. When Edgecombe was denied entry, he tried to shoot the lock out with a revolver. Mandy Rice-Davis called Ward, who was working at his clinic, and the osteopath in turn called Scotland Yard. By the time the police had arrived Edgecombe had fled. He was later arrested at home and charged with attempting to murder Keeler.

Unsurprisingly, Ward asked Keeler to keep her distance in the future. Feeling dejected, Keeler decided to lift the lid on certain goings on in Ward's apartment. Keeler was introduced to John Lewis, the former Labour MP for Bolton, who hated Ward, believing he had led his wife astray. Keeler revealed to Lewis that Ward had asked her to find out about the delivery dates of nuclear warheads to West Germany from Profumo. This clearly implied that Ward was working for the Soviets.

On 2 January 1963 Lewis contacted MP George Wigg, the Opposition expert on intelligence matters. A veteran of both world wars, Colonel Wigg held a grudge against Profumo and immediately saw a means to destroy the Secretary of State for War. He began a private investigation into the matter.

Meanwhile Keeler was approached by and sold her story to the *Sunday Pictorial*, giving them the handwritten note to her from the Secretary of State that had been written on 9 August 1961.

"We won't detain you long, Miss Keeler. Just until all the American V.I.P.s are out of the country"

Cartoon depicting President Kennedy's visit to Britain at the height of the Profumo Affair, 30 June 1963. (Carl Giles, the Sunday Express, *30 June 1963, the British Cartoon Archive, University of Kent, © Express newspapers)*

Before the newspaper published the account, Stephen Ward caught a whiff of it and strongly advised the newspaper to drop the story, which – he claimed – was inaccurate and would lead to a very costly libel suit.

At the time newspapers were very wary about running such stories as recent libel cases had seen record payments. The story remained under wraps until 8 March 1963, when an American journalist, Andrew Roth, gave a thinly disguised account of the scandal in the *Westminster Confidential*, which was widely read by MPs. At this point Profumo was questioned by his superiors, but he denied the allegations and said that he would take legal action against anyone who linked his name to the story.

A few days later, on 14 March, Johnny Edgecombe's trial opened at the Old Bailey. He was charged with the attempted murder of Christine Keeler who, in a bizarre twist, fled Britain and headed for Spain to avoid the spotlight.

The *Daily Express* newspaper saw an opportunity here and very cleverly ran a story featuring a photo of Profumo and his wife on one side of the page, declaring he had threatened to resign over a matter of government policy, and a large photo of Keeler on the other side of the page, with the story that she had fled to Spain and not turned up for the Edgecombe trial. Although the stories were apparently unconnected, for those in the know, it showed that the press was aware of the story and was just waiting for the right opportunity to pounce.*

On 21 March 1963, George Wigg decided that the time was right to deliver his attack. He took part in a debate about national

---

* This is a common trick by newspapers. Next time you see an article about a scandal with persons unnamed for legal reasons, look to see who else is on the page – there is a chance the stories are connected!

security which had been provoked by the imprisonment of an Admiralty clerk, William Vassall, on charges of espionage. During the debate, Wigg stood up, and using his parliamentary privilege, which allows an MP to ask any question in the House without fear of legal action, asked the government to deny the well-known rumours involving a member of the cabinet.

The Prime Minister was woken in the early hours of the morning by the Conservative Party's 'Chief Whip', Martin Redman, who explained the allegation. Both Macmillan and Redman felt that Profumo needed to make a statement on the subject before the press got themselves into a frenzy over Wigg's remarks.

The evening before, Profumo had gone to bed, taken the telephone off the hook and popped some sleeping pills. When he could not be summoned on the telephone a car was sent for him and he was literally dragged out of bed and made to draw up a statement. At 11.00am Profumo went into the House of Commons and committed political suicide. He lied to the House.

Profumo admitted meeting Keeler and being on friendly terms but denied any impropriety whatsoever in his acquaintance with her. He finished his statement with the threat of legal action if the allegations were made or repeated outside the House of Commons. Amid cheers from his own Conservative Party, Profumo left the House as if in triumph. His safety appeared all the more secure when a reporter tracked Keeler down in Spain. On 25 March the *Daily Express* published an interview with Keeler in which she confirmed Profumo's denials of any impropriety.

George Wigg, seething at Profumo's apparent escape, appeared on a current affairs programme and spoke about a continued threat to national security. This programme marked a shifting of strategy by Wigg. He had tried a direct assault on Profumo but failed.

Instead he kept hammering away at the angle that national security had been compromised. The day after the programme he was contacted by Stephen Ward, who convinced him Profumo had lied. Eventually Wigg managed to convince the leader of the Opposition, Harold Wilson, to meet with Macmillan and urge him to open an inquiry into the business.

Finally on 31 May there was such a body of evidence that the *People* newspaper informed Macmillan it was going to expose Profumo as a liar. The Secretary of State for War at last decided to come clean, and, after talking the matter through with his wife, offered his resignation to the Prime Minister, who accepted. On 5 June 1963 Profumo entered the House and admitted that he had lied. In so doing he ended his political career.

As the Profumos went off into hiding the media spun round looking for someone on whom to vent the nation's wrath. They were led to the door of Stephen Ward. Tipped off by MI5, Special Branch had been investigating certain activities at Ward's apartment. Behind the scenes of Profumo's affair was a lurid tale of high-class orgies and call girls – and all roads led back to Ward as the procurer of girls for these parties. On 8 June Ward was arrested and charged with living on the earnings of prostitutes – in other words they accused him of being a pimp.

Between Ward's trial and an inquiry made by Lord Denning into the security aspects of the matter, the country was left rocking by an unbelievable exposé of debauchery at the highest levels of British society. Giving evidence to the Denning Inquiry, Mandy Rice-Davis lifted the lid on the infamous 'Man in the Mask' orgy, where a prominent personality willingly allowed himself to be flogged and humiliated at party hosted by Mareilla Novotny, who claimed to have had an affair with Jack Kennedy. There was enormous speculation about the identity of this masked man, who was variously rumoured to be a senior member of the royal family, another cabinet minister, or a prominent, anglophile Hollywood actor.*

Although Denning found the business sordid, he concluded that there had been no risk to security. With Profumo cleared of any wrongdoing, other than having lied and committed adultery, the axe fell on Stephen Ward. His trial was a real hatchet job now famous for a quote made by Mandy Rice-Davis. When told Lord Astor denied her claim that he paid her for sex, she replied: 'Well, he would, wouldn't he?'

With his friends deserting him in droves, Ward resorted to suicide on the last day of the trial. He took an overdose and died three days later on 3 August 1963.

Perhaps the most scandalous aspect of the whole affair is the role of MI5 throughout. The boss of the security service, Roger Hollis, knew all about the Profumo–Keeler–Ivanov affair but did not come forward at any point and inform the government that Profumo had lied to them. Completely contrary to the claims being made by Keeler, that Ward was trying to get secrets for the Russian, it seems that Ward was working for MI5 and that the security service were trying to get Ivanov to defect to the West. To achieve this Keeler was used as what they call a 'honey trap' against Ivanov. The speculation is that the original plan was for Ward to fix Keeler up with Ivanov and to get him to defect or at least pass secrets.

Profumo's involvement was pure unlucky coincidence, but one which MI5 tried to turn to their advantage. Ward met with MI5 and told them the Soviet agent was asking Ward to find out if

---

* The FBI looked into the Profumo Affair after rumours of links back to President Kennedy. The investigation was codenamed *BOWTIE* and is available at the FBI's website to download.

nuclear weapons were going to be sent to West Germany. It seems probable that between MI5, Ward and Profumo, Keeler was being fed false information to pass on to Ivanov. If this is the case they made a real hash of it as Keeler baulked at the idea of being involved in a spy game.

If MI5's involvement was as deep as is widely reported, it is even harder to fathom why the security service threw Stephen Ward to the lions and closed ranks to protect Profumo. Was it a case of 'The Establishment' looking after its own?

Probably.[84]

OPERATION *RANCH HAND*

To deny jungle cover and food crops to the Vietcong, between 1961 and 1971 the United States sprayed about 80 million litres of poisonous defoliants over the Vietnamese countryside. Of these defoliants the most famous was Agent Orange. Over 45 million litres of this poison was sprayed over roughly one tenth of the country.

Aside from killing off large portions of countryside, Agent Orange is believed to have caused some extremely nasty side effects to the humans who came into contact with it. Agent Orange was a 50:50 mixture of the chemicals 2,4-D and 2,4,5-T. The latter component was found to contain the contaminant TCDD, regarded as one of the most toxic chemicals known to man. The military then sprayed the agent in an undiluted state, which made it about 25 times stronger than the manufacturer's recommendation.

Although the risk of dioxin poisoning was known from the start of the operation, no one appeared too concerned about the damage it might cause because the chemical agents were being used against an enemy. Apparently it did not occur to anyone that US troops and innocent civilians might come into contact with the chemical too.

The idea of using chemical herbicides first arose in 1961. American personnel in South Vietnamese aircraft conducted trials, which gained the support of South Vietnam's President Diem. The South Vietnamese were already burning crops to deny food to their enemy; Diem urged the US to speed things up by deploying chemicals.

From the start the US Department of Defense was in favour of expanding the programme, but it was aware this programme might cause adverse reaction around the world – although the US administration could cite the earlier example of the British using defoliants against insurgents' food crops in Malaya.

To begin with the US decided not to go for crop-growing areas, and agreed to target transport routes only. This tactic could be justified on the grounds of denying cover to would-be ambushes and was not thought to violate any international law. There was a precedent set by the French troops in Vietnam a decade before, who burned off all vegetation along important roads. Chemicals were seen as another way to achieve the same result.

On 30 November 1961 President John F. Kennedy approved the start of Operation *Ranch Hand*. Initially all targets had to be approved by the Oval Office, but after a year of missions, target approval was delegated to the commander in South Vietnam.

Meanwhile President Diem continued to advocate using herbicides for crop destruction. On 2 October 1962 President Kennedy authorized restricted crop spraying. Still wary of the indiscriminate nature of this tactic and possible adverse publicity, only South Vietnamese personnel and equipment carried out chemical attacks on crops.

As the war escalated and Operation *Ranch Hand* was expanded to target crops, the Americans were still so sensitive that *Ranch Hand* aircraft were given South Vietnamese markings when on crop missions. By the end of 1965, as US commitment grew, the controls on *Ranch Hand* operations were relaxed and US aircraft even started missions against Vietcong assets over the border in Laos.

In fact Operation *Ranch Hand* was only the aerial component of an overall herbicide programme, which was known as Operation

Trail Dust. Most of the aerial spraying was done from modified C-123 transport aircraft and helicopters. However, herbicides were also sprayed by soldiers on the ground and out of the back of trucks. Even the navy was involved, with riverboats spraying herbicide along the river banks. *Ranch Hand* missions remained the mainstay of the programme and its operations steadily increased, peaking in 1967 when the unit sprayed 1.7 million acres.

The first big condemnation of the programme came with the Cha La incident in 1964. A *Ranch Hand* aircraft accidentally sprayed the friendly village of Cha La and destroyed its crops. The *Washington Post* ran the story and called for the end of herbicide use in the conflict. In 1967 two reports by the think-tank Rand Corporation also cast doubts over the strategy. The reports claimed that the use of herbicides had done little to affect Vietcong rice supplies, but had harmed civilians and was therefore alienating the rural South Vietnamese population from the government. In both the *Washington Post* article and the Rand Corporation reports, it was pointed out that spraying chemicals was too indiscriminate in a guerrilla war where the Vietcong frequently mixed with innocent civilians.

These were only some of a number of calls to end the *Ranch Hand* missions. By 1969 political expediency caused President Nixon's administration to look for a way to put an end to *Ranch Hand*. That autumn a scientific report demonstrated that high doses of a component of Agent Orange could cause stillbirths and birth defects in mice. On 15 April 1970 the chemical 2,4,5-T was banned in the United States after the Surgeon General issued a warning that its use might be hazardous to health. Although the military wanted to continue using Agent Orange, the Defense Department banned its use in April. The military instead turned to another defoliant, Agent White. *Ranch Hand* did not come to an end until 7 January 1971.[85]

People now wanted to know the ecological cost of *Ranch Hand*. The sheer quantities of herbicide used were staggering:[86]

Agent*	Years used:	Estimated litres sprayed:
Pink	1961; 1965	50,312
Green	Uncertain	31,026
Purple	1962–65	1,892,773
Orange	1965–70	45,677,937
Orange II	1968–?	Unknown (3,591,000 sent to Vietnam)
White	1966–71	20,556,525
Blue (powder)	1962–64	25,650
Blue (H$_2$O solution)	1964–71	4,715,731

The area affected by the programme was also astounding:[87]

Year	Acres Treated
1962	5,724
1963	24,920
1964	93,869
1965	221,552
1966	845,263
1967	1,707,784
1968	1,696,337
1969	1,519,606
1970	252,989
1971	3,346
Total:	**6,371,390 acres (25,784,206 km^2)**

---

* Agents were named for the coloured bands found on the containers.

It should be noted that the above figure does not take into account some areas being sprayed multiple times. It is estimated that about 12 per cent of the total area covered by *Ranch Hand* had received triple coverage. As a result mangrove areas in the southern part of South Vietnam were devastated, with 36 per cent destroyed.

However, in 1974 a three-year study by the National Academy of Sciences revealed that they had found no direct evidence of human health damage from herbicides. They had found second-hand evidence that herbicides had caused fatal respiratory problems in children, but – presumably – with the children no longer alive, no positive evidence could be ascertained.

As the veterans came home the government's controversial use of defoliants continued to stay in the news and legal challenges for compensation were filed. In 1984 chemical companies that manufactured Agent Orange refused to admit that there were any harmful side effects, but paid $180 million to US veterans of the conflict who claimed that their health had been affected by exposure to the substance.

In 2004 the Vietnamese Association for Victims of Agent Orange/Dioxin (VAVAO) attempted a legal challenge against several US companies for developing the chemicals that they claimed had caused cancers and other illnesses, not to mention birth defects and severe illnesses in as many as 150,000 children in Vietnam.[88] The suit was dismissed in March 2005 after the judge concluded that Agent Orange was not considered a poison by the international community at the time it was used and that therefore there was no case to answer.

DRAFTING ALI

LIKE most eighteen-year-old Americans that year, in 1960 Cassius Marcellus Clay registered for the draft. Two years later he became eligible and, on 24 January 1964, was ordered to undertake a military qualifying examination.

As a young professional boxer and the gold medal winner of the 1960 Olympic Light Heavyweight competition, Clay had no trouble passing his army physical. However, when confronted with a mental aptitude test, Clay failed miserably, attaining an IQ score of just 78, which placed him in the 16th percentile of potential draftees.

The pass mark was 30%. Anyone could flunk an examination, especially if it was to avoid military service, so Clay was recalled to sit the examination two months later. Under the watchful eyes of three army psychologists he failed again and on 26 March 1964 was classified 1-Y – 'not qualified under current standards for service in the armed forces'.

This would have been all well and good had not Clay just become the youngest ever heavyweight boxing champion of the world. On 25 February 1964, Clay shocked the sporting world by beating Sonny Liston, the self-professed 'baddest-man-on-the-planet'. Shortly after the victory, the boxer then announced that he was a member of the Nation of Islam group and no longer wanted to be known by his 'slave name' Clay. Henceforth he became first Cassius X, then Muhammad Ali. Against this background, when

Ali – the best fighter on the planet – was declared unfit for military service, there was uproar.

The army defended its decision, saying that it needed recruits capable of learning new skills and that the current examination process should be respected. When people asked if Ali was not intelligent enough to peel potatoes, Secretary to the Army Stephen Ailes asked a question of his own: should Ali be drafted simply because of his national prominence?

Ali was understandably embarrassed by the public discussion of his low IQ, telling reporters: 'I said I was the greatest, not the smartest.'[89]

And so the matter rested until, in 1966, the escalation of the Vietnam War caused the government to lower the entry requirement for the draft. The pass mark changed from 30% to 15% making Ali eligible. On 17 February 1966, Ali was reclassified 1-A – fit for service.

The heavyweight champ first heard of this when a local news truck arrived at the front of his house for his comment. Then the telephone started ringing and Ali was caught on the back foot. He was bombarded with questions with the simple aim of goading him into making a headline-grabbing statement. Eventually it came. When asked 'What do you think of the Vietcong?' Ali replied: 'Man, I ain't got no quarrel with the Vietcong.'[90]

That was the knock-out punch line they had been waiting for. Already widely despised as a loud-mouthed black Muslim, Ali – the Louisville Lip – was now thrown to the wolves as an unpatriotic and cowardly draft dodger.

On 17 March 1966 Ali appeared before the draft board and applied for conscientious objector status. The request was denied but then sustained on appeal six weeks later. On 23 August Ali's appeal was heard by hearing officer Lawrence Grauman. At the start of the hearing Ali handed over a letter outlining his religious beliefs with an account of how he had converted to the Nation of Islam. In a statement to the hearing, Ali said that he realized this stand would cost him the support of the American public and would cost him millions of dollars in earnings, whereas if he had had no conscience, he could have joined the army and enjoyed an easy war performing at army boxing tournaments.

Somewhat unexpectedly, Grauman accepted Ali's argument and ruled that he was of good character and was sincere in his objection to war in any form. He recommended that Ali's claim be sustained. This decision caused an even bigger backlash. Based in large part on an investigation by the FBI, the Department of Justice wrote to the Appeal Board opposing Grauman's decision.

In order to qualify for classification as a conscientious objector, Ali would have to satisfy three basic tests:

1. that he was conscientiously opposed to war in any form
2. that his opposition was based upon religious training and belief
3. that his objection was sincere.[91]

The Department of Justice argued that Ali was not opposed to 'war in any form' but was only selectively opposed to certain wars, and that his objection was limited to service in the Armed Forces of the United States. Furthermore the teaching of the Nation of Islam was deemed to be political and racial rather than religious. Despite Grauman's recommendation, the Department of Justice wrote a letter to the Appeal Board, advising it that Ali's conscientious objector claim should be denied.

While these wranglings were taking place, Ali's career was badly affected. In upholding his claim to be a conscientious objector Ali did himself no favours in his fight with Ernie Terrell, which even in the bloody annals of pugilism left a bad taste in many a mouth. Terrell insisted on calling Ali by his birth name, Cassius Clay. On 6 February 1967, Ali entered the ring and punished Terrell for 15 rounds. It was as if he deliberately refused to knock Terrell out so he could prolong the agony over the full distance of the fight. In between the flurries of punches, Ali could be heard taunting Terrell: 'What's my name, Uncle Tom? What's my name?' These were hardly the actions of a man of peace.

A month after the Terrell fight, on 6 March the Appeal Board voted to retain Ali's 1-A classification. Soon Ali would have to decide between the army or prison. Although many believed that Ali would eventually choose the army over prison, the fighter's increasingly hard-line stance should have left them in no doubt: 'Why should they ask me to put on a uniform and go ten thousand miles from home and drop bombs and bullets on brown people in Vietnam while so-called Negro people in Louisville are treated like dogs?'[92]

On 28 April Ali arrived at an induction centre in Houston, Texas. He went through the formalities of registration and a physical examination, then after lunch was taken with 25 other young men into the 'ceremony room' where the induction process would be carried out.

It was a simple affair. After a brief prologue, each candidate's name was called out and the candidate was required to take a step forward signifying acceptance of the call to arms. When the name 'Cassius Marcellus Clay' was called out, Ali stood motionless. When it became clear he would not step forward he was taken into an adjoining room and cautioned that his refusal to accept induction was a criminal offence punishable with up to five years in jail and a $5,000 fine. Ali declared that he was aware of this and returned to the ceremony room where his name was again called. Ali stood still.

Within an hour of Ali's refusing to take his step forward, the boxing authorities of America stripped him of his heavyweight crown. On 8 May Ali was indicted by a Federal Grand Jury in Houston. He was released on $5,000 bail on the condition that he did not leave the continental United States. Although not yet in jail, banned from boxing in the States, he was now unable to earn a livelihood by fighting abroad. The greatest boxer in the history of the sport was to be robbed of his best years in the ring.

The legal battle now began. Ali was given every indication that if he backed down he would be given a non-combat role, entertaining the troops. Some felt Ali had backed himself into a corner and could not, or would not, allow himself to lose face. The Nation of Islam strongly denied putting pressure on Ali to turn him into a martyr for their cause. However their actions look less than sincere in the light of their suspending Ali from being a Muslim for a year. With the gravy boat empty – what need did they have for a former champion?

On 19 June Ali went to court and was found guilty of not accepting the draft. He was sentenced to the maximum five years and fined $10,000. The assistant United States attorney, Carl Walker, who presented the government's case against Ali, gave an interesting insight into the political motivations at work during the trial. Walker was responsible for prosecuting a large number of draft evaders, but, to the best of his knowledge, the Ali case was the only time that the recommendation of conscientious objector status was turned down having been recommended by the hearing examiner.[93]

At the time America was a divided nation. On the one hand there was a very conservative establishment, which had come through the Second World War and saw itself in real danger from communist menace. On the other hand the mid- to late 1960s was a time of civil-rights movements, The Beatles had invaded, youth culture had exploded in a way never before seen and opposition to the war in Vietnam was flourishing into a fully fledged peace movement. Everything about the American way of life was being questioned and, in the minds of many conservatives, Ali's refusal to be drafted was the apex of an anti-social tidal wave threatening to destroy the very fabric of society.

In the ensuing legal action, the court had to acknowledge that blacks were underrepresented on draft boards. The government's case also received a setback when it was revealed that the FBI had monitored telephone conversations involving Ali. On 28 June 1971 the United States Supreme Court reversed his conviction on a technicality, clearing his way to begin a comeback which culminated in his 1974 'Rumble in the Jungle', where he sensationally regained

"Your call-up papers, Muhammad!"

Cartoon published as Muhammad Ali's case as a conscientious objector was to be reconsidered at a Kentucky Selective Board. (Jak [Raymond Jackson], the Evening Standard, 8 February 1967, the British Cartoon Archive, University of Kent, © Solo Syndication/Associated Newspapers)

the title from George Foreman in Zaire.[94]

By 2005 Muhammad Ali's rehabilitation was completed when President George W. Bush awarded him America's highest civilian honour – the Presidential Medal of Freedom. His citation read:

> One of the greatest athletes of all time, Muhammad Ali produced some of America's most lasting sports memories, from winning the Gold Medal at the 1960 Summer Olympics to carrying the Olympic torch at the 1996 Summer Olympics. As the first three-time heavyweight boxing champion of the world, he thrilled, entertained, and inspired us. His deep commitment to equal justice and peace has touched people around the world. The United States honors Muhammad Ali for his lifetime of achievement and for his principled service to mankind.[95]

ACT V

'EVEN IN OUR ENLIGHTENED TIMES?'

MURDER AT LILLEHAMMER

FOLLOWING the kidnapping and death of 11 of their athletes during the 1972 Munich Olympics, Israel decided to strike back at the Palestinian 'Black September' terrorists who had planned and enacted the outrage.

With the backing of Israeli Prime Minister Golda Meir, teams of Mossad agents were sent out to take the war to the terrorists. The plan was not simply to kill them, but to use terror tactics against them and to make their kills as spectacular as they were unexpected. After Munich it was quite simply a case of 'an eye for an eye'. These missions are now known under the collective title Operation *Wrath of God*. There were numerous teams involved, each working on hit lists provided by Israeli secret service chiefs.

Of all the people selected for assassination, perhaps the number one target – and certainly one of the most high-profile figures – was Ali Hassan Salameh, nicknamed the Red Prince. The Palestinian-born Salameh was thought to be chief of operations of the Black September group. He was young, and extremely popular for his playboy image and penchant for fast cars and beautiful girls. He was close to PLO leader Yasser Arafat and was tipped by many as his successor. He also maintained on–off links with the CIA, although as an ally of Israel the United States kept this information very close to its chest.

Salameh was extremely well guarded, but in July 1973 there were reports that he was in Scandinavia. A Mossad team was sent to investigate and travelled from Stockholm to Oslo, then on to the Norwegian town of Lillehammer.

Having identified their man, the team organized an assassination. The target was monitored and followed. On 28 July Salameh was seen to leave his apartment with a young woman. The couple went to the cinema and watched the film *Where Eagles Dare* – the well-known war movie staring Clint Eastwood and Richard Burton. As the couple left the cinema they were followed by a group of Israeli agents.

They caught a bus and were walking back to the apartment when a white Mazda pulled up in front of them. A male and female Israeli agent jumped out of the Mazda and opened fire. Struck repeatedly in the stomach, the target fell to the ground where he was finished off. In all he was hit with 14 bullets. As his female companion started screaming, the Mossad agents jumped into their car and sped off.

The only trouble was they had got the wrong man. The man they had identified as Salameh was in fact a completely innocent Moroccan waiter named Ahmed Bouchiki and the woman was his pregnant wife, Turil.

Norwegian police were quickly on the trail of the Mossad agents. With a population of just 20,000 souls, the good citizens of Lillehammer had indeed noticed the arrival of a dozen or more Israelis and had watched them hanging around outside Bouchiki's home. As the Mossad agents fled to Oslo and a flight out of the country, Norwegian police were already hot on their trail. Within a few days, six of the Mossad team were in custody and – rather than acting like the élite secret agents we might imagine – between them they talked quite freely about what they were doing and their links to the Israeli government.

The Israeli government had not wanted any mistakes – in other words no civilians hurt. At the same time they wanted to be able to deny any involvement. The six agents blabbed and Norwegian police were even able to recover a key to a safe house in Paris. When this key was passed on to the French police, it in turn revealed a number of safe houses in Paris, which linked the Lillehammer team members with other *Wrath of God* operations.

The whole cloak of deniability was breathtakingly shattered and caused a public relations disaster from which Mossad would take years to recover.[96]

'GOTCHA!'

A CYNICAL view of the 1982 Falklands Conflict is that it was a classic example of two unpopular governments resorting to violent jingoism in order to direct attention away from failed domestic agendas. It also scandalously robbed the British public of the chance to watch Argentinean football stars Ossie Ardilles and Ricky Villa play in the 1982 FA Cup final for Tottenham Hotspur. However, on a more serious note...

At 11:00am on 30 April a 'total exclusion zone' was established by the British within a 200-mile radius of the Falkland Islands. Four days before, the Argentine *General Belgrano* had left Ushuaia with an escort of two destroyers on a course to intercept the British naval task force.

On 1 May the three Argentine ships were picked up by the British nuclear submarine HMS *Conqueror* and tracked. Although it was outside the limits of the exclusion zone the commander of *Conqueror*, Chris Wreford-Brown, was concerned that the *Belgrano* might be able to reach a position from which it could cause havoc with the task force unless he attacked. His concern came at a time when British intelligence was warning that the Argentines were about to launch a full-scale attack on the task force. A decision was taken by the government and *Belgrano*'s fate was sealed.

The following day, at 18:56pm GMT *Conqueror* fired a salvo of three torpedoes at the cruiser *General Belgrano*. After a 57-second run, Wreford-Brown saw an orange fire-ball as the first torpedo struck the ship; five seconds later he witnessed a second explosion and a large spurt of water or steam. By the time of the third explosion he was no longer waiting to see what had happened but was busy plotting his way out of danger.

On board the *Belgrano* there was pandemonium. The first torpedo had blown the bow of the ship off. The second punched through the armour plating and blew up, knocking out the ship's electrical power. Although the bulkhead doors were secure, the ship began listing heavily. About 25 minutes later Captain Bonzo ordered his crew to abandon ship. In total 323 Argentine crew were lost in the attack, the

This cartoon of Margaret Thatcher was published in August 1984 when confidential documents about the sinking of the Belgrano *were leaked. (John Kent, the* Evening Standard, *20 August 1984, the British Cartoon Archive, University of Kent, © Solo Syndication/Associated Newspapers)*

majority of whom were killed by the second explosion, which took out several mess rooms.

Although the mission was a success – the Argentine Navy kept well away from the Falklands for the rest of the war – the sinking of the *Belgrano* left a bitter taste. The early edition headline in the popular tabloid *The Sun* infamously read: 'GOTCHA!' Later editions were toned down as the reality of the situation sank in. Hundreds of young men were either dead or adrift in the bitterly cold South Atlantic, desperately praying for rescue.

When it was later revealed not only that the *Belgrano* had been attacked outside the exclusion zone, but that it was in fact sailing away from the islands at the time of the strike there was a wave of outrage. Sure enough the British had changed their rules of engagement to allow *Conqueror* to attack the *Belgrano* outside the exclusion zone and this decision had been personally authorized by Prime Minister Margaret Thatcher, who received criticism for the attack long into her premiership. The sinking was labelled as somewhere between an act of piracy and a war crime, or both.

In the fullness of time it appears the British were justified in sending the *Belgrano* to the bottom. In a TV interview more than two decades after the sinking Héctor Bonzo admitted that he was still under orders to attack the British fleet wherever he found it and that he was anxious to do so.[97] His westward movement on the morning of 2 May was only a temporary measure to get the *Belgrano* into a better attacking position – not back to Argentina.*

---

* One final irony is that the *Belgrano* had been sold to Argentina by the United States. In US service the *Belgrano* had been named USS *Phoenix* and was a survivor of the 1941 Japanese Pearl Harbor attack.

THE BABY SNATCHERS

I N many respects, the British recapture of the Falkland Islands did Argentina a big, albeit backhanded, favour. If the ruling military Junta led by General Galtieri had got away with seizing the islands, it would probably have remained in power for much longer and the dark age of military rule would have been allowed to continue. But with the loss of face – perhaps even humiliation is not too strong a word – Galtieri and Co. were ousted and democracy was allowed to make a welcome return to the country.

The Junta's stewardship of Argentina had lasted from 1976 to 1983. During that time the military dictatorship carried out 'the Dirty War' – a scandalous, massive and indiscriminate campaign against so-called subversives and terrorists, including thousands of labour activists, members of the clergy, human rights campaigners, scientists, doctors and leaders of opposition parties – all of whom were outlawed.[98]

This campaign consisted of brutal and systematic detention, horrible torture and in some cases the literal disappearance of victims – disappearance being a euphemism for murder. Although official estimates put the figure of *los desaparecidos* (the disappeared) at around 9,000 people, human rights groups claim that the figure is much higher – perhaps as many as 30,000. Taken from their homes by military snatch squads, blindfolded and beaten, the victims of the regime were taken to secret detention

232

centres, like the notorious one at the Navy School of Mechanics (ESMA) in Buenos Aires.

As is generally the case, when freedom is restored to an oppressed people there follows a period of recrimination. In 1983 the incoming Argentinean president, Dr Raul Alfonsin, formed the National Commission on the Disappearance of Persons (CONADEP) to investigate the fates of the thousands who disappeared during the Junta rule. The commission was to collect evidence concerning these events, and pass the information to the courts in those cases where crimes had been committed.

After hearing thousands of horrific testimonies, CONADEP published its report, which it entitled *Nunca Más* ('Never Again'). Following this damning report, members of the Argentinean military went on trial for numerous human rights abuses.*

Much to the dismay of groups looking for justice, these individuals were later pardoned by President Carlos Menem in 1990 as a part of a policy to end the recriminations and put Argentina's past behind it. A former prisoner of the Junta himself, Menem argued that his five years in custody gave him the moral authority to make this pardon and pointed out that the Junta had involved so many people in its crimes that the country would tear itself apart trying to persecute everyone.

Despite the pardon people still wanted answers and one question reigned above all others: what had happened to the missing children taken in at the time of their mothers' abduction or to the estimated 500 babies born to expectant mothers in custody?

The answer to this question proved to be a harrowing revelation. Many abducted women were pregnant at the time of their capture.

---

* The report makes fascinating, though upsetting reading. See www.nuncamas.org.

In fact there were so many that the Junta established maternity clinics in some of the bigger detention centres. If what we are led to believe is true, the treatment of the mothers was barbaric in the extreme. The pregnant women were handcuffed and tied to tables, hooded or blindfolded and gagged. Their babies were often born through Caesarean section and then taken away minutes after their birth. In many cases the mothers were then murdered – most commonly shot and then either incinerated or buried under a sports field. Outrageous as it may seem, others were disposed of in so-called 'death flights' where the women were drugged, stripped naked and then pushed out the back of Hercules transport aircraft while flying over the sea.[99] After all, it's hard to prove a crime without a body.

As for the babies, the government found itself in a quandary. If the orphaned children were returned to their mothers' relatives, they would no doubt grow up into dangerous rebels, hell bent on revenging their murdered parents. To prevent this, instead of returning the babies to their relatives, they had them illegally adopted by childless military families. Rather than rebels, by falsifying the birth certificates of these children the regime hoped to create a race of future model citizens. The fact that some of these children were treated as war booty, adopted and unwittingly raised by the very people who had murdered their mothers, was sickening to say the least.

The policy also extended to infants whose parents who were arrested after their birth. An often-cited example of this is that of the Poblete family. The father, José, was a Chilean lathe operator, who had lost both legs in a car crash. While recovering in a Buenos Aires clinic, José Poblete met his disabled wife Getrudis. Both were members of the dissident Christians for Liberation movement and it was this that led to their arrests on 28 November 1978. Arrested with Getrudis was the couple's eight-month-old daughter Claudia Victoria. As the two were put into a patrol car their house was looted by police who loaded their valuables onto waiting army trucks.

A month later Getrudis was allowed to telephone her mother. Naturally she asked for news of her daughter. Before anything could be said a gruff male voice cut into the call and said, 'Watch your language. Your daughter is better off than the rest of her companions. We are not in Russia here.'[100] The telephone line went dead. And that was the end of the Poblete family as far as the outside world was concerned.

Not much is known of the parents' fate, except that José Poblete was brutally tortured. Some time in 1979 witnesses recalled hearing he was to be 'transferred'. Two days later they found his wheelchair abandoned in the corner of a parking lot. His wife was last seen on 28 January 1979.

It is believed that their daughter remained at the El Olimpo camp for two days after her abduction. She was then taken and adopted by Lieutenant Colonel Ceferino Landa, a colleague of her parents' killers. She was raised as Mercedes Beatriz Landa, and it was not until February 2000 that her real grandmother tracked her down and revealed her true identity.

Despite the CONADEP report, initially there was no hard evidence of the baby abduction programme. However a group called the Grandmothers of the Plaza de Mayo, an organization founded by the grandmothers of the missing children, continued to lobby the government for answers. Taking advantage of medical advances, the Grandmothers of the Plaza de Mayo began to compile a genetic database of blood samples to help trace orphaned children, collecting samples from blood relatives on both sides of the child's family.

Such revelations have caused understandable anguish among the young adults and some refused to take DNA tests to protect the surrogate adoptive parents from arrest. It is a distressing paradox that highlights the evil of the military regime – first the state murdered their real parents, then it wanted to arrest their adoptive ones. This is again perhaps best highlighted by Claudia Poblete, who appeared as a witness for the defence for her adoptive parents in June 2001, telling the court that she had lived with them believing they were her parents for 22 years and how could she do anything but love them?

There were also important legal implications to the research carried out by the Grandmothers group. Following their lead an investigation into the missing babies began in 1996.[101] In July 1998, Federal Judge Roberto Marquevich ordered General Jorge Videla – head of the first military Junta – to be arrested and held in custody pending trial in connection with the theft of babies born in army detention centres. Videla was incarcerated for two weeks but then transferred to house arrest because of his health. In September 1999, Judge Adolfo Bagnasco indicted the other surviving member of the first military Junta, Admiral Emilio Massera, on similar charges.

Key to the defence of these two men, and many others waiting in the wings, was whether or not they were covered by the 1990 presidential pardon. Prosecutors argued that, because the original human rights trials did not include charges of baby theft, the new charges were not covered by the amnesty. This argument continued back and forth until at last on 5 September 2006 the Federal Court ruled that the presidential pardon granted to Videla in 1990 was unconstitutional. At his advanced age, will the ruling be too late to see Videla put to rights?

KAL 007

HERE we present one of the biggest military scandals of the 1980s, and one that should be enough to put nervous fliers off for life. It is one of those tragedies that, rather than being healed, has been made worse by the passage of time. Like all disasters it is surrounded by an ever-thickening mist of controversy and conspiracy.

On 31 August 1983 Korean Air Flight KAL 007 took off from New York's John F. Kennedy International Airport destined for Seoul with a stop-off at Anchorage, Alaska. It was carrying 269 passengers and crew, among whom was Lawrence McDonald, a US congressman. Unbeknown to the passengers – and presumably the crew – the aircraft went off course and cut across the Kamchatka Peninsula, bringing it into Soviet airspace.

In the Cold War era, US RC-135 spy-planes often hovered around Soviet airspace, monitoring response to air incursions. Believing KAL 007 was such an aircraft, the Soviets scrambled fighters to intercept the intruder.

It wasn't the first time a Korean airliner had blundered into Soviet airspace. In 1978 KAL 902 was fired on and forced to land by Soviet jets. This time the civilian airliner was not so lucky. After firing a warning shot from his cannon – which the crew presumably never saw – Soviet pilot Gennadiy Osipovich fired two missiles from his SU-15 at the passenger jet.

237

Details are hard to come by, but at least one of the missiles hit the plane, causing the loss of at least one engine and cabin decompression. As howling winds sucked through the cabin the pilots performed an emergency descent to get below 10,000 feet and radioed air traffic control in Tokyo for instructions. From that point on, very little is certain ... except that none of the 269 passengers and crew have ever been seen again, Congressman McDonald included.

When news of the shooting down occurred there was predictable outrage. All round the world the loss of so many civilians was greeted with complete shock. US President Ronald Reagan condemned the action as a 'massacre'. In their defence the Soviets claimed that they believed the aircraft had been a US spy-plane and that they had tried to warn it off before firing. Many later speculated that the United States had deliberately sent the aircraft off course in order to test Soviet defences. Certainly when the airliner was detected by the Soviets, their missile defences lit up like a Christmas tree on US scanners. Although many have subscribed to this conspiracy theory, there is certainly no proof.

One of the most tragic aspects of the outrage is that many grieving families have yet to have key questions answered about the airliner's last moments. For 11 years the Soviets claimed no knowledge of the airliner's two 'black box' recorders. It was not until President Yeltsin revealed their existence in 1991 that they were forthcoming. Even then there were big questions left to answer, which only served to thicken the growing mystery surrounding the incident.

The cockpit voice recording lasted for only 1 minute 25 seconds after the missile attack. The pilot is heard reporting a loss of cabin pressure and stating that he was descending to 10,000 feet –

standard procedure in such an event. He is also heard asking Tokyo air traffic control for instructions or directions, the recording is not clear enough to distinguish which.

If, as the Soviet pilot reported, the target was destroyed then that would perhaps explain why the flight recording suddenly stopped. However, immediately after the disaster, it was revealed that KAL 007 was on the radar screens for 12 minutes after the strike. So what happened to the remaining ten minutes of the recording? Had the tape been doctored by the Soviets for some reason and, if so, what were they trying to hide?

Without wishing to lend too much credence to the argument, one of the more interesting theories is that the aircraft made a successful landing somewhere on Soviet territory. There are in fact some who believe the surviving crew and passengers were taken prisoner by the Soviets and are still languishing somewhere in the former superpower's territory – although that does take an astonishingly large leap of faith to accept.*

Although a touch macabre, there is a perplexing mystery surrounding the issue of the human remains. According to Soviet sources the aircraft hit the water travelling at such high speed that it – and everything inside – was torn to shreds. Explaining the lack of human remains, the Soviet authorities speculated that whatever human remains survived the impact must have been devoured by greedy cuttlefish.

The only body parts ever officially recovered were located not by the Soviets, but by Japanese fisherman working in international waters. Two unidentifiable bodies and other human remains

---

* The International Committee for the Rescue of KAL 007 Survivors, Inc. was formed in 2001 to bring about the rescue and return home of any survivors from the airliner.

amounting to 13 out of 269 people are not much at all when similar incidents are considered. Take for instance the Air India Flight 182 which exploded over the Atlantic south of Ireland in 1985. The aircraft had been travelling at 31,000 feet when a terrorist bomb knocked it out of the sky. In that case 132 bodies were recovered and identified.

It has been suggested that the human remains found by the Japanese fisherman may have been from the result of the initial decompression in the passenger cabin. Other fragments recovered also came from inside the passenger cabin – there were for example no pieces of luggage from the hold of the aircraft. Is it possible that the Soviets did find human remains but kept this a secret? They did, after all, lie about not having the black boxes.

Whatever the truth about the matter, the shooting down of the airliner remains one of the darkest incidents of the Cold War and was, as President Reagan announced at the time, an 'act of barbarism'.

SATANIC OPERATION

France has been alarmingly quiet for too long in these pages. The last time we heard of a French scandal was back in the days of red trousers. Making a welcome return, here are the French again, leaping like a hare out from the undergrowth of history straight into the onrushing headlamps of global condemnation.

On the evening of 10 July 1985 there was a party atmosphere on board the Greenpeace protest ship *Rainbow Warrior*. Having travelled to New Zealand, the ship was anchored in Marsden Wharf, in Auckland's Waitemata Harbour. The Greenpeace activists on board were preparing to lead a flotilla of yachts to French-controlled Mururoa Atoll to protest against nuclear weapons testing. The crew had been having a meeting to discuss tactics in their forthcoming protest and also celebrating a crew member's birthday with a cake and some beers.

The meeting broke up about 11pm and the crew split up. Some remained talking, finishing off the last of the beer; others returned to their cabins and went to sleep.[102] At about 11.50pm there was a dull thud that felt as though a tug had collided with the Greenpeace ship. The generator went out, and for a few seconds before the emergency lighting came on, the ship was plunged into darkness. Some of the crew ran up on deck, while others went to see what the trouble was.

Two minutes later, those on deck saw a flash of blue light below the surface near to the ship and felt the force of an explosion.

Those already on deck jumped onto the wharf to safety and watched in disbelief as the *Rainbow Warrior* began to sink before their eyes.

As the activists stumbled around in shock at what had just occurred, it became apparent that one of their crewmates was missing. Photographer Fernando Pereira had last been seen in the mess at the time of the first impact, but had not been sighted since. New Zealand Navy divers went onto the wreck, and at about 3.00am returned with Pereira's body. They had found him face down in a cabin. Although no one can be exactly sure what happened, it is believed he had gone to retrieve his cameras and had been caught by inrushing sea water after the second detonation.

New Zealand Prime Minister David Lange quickly condemned the explosion as 'a major criminal act'. A massive police investigation was launched to find the cause of the sinking and establish if the death of the photographer should be treated as murder.

The public's response to an appeal for information yielded immediate results. Following interviews with the crew the police said they wanted to interview a Frenchman who had visited the ship earlier in the day. Reading this in the press, a customs officer called Frank McLean reported an unusual incident involving a French crewed yacht, the *Ouvéa*. This yacht had been docked in Whangarei but had left on 9 July.

What was strange about it in McLean's opinion was that the three crewmen had brand new passports, all of which were lacking the usual creases and signs of wear one would expect. He also reported that the three men were distinctly military in their bearing. When McLean checked the vessel he also became suspicious that there was no photographic equipment on board despite one of the men telling him he was a photographer.

Shortly after the bombing these three men were brought in for questioning but were then released as there was insufficient evidence to hold them. The passenger on the yacht, another Frenchman, was also questioned but then released due to lack of evidence.

There were other reports of unusual activity reported to the police. At 7pm on the evening of the incident two strangers had been spotted carrying an inflated Zodiac rubber dinghy, which struck them as being unusual for its light grey colour. At 9.30pm another witness drinking at a boating club had seen a man get out of a Zodiac rubber dinghy, jog down the road, and then return driving a white camper van. He watched as the man and someone else took a large bundle out of the dinghy and loaded it into the camper van. Thinking this was suspicious, he telephoned the police and made a note of the van's registration plate.

The camper van was traced to Newman's car rentals and the staff warned to alert the police when it was returned. Sure enough, on 12 July a married Swiss couple, Sophie and Alain Turenge, came into the airport branch of Newman's with the white Toyota Hiace. They said they were going home early and asked for a part refund for the early return of the vehicle.

While staff kept the couple talking the police were called. A detective was sent to the airport and the couple were brought in for questioning. It was very quickly realized that both were travelling on false passports. In fact, their identity was established as Major Alain Mafart and Captain Dominique Prieur, both of whom were agents of the DGSE (Direction Générale de la Sécurité Extérieure), part of the French secret service.

Meanwhile an investigation of the wrecked Greenpeace ship revealed a huge hole measuring 6 by 8 feet in the side of the vessel. The fact that the metal had been pushed inward indicated that an explosive device had been placed on the outside of the ship's hull. A second device appeared to have damaged the propeller and rudder. Sure enough, fragments of limpet mines not used by New Zealand's armed forces were found attached to the hull.

Putting together the evidence it appeared the *Ouvéa* had been used to transport explosives and French agents to New Zealand. This was reinforced by the discovery of fingerprints from the captured agents on documents taken from the *Ouvéa*. After the crew of the *Ouvéa* had been questioned they and their boat disappeared – literally without trace. New Zealand police concluded that the yacht had been scuttled mid-ocean and the crew had been taken off by a French submarine.

With a clear motive established – the fact that *Rainbow Warrior* was heading for French waters to protest against their nuclear tests – and the clumsy trail of evidence left behind, New Zealand pointed an accusing finger at the French government who they believed were behind the attack. Such an accusation caused an almighty international row and led to strenuous denials from the French government – denials which no one outside France seriously believed.

In truth it was so glaringly obvious that the French were behind the attack that President Mitterrand was obliged to order an inquiry into the matter on 8 August. It reported that although six agents from the French secret service, DGSE, were in New Zealand at the time, they were on an intelligence-gathering mission against Greenpeace and did not commit the attack. When received this report appeared as credible as a chocolate kettle, and it was immediately followed by a second inquiry headed by the French Defence Minister, Charles Hernu.

While the French newspaper *Le Monde* accused Mitterrand of being behind the mission, a scapegoat was required. Hernu interviewed the head of DGSE, Admiral Lacoste, and asked him to explain himself. The investigation became farcical when Lacoste refused to answer certain of the Defence Minister's questions, citing the need for secrecy to protect his agents' lives. Lacoste was sacked and Hernu resigned.

On 21 September French Prime Minister Laurent Fabius came clean and admitted that the DGSE had been ordered to neutralize *Rainbow Warrior*. Ironically enough, Fabius was one of the few people mentioned so far who didn't have prior knowledge of the attack.

New Zealand was understandably enraged by the whole business. As some pointed out, there are a lot of New Zealanders buried in war cemeteries in France – were they to be repaid by French saboteurs attaching limpet mines to a ship and killing an innocent man?[103] There were also international implications to the affair. Pereira was a Dutch citizen and *Rainbow Warrior* was registered in Great Britain. Clearly France was in line for some major criticism.

Meanwhile, on 4 November, the trial of Prieur and Mafart began. At an earlier hearing the two had pleaded not guilty to charges of arson, conspiring to commit arson and murder. However, to avoid prolonging France's embarrassment, the pair caused surprise by pleading guilty to a lesser charge of manslaughter. New Zealand's Solicitor General, Paul Neazor, QC, accepted the plea as it could not be proved the French agents were personally to blame for placing the explosive devices, nor that they intended to kill. They were each sentenced to ten years' imprisonment.

Perhaps the most scandalous aspect of the case is yet to arise. Neither Mafart nor Prieur served anything like their full sentence before they were allowed back to France. While most of the world condemned them, a sort of siege mentality developed inside France and calls were made to put economic sanctions on New Zealand to secure the agents' release. New Zealand stood to suffer very heavily if France used its influence on the European Community to impose greater tariffs on New Zealand lamb, butter and other agricultural produce.[104]

The growing perception that the agents were heroes was reinforced by the sending of gifts to them in gaol. As they faced their first Christmas in prison, French politicians sent them presents of cognac and wine.[105]

A solution to the dispute was offered by Dutch Prime Minister Ruud Lubbers, who suggested that both parties should go to the UN. New Zealand demanded an apology, $9 million compensation and a ruling that France would not try to oppose New Zealand exports through the European Community. There was some haggling over the price, but eventually France agreed to pay $7 million and apologize for its violation of New Zealand and international laws.

In return for this – and this caused a lot of anger – New Zealand agreed to transfer Mafart and Prieur to the custody of the French military authorities on the French Polynesian island of Hao where they were to remain for three years. Although kept away from the media, the two agents were able live quite normally.

Two years later, Mafart returned to France claiming that he had a health condition that required attention in Paris. Prieur also returned to be at her dying father's bedside. Needless to say, in both cases that was the end of their punishment.

While Prieur was last heard of giving birth to a child and leaving the service, in 1988 Mafart was promoted to the rank of lieutenant colonel, then in 1991 was awarded the French Legion of Merit. Although this award was bestowed routinely on service personnel who had completed 14–18 years' service, it was interpreted by many as being a reward for his part in Operation *Satanic* – the French codename for the mission.

With the passage of time some of the details in the mission became much clearer. In 2005 the French newspaper *Le Monde* received a 23-page, handwritten report dated 8 April 1986, which had been prepared by former DGSE chief Admiral Pierre Lacoste on the orders of incoming President Jacques Chirac's Defence Minister, André Giraud. Until the publication of this hitherto secret report, the official line was that Mitterrand had not given the order to sink the *Rainbow Warrior* and that the decision was made solely on the authority of Charles Hernu under pressure from elements within the French Navy.

Although the report is not conclusive proof, Lacoste clearly states that Mitterrand did know about the mission and gave them a green light to go ahead with it.[106]

In 2006 Xavier Maniguet, a doctor and French Navy reservist, revealed that he had been part of the mission. He confirmed earlier suspicions that the *Ouvéa* was used to smuggle explosives and diving gear into New Zealand. His part in the operation was to pose as a playboy who had chartered the yacht and its three-man crew. Maniguet was arrested along with the three crewmen who had been picked up because of their suspicious passports. He was released after a night of questioning by the New Zealand police.

Cartoon by Kal [Kevin Kallaugher] published in The Observer, *1 September 1985. (The British Cartoon Archive, University of Kent, © Kevin Kallaugher)*

Maniguet said that Mafart and Prieur collected the sabotage equipment from the boat and passed them on to a third team – the agents who actually placed the charges on the Greenpeace ship, and who escaped from New Zealand without detection. According to Maniguet, the pilot of the Zodiac dinghy that took the two divers to a drop off point from which they swam to the *Rainbow Warrior* was former DGSE agent Gérard Royal. However, according to Royal's younger brother Antoine, the agent was actually the man who placed the limpet mines on the hull of the ship.[107]

It appears that the DGSE had a history of dirty tricks against protest ships and had developed special bacteria to contaminate the fuel lines of *Rainbow Warrior*. However, Defence Minister Hernu wanted to make a big splash and ordered them to blow the ship up.

Under pressure from Hernu for speedy results, the mission was not properly thought out. The only information the sabotage team had on Greenpeace was from the agent Christine Cabon whom the DGSE had planted in the organization as a mole under the name Frederique Bonlieu. Although Cabon was able to give the team helpful background information, there was little of operational use.

Mafart was in charge of planning. He argued that a bomb should be placed on the propeller shaft of the ship, which would have been enough to cripple it. However, Mafart claims that Hernu put pressure on DGSE bosses to actually sink the vessel. It was therefore decided to place a small charge to knock out the engine and to scare everyone off the ship. The second charge would then detonate two minutes later and blow a hole in the ship below the water line, causing it to sink.

To achieve the best results, Mafart revealed that the saboteurs obtained a set of blueprints for the vessel and worked out where to place the charges so they would not hit cabins. There was – he says – absolutely no plan to harm anybody, pointing out that if they had wanted to kill the crew they could have easily bombed the ship while it was out in the ocean.

Another problem facing Mafart was the strange insistence that the team use four-hour timers on the mines rather than the usual 24- or 48-hour ones. If these longer timers had been used all the agents would have been able to evacuate the country before the police were alerted.

In the event, Mafart woke up the morning after the bombing and was horrified to learn that one of the Greenpeace crew had been killed. From their room in the Hamilton motel, Mafart and Prieur made an emergency call back to DGSE for guidance. Inexplicably they could not get through to their case officer. Feeling abandoned, the two agents added up their options and decided to use their Swiss passports and fly out of the country.[108] Next thing they knew, they were facing a murder charge.

The moral of our story is that although peace protestors might at times be a nuisance, governments can't go blowing things up just because life is being made difficult for them. The net result of the attack – other than the consequent wave of protest – was that Greenpeace received a great deal more public support and an increase in donations, including compensation from France, which allowed them to replace the vessel.

In conclusion, if it had not been for the tragic death of a peaceful civilian, the whole affair could be described as more Inspector Clouseau than James Bond.

IRANGATE

IN the Iran–Contra Affair of 1986* we find a perfect scandal, right up there with Dreyfus and Profumo. It is a complicated business involving a series of illegal acts that were put into motion by the highest authorities in the land. It just goes to show how far a government will go to circumvent the rule of law.

Since 1981 the United States had been sponsoring anti-government 'Contra' rebels against the socialist Sandinista government of Nicaragua. This sponsorship was part of a long-term strategy to prevent Latin American countries going the way of Cuba and letting the Soviets in. However, in 1982 a Democrat-controlled Congress introduced a number of control measures – notably the Boland Amendment – which limited Republican President Ronald Reagan's scope to act abroad without informing Congress. It also specifically prohibited the CIA from funding any overthrow of the Nicaraguan government.

When the Boland Amendment kicked in, Reagan instructed his National Security Advisor, Robert McFarlane, to keep the Contra movement alive 'body and soul'. Interpret that statement how you will. In February 1984 McFarlane suggested inviting other countries to support the Contras on behalf of the US. CIA Director William

---

*   Otherwise known as 'Irangate'. Ever since the 1972 Watergate scandal, Americans have added the suffix 'gate' to anything vaguely scandalous, hence Iran-gate and, the author's personal favourite, Monica-gate.

Casey agreed with the plan and recommended several potential sponsor countries, including Saudi Arabia, which agreed to contribute $1 million a month. McFarlane used a trusted assistant on the National Security Council (NSC) staff to set up a covert bank account for the money transfers. His name was Lieutenant Colonel Oliver North.

North soon became America's handyman in all dealings with the Contras. In addition to his third-country deals, North raised millions from wealthy American fundraisers through tax exempt organizations and Swiss bank accounts.* Casey teamed North up with retired Air Force Major General Richard Secord, who helped broker arms deals for the Contras. In September 1985 North approached Felix Rodriguez – an ex-CIA operative fighting communist guerrillas in El Salvador – and set up a deal with the Salvadoran Air Force to use its air base at Ilopango for Contra missions.

While this illegal covert activity was underway, the US also got involved in an interesting three-way negotiation with Israel and Iran. In May 1985, Michael Ledeen, a part-time NSC consultant, obtained Robert McFarlane's approval to meet Israeli Prime

---

* There is continued speculation that drug money was used to finance the Contras and that the emergence of crack cocaine in Los Angeles was somehow related to Contra sponsorship schemes. (See *The Contras, Cocaine, and Covert Operations* at the National Security Archive Electronic Briefing Book No. 2, www.gwu.edu/~nsarchiv.) Such allegations were strenuously denied in a CIA press release of 29 January 1998:
'The Central Intelligence Agency's independent statutory Inspector General (IG) is nearing completion of a seventeen-month investigation into allegations in *The San Jose Mercury News* that the CIA supported efforts by the Nicaraguan Contras to bring cocaine into the United States to finance their operations. The IG's investigation has found no evidence that would substantiate the *San Jose Mercury News* allegations that the CIA had any involvement … in cocaine trafficking in California to raise funds for the Nicaraguan Contras.'

Minister Shimon Peres. The meeting was ostensibly about sharing intelligence on Iran, but during the meeting Peres mentioned that the Iranians had asked to buy artillery shells from Israel. Peres told Ledeen that Israel would only make the sale if the US agreed to the deal. Ledeen said he would discuss the matter with McFarlane.

This request raised some interesting questions about US policy towards Iran. Since the 1979 American embassy siege in Tehran, the US had outlawed the sale of American weapons to Iran from any source. It had also fingered Iran as a sponsor of international terrorism. At the time there were six American hostages held in Beirut, including William Buckley – the CIA Beirut station chief. The hostages were held by groups with links to Tehran. If the hostages were going to be released, Iran would have to be involved somewhere down the line. At the same time, increased Soviet influence in Iran was a concern, as was the Iran–Iraq War. If the US did not help Iran in the war, there was a danger that Iraqi dictator Saddam Hussein's territorial ambitions might destabilize the entire region. The intelligence community therefore called for closer relations with Iran.

On 3 July 1985 McFarlane met David Kimche, the Director General of the Israeli Foreign Ministry. Kimche suggested that moderates in the Iranian government would use their influence to obtain the release of American hostages in the Lebanon in return for military equipment. McFarlane passed the proposal to President Reagan who expressed interest and instructed McFarlane to explore it further.

Ledeen next informed McFarlane that Israel's principal Iranian contact, Manucher Ghorbanifar, could do a deal on the hostages for 100 American TOW anti-tank missiles. Although the CIA considered Ghorbanifar a shady Iranian businessman, Reagan remained interested in what he had to say. Ledeen was sent to meet Ghorbanifar directly.

On 2 August, McFarlane and Kimche met at the White House. Kimche put a slightly different spin on the proposal. If the US would not sell weapons to Iran directly, would it permit Israel to sell US-manufactured weapons to Iran instead? Furthermore, if the US agreed, would it then sell replacement stock to Israel?

McFarlane took the proposal to the President and also briefed Vice-President Bush, William Casey, Secretary of State George Shultz and Secretary of Defense Caspar Weinberger. Although the last two had difficulties with the deal, McFarlane went away believing he had a green light. The only thing that is really certain here is that nobody told Congress what was going on.

On 20 August 1985 Israel sent a first shipment of 96 TOW missiles to Iran, but no hostages were released. At a meeting in Paris on 4 September, Ghorbanifar explained that the missiles had gone to the wrong people. However, if 400 more TOWs were sent, he could arrange for one hostage to be released.

Rather than the Americans cutting their losses and walking out on the deal, on 14 September an Israeli-chartered aircraft arrived in Iran carrying 408 TOWs. McFarlane instructed the Israelis that if only one hostage was going to be released, they wanted William Buckley. Instead of the CIA man, Benjamin Weir was released in Beirut as it was claimed that Buckley was too sick to be moved. In fact, Buckley was already dead.

Despite disappointment with the results so far, Ledeen continued to meet Ghorbanifar, who suggested Iran might like to get some US-made anti-aircraft missiles. After much debate, Ghorbanifar's Iranian contact suggested a trade of 150 HAWK missiles, 200 Sidewinder missiles and 30–50 Phoenix missiles in return for all the hostages.

McFarlane was becoming very sceptical about the whole

arrangement and told Ledeen he was happy for more deals, providing live hostages were released before the delivery of further weapons. This didn't happen.

On 15 November Israeli Defence Minister Yitzhak Rabin met with McFarlane and asked if the US would replace a shipment of HAWK missiles that Israel was ready to send Iran. McFarlane agreed and assigned his NSC fixer, Oliver North, to ensure that the deal went smoothly. McFarlane then advised the President and Vice President Bush of the imminent transaction.

Rabin telephoned North on 17 November saying he was ready to go ahead with delivery as soon as the replenishment deal was worked out with the US. North had been instructed by McFarlane not to go over $14 million per order when working out the replenishment programme. Anything over that sum would have to be presented to Congress.

An unexpected problem concerned stock control. Did the US have enough missiles to replenish Israeli stocks? On 19 November McFarlane asked Weinberger to check the availability of HAWKs. Weinberger delegated the task to his military assistant, General Colin Powell, who came back with a negative answer. Weinberger, a lawyer by trade, telephoned McFarlane and told him that the transaction would be illegal without the backing of Congress. MacFarlane pressed on.

There was further trouble trying to get flight clearance in Europe. North brought his Contra arms man, Secord, to Europe to try to work out flight clearances for the missiles, but in the end only 18 HAWKs arrived in Iran. Not only were the Iranians expecting 80 missiles, they were expecting the improved I-HAWK version. Nor were they impressed by the Israeli 'Star of David' markings on the missiles. No hostages were released.

Fed up with bureaucratic wrangling, McFarlane resigned on 4 December and was replaced by John Poindexter. Ledeen was dropped and North took over full control of the Iran project. After more meetings with the usual suspects, North reported that the Iranians were now looking for 3,300 TOWs and 50 HAWKs for the release of all US hostages and one French hostage.

On 7 December there was a high-level meeting in the White House to decide what to do about the project. Shultz and Weinberger again voiced their opposition to the Iran arms sales. Poindexter was all for continuing. Reagan decided to send McFarlane as his envoy to London to meet with all the interested parties before deciding. Reagan was worried that if the US pulled out of the deal, Iran might go ahead and kill the hostages in revenge.

Early 1986 saw a new Israeli proposal. They proposed sending 500 TOW missiles to Iran in return for the release of all American hostages in Lebanon. Israel would then release certain Hezbollah prisoners in southern Lebanon. If all went as planned, Israel would then send 3,500 additional TOWs to Iran. Tehran would renounce hostage taking and the United States would replenish Israeli missile stocks. It sounded like the perfect deal.

President Reagan called a National Security Council meeting for 7 January to consider this new proposal. Again, Shultz and Weinberger opposed the deal, with Weinberger arguing that the deal violated the Arms Export Control Act. However, presidential adviser Edwin Meese said it was within the President's power to authorize the transfer of arms from the Defense Department to the CIA, and from the CIA to Iranians. Reagan was sold on it.

The first shipment of 500 TOW missiles was delivered to Iran on 18 February. The CIA then purchased TOW missiles from the US Army. Secord laid on a Miami-based aircraft charter company, which ferried the missiles to Israel. An Israeli charter plane then carried the weapons on to Iran. On 27 February 500 additional TOWs were delivered to Iran. Still no hostages were released.

It was decided that an American delegation should travel to Tehran to sort out the hostage situation face to face. McFarlane led the delegation and he brought along North. They travelled to Iran on an aircraft arranged by Secord and brought a goodwill offering in the guise of a pallet load of HAWK spare parts.

Not much came out of their three-day visit. The Iranians admitted they had little hope of getting the hostages released, but would try their best to get one or two out of Lebanon. The Americans left empty handed and realized that Ghorbanifar had been stringing both sides along.

To cheer McFarlane up, on the way home North told him a secret. North had added a little mark-up on what he charged the Iranians for the missile parts and had channelled the profits back into supporting the Contras! McFarlane didn't share his reaction with North, but his first thought was: 'Oh, shit'.

In June the Iranians discovered North's little mark-up. They had paid six times the list price for the missile parts! That said, they still wanted more missiles and, on 24 July, hostage Lawrence Jenco was released. His release was followed by the message that the Iranians would kill an American hostage if undelivered HAWK spare parts were not sent in return. North decided to use a new channel with the Iranians that cut Ghorbanifar out of the deal.

North turned his attention to the Contras and met a representative of Panama's General Noriega. On 31 August 1986 North emailed Poindexter telling him that in return for the lifting of an arms ban on Panama, Noriega would 'take care' of the

Sandinista leadership. North also suggested paying General Noriega $1 million from the profits out of the Iran sales in return for a Panamanian sabotage campaign against Nicaragua.[109]

Before much could be accomplished on this new front, things started to go very badly wrong, very quickly. On 5 October Nicaraguan troops shot down one of North's C-123K cargo planes carrying arms and supplies from El Salvador to the Contras. When Nicaraguan government troops reached the crash site they found an American survivor, Eugene Hasenfus, who admitted belonging to the CIA. North ordered his people out of Ilopango as fast as they could run.

Ironically, when the supply plane was shot down, Congress was on the verge of approving President Reagan's $100 million Contra-aid package. Although Hasenfus' disclosure caused a few wobbles, the administration received approval for funding on 17 October 1986. It appeared that Reagan had got away with it.

On 28 October 500 TOW missiles were delivered to Iran and on 2 November hostage David Jacobsen was released. Again, things seemed to be levelling out for the government.

Then Hezbollah decided that it did not like the idea of Iran and the United States getting cosy together and took two more American hostages to replace the ones it had released. Furthermore, Hezbollah leaked details of the deals to the press. On 3 November the Lebanese newspaper *Al-Shiraa* reported McFarlane's Tehran visit. The day after the article appeared this story was confirmed by Iranian Parliament Speaker Rafsanjani.

This was an unbelievable scandal. It wasn't long before the arms-for-hostages angle leaked out. Such a policy was directly at odds with a statement Ronald Reagan had made at a news conference on 18 June 1985, when he said:

Let me further make it plain to the assassins in Beirut and their accomplices, wherever they may be, that America will never make concessions to terrorists – to do so would only invite more terrorism – nor will we ask nor pressure any other government to do so.

Clearly the US government had some explaining to do.

At first Reagan came out with a straight denial. On 6 November he denied that arms had been sold. Then, on 13 November, he acknowledged that some weapons were sold to Iran, but stated that these had nothing to do with the release of American hostages.

Then came the big one. At noon on 25 November President Reagan announced that proceeds from the Iran arms sales had indeed been diverted to support the Contras, but that Poindexter had resigned and Oliver North had been reassigned to the US Marine Corps.

The United States illegally selling arms to a terrorist sponsor state and then using the money to illegally fund the overthrow of a foreign government – this was a scandal of the first degree, which almost destroyed Reagan's administration.

The fact that it did not do so is perhaps an even bigger scandal! Although President Reagan announced the creation of the Tower Commission to look into the affair, a criminal investigation of Iran–Contra began on 26 November by the FBI at the order of the Attorney General. As people threw themselves on their swords to protect the President, two men were thrown to the wolves: Oliver North and John Poindexter, both of whom were eventually found guilty of relatively minor charges. However, these convictions were overturned when it emerged that their Fifth Amendment rights might have been violated. In 1994, North unsuccessfully ran for the Senate as the Republican candidate in Virginia.[110]

Absolutely astonishing!

IRAN AIR FLIGHT 655

IN 1987 – a year after the United States illegally sold missiles to the Iranians – the US Navy deployed ships into the Persian Gulf in order to protect Kuwaiti oil tankers from attack by Iranian missile boats.

With the Iran–Iraq War raging around the Persian Gulf, there had been numerous incidents of vessels hitting mines or being struck, the most serious case being when USS *Stark* was struck in May 1987 by two Exocet missiles fired from an Iranian warplane.

On the morning of 3 July 1988, USS *Montgomery* observed seven Iranian Guard small boats with machine-gun and rocket mounts approaching a Pakistani vessel. Five more boats joined the first group, which appeared to be menacing merchant shipping. USS *Vincennes* was ordered to the area to support *Montgomery* and launched a helicopter to reconnoitre the scene. In the process the helicopter reported that it had been fired upon. In retaliation *Vincennes* and *Montgomery* closed in on the boats and engaged them.

This quickly developed into a high-speed surface battle which saw the *Vincennes* breach Iranian territorial waters. The tension on board increased when one of its guns became fouled and went out of action. To give the remaining gun a clear field of fire the ship was having to make some quite dramatic manoeuvres, lurching through the water in order to get a clear shot at the Iranian boats. On board the ship the manoeuvres sent loose equipment and books flying across the ship's combat information centre. At the same time Captain Rogers was listening out for news from his airborne helicopter, which had already reported coming under attack, and for information on an Iranian P-3 Orion patrol aircraft that his crew was tracking.

While all this was happening an unknown aircraft was picked up by the *Vincennes'* AN/SPY-1A radar. It was civilian Air Bus Iran Air Flight 655, which had just taken off from Bander Abbas airfield and was headed for Dubai carrying pilgrims en route to Mecca.

Petty Officer Andrew Anderson sent out an electronic IFF (Identify, Friend or Foe?) query and received the response 'commair' – a commercial airliner. When Anderson tried to confirm this on a list of scheduled flights he missed Flight 655 on the list apparently because it was dark where he was working, everything was being flung about in the boat chase and he got confused over the Gulf's four different time zones. Anderson tried the IFF again, but forgot to reset the range. This time he got a reply from a military aircraft still on the ground at Bander Abbas. The Iranian airliner was mistakenly reported as an F-14 Tomcat.

As the aircraft headed towards the two American ships it failed to respond to repeated challenges from *Vincennes* over both the military and international emergency distress frequencies. This is because the Iranian pilot was tuned into the air traffic control centre from where he had just taken off. The *Vincennes* could have broadcast on that frequency but did not do so.

The captain of the *Vincennes* was in a genuine dilemma. He had less than five minutes to decide whether or not to fire on this unidentified aircraft before it came into missile attack range. Bander Abbas was used by the Iranian military and Rogers had been warned to expect an increase of hostile activity around 4 July. Had the Iranian boats he was chasing called in air support?

More challenges were sent out by *Vincennes*:

Unidentified Iranian aircraft on course 203, speed 303, altitude 4,000, this is US Naval warship, bearing 205, 40 miles from you. You are approaching US Naval warship operating in international waters. Request you state your intentions...

Iranian fighter on course 210, speed 353, altitude 7,000 ft, you are approaching US Naval warship, operating in international waters. If you maintain current course you are standing into danger and are subject to USN defense measures. Request you change course 270 repeat 270...

Unidentified aircraft on course 207, speed 350, altitude 7000. You are approaching US Naval warship bearing 205, 30 miles from you. Your identity is not known, your intentions are not clear. You are standing into danger and may be subject to USN defensive measures. Request you alter course immediately to 270...

This cartoon depicts Ronald Reagan after the shooting down of Iran Air Flight 655. (Nicholas Garland, The Daily Telegraph, *the British Cartoon Archive, University of Kent, © Telegraph Media Group)*

> Iranian F-14 this is USN warship bearing 199, 20 miles. Request you change course 270 immediately. If maintain current course you are subject to USN defensive measures...[111]

Despite these warnings the aircraft continued to approach. At a range between 15 and 12 miles, the Tactical Information Coordinator on the *Vincennes* reported that the aircraft's altitude was decreasing. This was a terrible mistake and can only be explained if the Tactical Information Coordinator gave out the decreasing range of the aircraft and this was misinterpreted as a decreasing altitude.

Hearing this, Rogers added up all the factors. There had been no reply to the various warnings and now the unidentified aircraft – which his crew had reported as an F-14 – appeared to be diving in an attack run. Moments later Rogers ordered the launch of two Standard missiles. When the launch key was turned, the projectiles shot up out along their launch rails and 21 seconds later hit their target, which was blown out of the sky, killing 290 people, including 66 children.

The shooting down caused outrage around the world. The US government defended the action, stating wrongly that the aircraft was outside the commercial flight corridor and was flying at 7,000 feet on a descent towards the USS *Vincennes*. Although sorry for the loss of life, the United States was unrepentant and blamed the disaster on Iran. In light of the United States' reaction to the Soviet shooting down of KAL 007 in 1983, this response seems unpalatable to say the least.

When the incident was fully investigated the US did admit that mistakes had been made, blaming 'stress' and 'task fixation' for the tragedy. Another term bandied about by many analysts in this case was 'scenario fulfilment'. The crew of the *Vincennes* had put themselves in harm's way chasing the hostile boats into Iranian territorial waters. They had then increased their stress levels by continuing the pursuit, despite the malfunction of one of their main armaments. Then they had convinced themselves they were under attack by a hostile aircraft and were going to be attacked just as the USS *Stark* had been the year before. The result was that they saw what they expected to see – not what they were really looking at.

If at some point someone in authority had checked the data rather than listening to the excited shouting they might have realized it was a civilian airliner travelling in a recognized air corridor.*

Another victim down to the Fog of War.

---

* Although the Libyans were ultimately blamed for it, many believe that the 1988 blowing up of Pan Am 103 over Lockerbie was a direct retaliation for the loss of the Iranian Air Bus.

A PRINCESS IN LOVE

I<small>T</small> is the stuff of a scandalmonger's dream. A British cavalry officer and a beautiful princess fall into a doomed love affair – doomed because the princess happens to be married to the heir to the British throne and is mother to his two children – one of whom will one day be king. If it was a Hollywood script – no one would believe it. But, alas, it's all horribly true.

The affair between James Hewitt and Diana, Princess of Wales is thought to have begun some time in 1987. Diana was married to Charles, but was aware that her husband was following in the fashion of other Princes of Wales, by having an affair with his long-time love, Camilla, wife of Lieutenant Colonel Andrew Parker Bowles – the man of whom it is said 'he laid down his wife for his country'.

The affair started off when Captain Hewitt, then serving in the Life Guards cavalry regiment, met Diana at a party in 1986. Diana engaged Hewitt as a riding instructor and their relationship developed into an affair, which lasted until 1992 when Diana stopped taking his calls.

There is a certain irony that a member of the Guards – a man sworn in his duty to protect the royal family – was acting this way. In fact, by allowing himself to be seduced by the princess, Hewitt was committing a crime technically punishable by death – according to a British law of 1351 which reads '... if a man do violate the King's companion, or the King's eldest daughter unmarried, or the wife of the King's eldest son and heir ...'

In 1991, Hewitt was sent to Kuwait as part of the British contingent in Operation *Desert Storm*. While he was commanding a squadron of tanks in the Scots Guards, Diana wrote to him every day and sent the letters through Hewitt's mother.

The public first got an inkling of the affair while Hewitt was still in the Gulf. The *News of the World* ran the story on the front page – of which Hewitt saw a copy while out in the desert. Seeing their tank commander on the front page and reading that he was sleeping with the most famous woman on the planet must have been the source of some amusement for his men – not to mention envy.

Cartoon in The Daily Mirror, *4 October 1994.*
(The British Cartoon Archive, University of Kent, © Charles Griffin)

In 1992 Diana dumped Hewitt, who went on to sell his story to the press and later wrote a book called *In Love and War*. Diana later admitted the affair in a famous TV interview for the BBC's *Panorama* programme, saying, 'Yes, I adored him. Yes, I was in love with him. But I was very let down.'

The *Daily Mirror* was one of those in the forefront of popular opinion against the former guardsman. In March 1996, following a TV interview, the newspaper published Hewitt's car registration number, along with his home address and telephone number, and encouraged readers to get in touch with Hewitt and let him know exactly what they thought of him. Several thousand did so, forcing Hewitt to change his telephone number.[112]

The most outrageous stunt, however, was performed by the *News of the World*, which sent a knight in full armour on a white charger to confront Hewitt and arrest him for treason.

Hewitt's credibility went through the floor as he became the most loathed man in Britain. When he later decided to auction Diana's love letters to him after her death in 1997, his standing plummeted again. The 'Love Rat' was among the kinder phrases used to describe him in the press.

DRAFT DODGER-IN-CHIEF

For many Americans of a certain age, their lives are in large part defined by their response to the Vietnam War and in particular how they responded to the draft. It is for some almost as polarizing an issue as the North/South divide of the American Civil War.

It is true that while many submitted to the draft and served their country faithfully, many did everything possible to avoid being sent to the conflict in Southeast Asia. We have already seen how boxer Muhammad Ali's refusal to serve in the United States Army sent shock waves through American society, so imagine the furore that would be caused if later in life a prominent politician turned out to be a draft dodger. Welcome to the world of William Jefferson Clinton...

In 1992, the Governor for Arkansas, Bill Clinton, was in the running for the 1992 Democratic presidential nomination. As with all political elections in modern times, the candidates could expect every heartbeat and breath of their life to be trawled over by a combination of political opponents and prying journalists, all looking for the same thing: a scandal to fatally tarnish their election bid.

According to one senior member of Clinton's campaign team, George Stephanopoulos, a presidential candidate faced three big potential trip-ups:

Adultery: this was deemed survivable if the candidate could demonstrate that it was a discreet event very much in the past

Smoking pot: again, survivable, providing the candidate could prove it was something they had tried at college and that they had not liked it

Military service: The candidate didn't have to be a war hero, but any hint of draft dodging was a political suicide pill.

Clinton's campaign team were able to deal with the first two hurdles adequately enough and were not expecting any trouble with the third scenario, even though they were expecting Vietnam to come up in the election.

While Clinton had not gone to Vietnam, one of his rivals, Senator Bob Kerrey, was an ex-Navy SEAL, Medal of Honor-winning Vietnam hero. This did not bother the Clinton campaign team unduly as they believed that Clinton had fulfilled his obligation for military service by applying to join the University of Arkansas' Reserve Officers Training Corps (ROTC) programme, under the command of Colonel Eugene Holmes.

When Clinton entered politics he simply told anyone who asked why he didn't serve in Vietnam to contact Colonel Holmes, who assured them that Clinton received no preferential treatment.

The story was sound and the campaign team had no worries until in an interview with one journalist, Clinton described his avoiding the draft with a 1-A classification as a fluke. The journalist smelt a rat and decided to probe the story further. Unfortunately for Clinton, when Jeff Birnbaum of the *Wall Street Journal* asked Colonel Holmes about the Clinton case, the veteran changed his story. Holmes told Birnbaum that he felt Clinton's promise to join the ROTC was a pretext for avoiding the draft as it reclassified him 1-D.

A bigger blow was landed on 10 February 1992, when Mark Halperin of ABC News met Stephanopoulos and passed him an old letter written by Clinton in 1969. The first line Stephanopoulos read made him feel sick.

> Dear Colonel Holmes ... I want to thank you, not just for saving me from the draft ...[113]

The letter was genuine enough and appeared to show that Clinton had indeed pulled some fast manoeuvres to avoid being drafted.

When Clinton returned from his first year at Oxford in 1969 he enrolled in Law School and had applied for the ROTC programme which would make him exempt from the draft. However, once accepted for the ROTC programme, Clinton changed his mind about Law School and went back for a second year at Oxford.

Once back in England, Clinton wrote to Holmes and said that he was not going to take up the offer of joining the ROTC after all, but was going to take his chances with the draft instead. It went on to describe how opposed he was to the war and to the concept of drafting young men to serve in a war they did not believe in.

The reason for this change of heart was because an amendment in the law passed by President Nixon in October 1969 allowed students to finish their year at college before being drafted. Safe in the knowledge he could see out his year at Oxford, Clinton entered the December draw and drew a very high number in the draft lottery, which made it almost certain he would not be selected. Clinton was therefore safe until June 1970, by which time he would no doubt figure out another way of avoiding conscription.

In the meantime he organized and attended peace rallies and even visited Moscow and Prague, which led some of his more extreme critics to accuse him later of being anything from a communist spy to a CIA stooge!

Returning to the election campaign, the issue of Vietnam did not appear nearly as important to voters as it did to the press and the campaign teams. Clinton took the Democrat nomination and faced up against President George Bush (senior), who was standing for a second term.

Bush had an impressive war record, being a pilot in the Second World War. He had also just successfully fought the 1991 Gulf War. Of course, with the President of the United States the commander-in-chief of America's armed forces, the incumbent's men were going to compare Bush's record with Clinton's.

In September 1992 the spectre of Colonel Holmes returned to haunt Clinton. He put out an affidavit saying he believed Governor Clinton had deceived him in 1969 and accused him of applying to the ROTC only to obtain a draft deferment.

Holmes' statement was shocking. It said that although he accepted that many had tried to avoid service in Vietnam, they did not harbour ambitions of becoming the President of the United States. Holmes said that Clinton had come to see him in 1969 to discuss enrolling him in the ROTC programme at the University of Arkansas. Holmes was willing to oblige, not to help Clinton avoid the draft, but to give him the opportunity to become an officer in the United States Army. Clinton then went to Oxford and Holmes realized he had been duped –and, to make matters worse, Clinton instead turned out to be one of cheerleaders of the anti-war movement.

Unfortunately for Bush he was torpedoed by our old friend 'Irangate', when it was proved that the President – then Vice-President to Ronald Reagan – must have known that arms were being used to secure the release of hostages. As history records, despite the allegations of extra-marital affairs, drug taking and draft dodging, Clinton won the 1992 election by a landslide.

THE MYTH OF THE FLYING COW

O N a somewhat lighter note, in 1997 a bizarre story appeared in the *Hamburger Morgenpost* in Germany. It revealed a confidential report by the German embassy in Moscow to the Foreign Ministry in Bonn.

Apparently, the crew of a Japanese fishing boat had been arrested after being rescued by a Russian patrol boat. The shaken crew claimed that a cow had fallen out of the sky and had struck their wooden vessel with such force that it shattered the hull and caused them to sink. With this laughable excuse the Japanese were arrested and put in prison.

Several weeks later the Russian authorities checked the story and found that it was true – an air force source revealed that the crew of an Ilyushin cargo plane had stolen some cows as they wandered round the edge of a Siberian airfield. The cows were forced into the hold of the aircraft, which then took off.

Mid-flight the unsecured cows went berserk in the cargo hold and threatened to destabilize the aircraft. In a fit of desperation the pilot opened the tailboard and the crew shoved the cows out of the back of aircraft as they flew over the Ochotskische Sea near Sachalin Island at an altitude of 30,000 feet.

Credence was added to the story when it was confirmed by the German embassy to Reuter's news agency. However, journalist Susanne Höll reported from Moscow that she believed the story bore all the hallmarks of a well-perpetuated myth.

Höll pointed out similarities between the incident and a Russian film *Peculiarities of the National Hunt* in which a cow is stolen and hidden in a military jet. The story may also have had its origins in a communist-era joke about a Russian fisherman who was sent to a psychiatric hospital after reporting the loss of his boat due to a falling cow.

It appears the story reached the German embassy from the US embassy, which had told the story as a joke. A German diplomat had put the story on the info-net also as a joke, but before long it was being reported as verbatim.

A spokesman for the Russian Defence Ministry appeared to confirm Höll's findings. Vladimir Uvatenko commented: 'This is sheer nonsense. Not a single word is true.'[114]

THE MASSACRE OF CERMIS

THERE are a lot of things that can go wrong on a skiing holiday. It is a sport you enter into accepting a certain level of risk. That said, few people would have predicted that they would be struck by a US warplane while travelling in a cable car down from a ski slope. Unfortunately that's what happened to one group of skiers on their way back from the Cermis ski resort in 1998.

On 3 February Captain Richard Ashby was piloting an EA-6B Prowler jet near Cavalese in Italy. He was flying extremely low and apparently making a video tape of the flight. Travelling at more than 600 mph, Ashby performed a barrel roll and barely noticed the bump that was created when his jet slashed through a cable car line. As the plane sped away a cable car gondola plunged 340 feet, closely followed by several tons-worth of hook, which crushed the gondola flat and killed 20 skiers – if the fall had not already done so. A second gondola was left suspended for hours, but mercifully its emergency brakes kept it from falling.

There was complete outrage in Italy and suggestions that this was by no means an accident. Italian politicians called for an urgent inquiry and a ban on similar military exercises. The Italian communists went a step further and called for all Americans to be expelled from bases in Italy. It clearly appeared that the Americans had been, for want of a better word, showing off, treating the mission like a fairground ride.

Ashby and flight navigator Captain Joseph Schweitzer were not tried in Italy – much to the anger of the incensed Italians – but in the United States. In his defence, Ashby's lawyers said that the ski lift was not shown on the maps he was using. But then again, what did he expect to find in a region famous for ski resorts?

Although it was shown that Ashby broke both altitude and speed rules during the flight, both airmen were acquitted of manslaughter charges. They were instead found guilty of obstruction of justice because the video tape made during the flight had mysteriously disappeared.

Both Ashby and Schweitzer were dismissed from the services; Ashby also received a six-year custodial sentence. If he had been found guilty of manslaughter he could have gone down for a total of 200 years.

SMART BOMBS ARE STILL AS DUMB AS THEIR USERS

W E hear a lot about precision weapons these days; but a word of warning: although the bomb may land exactly where it was intended there is nothing to say that the aimer is pointing at the right target. Like any tool, precision weapons are only as smart (or dumb) as their users.

A classic example of this is the bombing of the Chinese embassy in Belgrade by NATO jets in 1999. On the night of 7 May, a B-2 Stealth bomber from Whiteman Air Force Base in Missouri took off, flew across the Atlantic and dropped four 2,000lb satellite-guided bombs on the Chinese embassy, believing it was a Yugoslav military supply headquarters. Three Chinese journalists were killed and a score of others were wounded. The attack was a sickening mistake which led to mass protests in China and hurt the NATO alliance diplomatically.

First things first. Let us rule out all speculation that the Americans deliberately targeted the Chinese embassy. There is nothing to substantiate such a heinous conspiracy theory. The target was selected for NATO by the CIA, which later categorically denied 'that the Chinese embassy was intentionally targeted or that anyone involved in proposing or reviewing the target nomination package was aware that the site was actually an Embassy'.[115]

No, according to a later CIA briefing, the United States bombed the Chinese embassy because of – you guessed it – 'systemic organizational problems'.

What? Is that some kind of service jargon for 'incompetence'?

In his statement of 10 April 2000 Director of Public Affairs Bill Harlow said:

One of the key findings of the Inspector General's investigation of this matter was that the CIA lacked formal procedures for preparing and forwarding target nomination packages to the US military. We have taken several steps to address the systemic organizational problems that contributed to the accidental bombing of the Chinese Embassy. These steps are classified and we cannot discuss them further.

With regard to individual officers involved in the process that led to the bombing, the principal shortcoming ... was the fact that numerous CIA officers at all levels of responsibility failed to ensure that the

Cartoon in The Daily Telegraph, *10 May 1999. (The British Cartoon Archive, University of Kent, © The Telegraph Media Group)*

intended bombing target – the Yugoslav Federal Directorate of Supply and Procurement headquarters – had been properly identified and precisely located before CIA passed a target nomination package to the US military for action.

The evidence shows that this was clearly a tragic accident ...

Apparently an intelligence officer had noticed that the maps the CIA were using were out of date before the bombing, but his query was not followed up. This must be the problem in the system that Harlow was talking about.

But as for what was really bad about the event – according to the 9/11 Commission report into the 2001 terror attacks on the United States, nervousness over making another mistake that month meant that the CIA pulled out of a cruise missile hit on Osama bin Laden in Afghanistan. Quoting from the report:

The decision not to strike in May 1999 may now seem hard to understand ... [but] the administration, and the CIA in particular, was in the midst of intense scrutiny and criticism in May 1999 because faulty intelligence had just led the United States to bomb the Chinese embassy in Belgrade during the NATO war against Serbia. This episode may have made officials more cautious than might otherwise have been the case.[116]

Now that's a scandal!

COFFINGATE

OUR next story begins in 1994, when seven Indian doctors serving in the peacekeeping force in Somalia were killed by a mortar attack in Mogadishu. An Indian pathologist, Lieutenant Colonel Danish, and Victor Baiza, a mortician contracted by the US government for the peacekeeping mission, together performed autopsies on the men, embalmed the bodies and sent the remains back to India.[117]

The remains were put into bodybags and placed into a large aluminium casket. This casket was not a coffin, but a transport case to get the remains home. Attached to the case was a note from Baiza explaining that the case would cost $2,000 if the Indians did not send it back.

The Indian military returned the case and greatly appreciated the dignified way the doctors' remains had been returned to them. They were so impressed with the aluminium casket that they decided they should get some of their own. Between 1995 and 1998 they corresponded with Baiza about purchasing the aluminium cases.

Where things started to go wrong was that they dealt with Baiza himself. He was not the manufacturer of the cases – the ex-military mortician was a private citizen who ran a funeral parlour in Texas. However, Baiza withheld details of his supplier. At no point did the Indian military think to seek out the manufacturers directly.

Sensing there might be a business opportunity in the offing, Baiza went into partnership with Fred Buitron and formed a company called 'Buitron and Baiza Casket and Funeral Supplies' on the back of the Indian enquiry. They inflated the earlier $2,000 price of the cases by 20 per cent, citing a downturn in the casket market as the US government was overstocked. Baiza also said he was factoring in additional costs because the Clinton administration had put trade sanctions on India following its nuclear tests in May 1998.

Just when it looked as though the Indians were going cold on the deal, in May 1999 a conflict broke out with Pakistan in the disputed region of Kashmir's Kargil heights. Inevitably there were casualties, and in India those who gave their lives fighting in such inhospitable reaches were considered martyrs by the general public. Treating the bodies of these martyrs with dignity became a very live issue – if that is not too ghoulish a pun – and the transfer case scheme was looked at again.

This time Baiza quoted a price of $2,663 per case. He travelled to New Delhi for negotiations and signed a deal on 28 July 1999 worth $1.5 million, to supply India with 500 cases and 3,000 bodybags. An initial shipment of 150 cases and 900 bodybags was set for 22 February 2000; the rest of the contract was scheduled to be fulfilled over the following eight months.

Within days of the first shipment's delivery, the Indian Ministry of Defence (MoD) realized that what had arrived did not meet their specifications. They had thought the caskets would weigh 18kg, but the ones Baiza delivered came in at 54kg, which the Indians found too heavy to lift.

The mix up came from a misinterpretation of the thickness of the casket, which was '18-gauge' not 18kg. Baiza stated that the 54kg casket was the standard issue used by the US. However, the Indian MoD scrapped the contract and withheld 10 per cent of their initial payment for the first shipment. Pleas by Baiza for the Indian MoD to consult with soldiers familiar with the transfer cases fell on deaf ears and the caskets were sent to a depot for storage.

And there they remained, until ... At the end of the Kargil conflict in July 1999, India's Comptroller and Auditor General (CAG) started to investigate what it thought were gross irregularities in defence procurement related to the conflict. Its investigation concluded that those employed in procurement were poorly managed, incompetent, highly corrupt, or a combination of all three.

All too often it found that the Indian MoD had not shopped around for best prices, had accepted inappropriate goods and had not introduced penalties for late delivery of goods. One of the most outrageous examples noted was the purchase of 52,000 pairs of multipurpose boots in 1999. When the shoes were delivered, 30,000 were considered too small for adult use – but the consignment was accepted anyway.[118]

When CAG investigators found out about the transfer cases they could not believe their eyes. They started an investigation of their own into the price of coffins, and contacted the Indian Commander of UN forces in Somalia. He told the CAG that the caskets were available for $172.

It was hard to explain the price of $172, unless that was a loan fee for the casket the Indians returned after the transportation of the doctors' remains from Somalia. When the CAG went looking for a figure they found that they could buy the caskets from at least three US suppliers and that the US Defence Supplies Centre of Philadelphia was able to get them at a price of $1,200 per casket. Why hadn't anyone at the MoD looked into this?[119]

·Delving deeper, the CAG was amazed to see that no test specimens had been ordered and that no price assessment had been carried out. The caskets were made out of top-quality aeronautical-grade aluminium – the same material used in the construction of aircraft engines. What on earth were the military doing using such a material for something that was going to be buried in the ground?

Clearly the CAG misinterpreted the use of the transfer cases – which were not intended for burial in the ground. Unfortunately for the MoD, the press caught wind of the story before such factors could be explained and the country erupted in an almighty wave of anger.

The story was broken by *The Times of India*. From the outside it looked as though corrupt officials had inflated the prices of the coffins to make a sizeable kickback. The thought of people making money out of the Kargil martyrs was shocking. The added fact that the coffins were too heavy to lift was simply too much.

There was uproar in the Rajya Sabha – the upper house of India's parliament – over the purchase of coffins for Kargil martyrs. The loud din of protest included such cries as 'coffin thieves'. The uproar was so great that the house had to be adjourned briefly before Defence Minister George Fernandes could stand up and read a statement, during which the Opposition staged a walk out.

For Indian state radio, the Opposition's anger was a genuine reflection of public feeling: 'The mood of the parliamentarians amply reflected the shock and anger felt by each and every Indian on these sordid revelations.'[120]

The coffin purchase was described as a scandal by Congress member Suresh Pachouri, who asked for Fernandes' resignation. In the face of all the evidence, Fernandes strenuously defended the deal, claiming that $2,500 was the going rate.

This scandal came at a bad time for Fernandes, who had only returned to office in October after previously resigning as Defence Minister when an internet news provider, Tehelka.com, secretly filmed politicians, army officers and bureaucrats as they appeared to accept bribes from reporters posing as arms traders. Although Fernandes was cleared of any wrongdoing, opposition politicians described his reinstatement as 'immoral'.[121]

Oddly enough, Fernandes was very popular in the army. He went to great pains to visit the troops in Kashmir, often riding to the front in army trucks with the soldiers and sharing the same rations that they had. It was this common touch that helped the Defence Minister survive a scandal that could have buried him ... but what a mess!

SINKING OF THE *KURSK*

O N 12 August 2000 the Russian Federation's nuclear submarine *Kursk* was on manoeuvres. We will never know precisely why, but a leak of hydrogen peroxide torpedo fuel caused an explosion in the forward torpedo room. Two minutes, 15 seconds later a chain reaction of other torpedoes exploding sent the Russian sub to the bottom of the Barents Sea and 118 men to their doom. Although most died during the explosions, because of a letter written by Lieutenant Dimitri Kolesnikov it is known that 23 men survived for some time in a waterproof compartment awaiting rescue. Eventually, probably within just 12 hours of the explosion, a combination of asphyxiation and an accidental flash fire finished them off while they were awaiting rescue.

It is impossible to describe just how big a blow the loss of the *Kursk* was to the Russian Navy. Since the end of the Cold War and the break-up of the Soviet Union, government cutbacks had reduced the armed forces to a mere glimmer of their former status. Even so the *Kursk* was a formidable weapon – it was the pride of the Russian fleet. According to a former captain of the submarine, Commander Viktor Rozhkov, the *Kursk* should have been unsinkable. 'I couldn't get my head round the idea that the *Kursk* could sink,' he told a TV interview. 'It couldn't, that just couldn't happen ... You can't take the *Kursk* out even with a torpedo. Yes, there may be some damage, but she'll always be [able] to come to the surface.'[122]

But nonetheless, the *Kursk* had sunk and was 350 feet underwater on the floor of the Barents Sea. Russian divers found the submarine but were unable to open its hatches. Rumours flew round that tapping had been heard from the crew trapped inside, but no one knew how long the oxygen supplies inside the *Kursk* would last.

The Russian Navy's inability to mount a rescue mission without outside help was particularly humiliating. So, as in the darkest days of the communist era, the Russian Navy sat on its hands, put a blanket over its head and did nothing. It was like the Chernobyl disaster, when the Soviet leadership simply pretended to the world that nothing had gone wrong.

Offers of help from the United States and European countries were seen as a mixture of gloating and attempted espionage. Hopelessly misjudging public opinion, President Putin remained on holiday at a Black Sea resort. While the naval hierarchy grimly predicted the worst for the crew of the *Kursk*, Putin was seen on TV enjoying a barbecue. It was just like being back in the bad old days of the 1980s again.

Perhaps the most shocking incident relating to the disaster was captured on live TV when a woman haranguing the Russian Deputy Prime Minister for news of the sinking appeared to be injected with tranquillizers by a female agent. The protester collapsed seconds later and was led away. This really was like the old days.

The mother of one of the *Kursk* sailors, Nadya Tylik later released a statement which said she was the protestor and that she had only been given medicine for her heart. Some doubt was cast on this claim when foreign journalists were not allowed to interview her for verification.

This Paul Thomas cartoon, the Daily Express*, 25 August 2000, is a very caustic comment on the action of Putin's government following the sinking of the* Kursk. *(The British Cartoon Archive, University of Kent, © Express newspapers)*

Eventually the Russian government relented and allowed help from British and Norwegian rescuers, who reached the scene on 19 August. The following day, eight days after the explosions, British divers reached the submarine's escape hatch. They quickly realized that the compartment was already flooded and the crew were dead.

To deflect any culpability away from cutbacks, incompetence and faulty equipment, the Russians blamed the United States for the disaster. They said that two American submarines had been monitoring the *Kursk* and that one of these had collided with it. This was not entirely implausible and the Russians held on to this argument for two years after the disaster before finally admitting that the torpedo fuel was most likely to blame.

A CAREER ON THE ROCKS

REMAINING on the subject of naval accidents, on 7 July 2002 Britain's Royal Navy suffered one of its most humiliating episodes in modern history when the Type 42 destroyer HMS *Nottingham* struck a rock 375 miles off Australia. The accident left the ship requiring a £42 million refit and led to the court martial of the ship's commanding officer and three other senior members of the crew.

To reconstruct the event, HMS *Nottingham* was en route from Cairns, Australia, to Wellington, New Zealand. A few minor detours were added to the route so that the crew might do some sightseeing. On the list of wonders to behold was Lord Howe Island, a volcanic outcrop in the middle of the Tasman Sea.

Nottingham was scheduled to pass the island just before nightfall on Sunday 7 July, but earlier in the morning a member of the crew had had an accident that required hospital treatment. The only place within helicopter range was Lord Howe Island, so the injured person was taken there and then flown on to a hospital in Sydney.

The ship reached the island in the afternoon and, as the weather was fine, a landing party went ashore to have a look round and thank the islanders for helping them care for their crewmate. Hearing that a party was coming over, Clive Wilson, the marine services manager on the island, provided drinks and food, hoping to meet the ship's captain.

Hearing this, the captain, Richard Farrington told Wilson he would come over once the party returned. He would then take the ship's Lynx helicopter back to HMS *Nottingham* later on.[123] While he was ashore the weather began to turn nasty and by the time Farrington headed back to the ship, the conditions were bad enough to force *Nottingham* into changing course to allow the helicopter to land.

With the helicopter safely aboard, *Nottingham* set off. In Farrington's absence, executive officer Commander John Lea, officer of the watch Lieutenant James Denney and navigator Lieutenant Andrew Ingham together made several changes in course, plotting a new course around the east of the island. Unfortunately, while they were working out this route a junior officer placed a navigational pointer on the map, which obscured a submerged hazard known as Wolf Rock.

As HMS *Nottingham* got underway Denney thought he saw what appeared to be the reflection of moonlight on the water. In response to his question, 'What the hell's that?,'[124] Ingham rushed to check their position on the chart and only then did he realize that they were heading straight for Wolf Rock.

It was too late. Seconds after Ingham understood the danger, HMS *Nottingham* struck the rock – the first ship to do so since 1837.

As the rock tore a 160ft gash in the *Nottingham*'s side, Farrington had only been back on the ship a matter of minutes. He felt a series of heavy judders and immediately realized that the ship had collided with something. He described the horror of the moment to journalists: 'I prayed to God it was a container, or even God forbid a small boat or something. I had no idea it would be the world's biggest rock ... It is the worst feeling in the world.'[125]

Farrington rushed up to the bridge and saw that his ship was being engulfed in white water. There was a heavy swell which was repeatedly lifting the ship up and dropping it down on the surface of the rock.

Assessing the situation, Farrington added up whether it was best to get off the rock and run the risk of sinking, or remain on the rock and hope the swell did not break the back of the destroyer. It was a tough call with 253 lives in his hands, but he decided to reverse off the rock in case it broke the ship in two.

Meanwhile water was pouring into exposed compartments including the Sea Dart missile magazine and one of the ship's messes. The vessel could well have sunk had not the crew managed to stem the worst of the flooding. Working in near darkness, chest deep in water, chief petty officers Robert Hunt and Chris Mullen and three crew members were later awarded the Queen's Gallantry Medal for their efforts below decks, shoring up bulkheads through the night. An MBE was also later awarded to Lieutenant Commander Ian Grove for the part he played in preventing the ship from sinking. By 11pm the ship was safely anchored and a salvage operation well underway.

However, Farrington could see stormy waters ahead for him and his crew. When the story hit the press, it was first presented as a dramatic sea adventure, but then the vultures started to circle in the hunt for scraps of a scandal. Farrington was described in many newspapers as sipping wine with the local harbour master while his ship ran aground. Of course, this was not strictly true, but by then the damage to his reputation was done. When asked what he thought the repercussions of the incident would be, he told Australian TV: 'It is inevitable. The sun comes up in the morning, you run your ship aground, you get court martialled.' And sure enough he was, along with Lea, Denney and Ingham, all four men facing a maximum sentence of two years in prison.

The court martial took place on 11 September 2003 in Portsmouth Naval Base. Farrington was charged with being negligent for failing to properly delegate command of the ship to his executive officer. Although the panel recognized that he bore no responsibility for the actual collision, it found Farrington at fault for not going over the navigation plan before going ashore, and leaving it to Ingham and Lea who were not considered experienced enough to handle such a task. If Farrington had gone over the charts with his subordinates the panel thought that he would have been able to bring any potential navigational hazards to their attention – big rocks included.

Farrington pleaded guilty to this charge. Denney, the officer of the watch on the night in question, admitted negligently causing the crash and Lea and Ingham also pleaded guilty to negligence in allowing the ship to be stranded.

Before sentencing, the president of the panel, Commodore Wilcocks, told the four defendants: 'This instance has undermined the high reputation of the Royal Navy and caused significant embarrassment, wasted resources, and took an operational warship out of active duty for a long period.' However, Farrington and Lea were also praised for their conduct after the accident. Wilcocks added, 'We would also like to acknowledge the immense courage and professionalism displayed by all of the officers and ratings in HMS *Nottingham* to save your ship from loss.'

When the verdicts were read, Commander Farrington received a reprimand, Lieutenant Ingham was given a severe reprimand, and Lieutenant Commander Lea and Lieutenant Denney were dismissed from their ships. Speaking after the verdict, Commander Farrington said, 'This incident reminds us all that the sea is an unforgiving master'.

THE BROTHEL BILLS SCANDAL

I T started out as an investigation into claims that US Defense Department employees had run up millions of dollars of debt on unpaid, government-issued credit cards. By the time the Government Accounting Office (GAO) had finished with the armed forces, it was clear that very serious abuses of these credit cards were taking place, including payments to prostitutes.

In a bid for greater efficiency, the Defense Department allows credit cards to be issued to service personnel to enable them to purchase certain supplies and services. There are two types of credit card issued – one for travel expenses and another for purchasing.

The cards are billed to the individual, who then claims the money back as expenses. However, what the GAO found was that, once reimbursed, some personnel were not paying off their credit cards. In fact they found that 46,000 Defense Department employees had defaulted on $62 million of payments in travel expenses charged to the government cards.

In the course of what became multiple investigations into credit card use among the military, the GAO began to uncover a pattern of illegal use of credit cards for purchasing personal items and services.

Between October 2000 and March 2002, the GAO survey found 1,180 US Navy transactions for personal items totalling $206,700. In the summer of 2001 the GAO had already found that 200 US

Army personnel had withdrawn $38,000 from ATMs which were spent on lap dancing and strip clubs near military bases. The GAO then found naval personnel guilty of similar abuses, apparently using the cash to tip dancers, waitresses and bartenders. The investigation also recorded the use of government credit cards in legal brothels where the payment for 'services rendered' had been disguised as restaurant charges.[126]

Examples of improper credit card use noted in the GAO report on US Navy expenses included:

- $13,250 in 80 transactions at two Nevada brothels
- $20,800 for 199 purchases at two jewellery stores
- $28,700 for 247 transactions at three adult clubs
- $34,250 for 80 gambling transactions
- $38,300 for 72 cruises
- $71,400 for 502 purchases of tickets to events, including *The Phantom of the Opera*, Yankees and Atlanta Braves baseball games and Lakers basketball games.

The US Army came out equally badly when investigated. Some of the worst examples of army spending included:

- $7,373 for closing costs on a house
- $4,100 to Budget-Rent-A-Car for purchase of a used automobile
- $2,278 to Spearmint Rhino adult cabaret
- $1,253 for internet gambling
- $4,704 in ATM withdrawals
- $8,709 to Wal-Mart supermarket
- $1,058 to Dream Girls escort services
- $5,192 for reservations for four people on Celebrity Cruises' Bahamas & Caribbean cruise
- $3,998 for accommodation for four nights during Rose Bowl tour

- $1,395 to Louisiana Superdome for 45 tickets to Essence Music festival
- $826 for Georgetown Prep Tennis Club membership
- $491 for automobile insurance
- $172 to Victoria's Secret – women's lingerie
- $275 to Sunshine Entertainment personal escort service.[127]

After these reports, and at the request of US Representatives Jan Schakowsky, Steve Horn and Senator Charles Grassley, the GAO examined the use of government-issued travel and purchase credit cards by US Air Force personnel. The GAO visited air force bases at different locations across the US including Nellis (Nevada), Hill (Utah), Travis (California), Edwards (California) and Lackland (Texas).

Although the US Air Force report came out better than the US Navy and Army investigations, it still found that low- to middle-income enlisted personnel were the most susceptible to making improper charges to their cards.

The report noted that cards were given out quite freely and that no checks were made on the bearer's credit history. Many bearers had significant financial problems including credit card debt, foreclosed home mortgages and even, in some cases, bankruptcy. The report recommended that some form of credit check be carried out before cards were issued, as those people with a poor credit history, who might have been refused credit by commercial institutions, were most likely to misuse government credit cards.[128]

Some of the more irregular purchases noticed by the report included:

- $2,141 for entertainment – dinner party and show for 18 people at Treasure Island Hotel and Casino, Las Vegas; including $800 of alcohol

- $1,935 for two reclining rocking chairs with vibrating massage feature
- $375 taxidermist bill for mounting a 'road kill' mule deer head, represented as for educational purposes
- $595 for a leather laptop case for a brigadier general
- $2,016 for civilian clothes for military assistants
- $2,948 for costumes for an air force regional band
- $2,443 for down payment on a $10,000 sapphire ring at E-Z Pawn
- $1,696 for physical fitness clothing and fleece jacket for drill instructors
- $828 for blazer and dresses for participants at an awards ceremony
- $5,500 for 50 Samsonite Pullman suitcases
- $796 for bottled water
- $540 for 12 pairs of 'paratrooper goggles' but in fact Oakley sunglasses
- $14,664 for briefcases and flight bags.[129]

In a second report on the air force, this time looking into the alleged abuse of travel cards, the GAO found that many cardholders made inappropriate purchases, including:

- $31,000 spent on 70 transactions with cruise liner companies
- $14,000 on 79 transactions linked with online gambling
- $31,000 on 223 transactions relating to the purchase of tickets to sports events and concerts, including the Dallas Cowboys, Backstreet Boys and Janet Jackson
- $32,000 on 187 transactions relating to so-called gentlemen's clubs, including Spearmint Rhino, Cheetah's Lounge and Déjà Vu Showgirls
- $1,000 on three transactions in legalized brothels: 40 Bar Ranch and Madam Butterfly.[130]

So that's where all the money goes!

THE SULTAN OF SPIN

HE was like a cross between the captain of the *Titanic* and a hard-pressed customer complaints manager. Without further ado, we hereby introduce Muhammad Said al-Sahaf, Saddam Hussein's Information Minister during the 2003 war.

Throughout the war, this quick-tongued mouthpiece of Saddam's murdering regime was responsible for some of the most outrageous, blatantly false pieces of wartime propaganda since the British announced that they had filled the English Channel with man-eating sharks imported from Australia to eat shot-down German pilots.*

With Western news agencies feeling themselves duty bound to report the Iraqi side of every news story, audiences were treated to Sahaf's freakish press conferences. Strangely engaging in his black beret and military uniform, the Iraqi Information Minister's well-worked diatribes included such prize gems as: 'It has been rumoured we have fired Scud missiles into Kuwait. I am here now to tell you, we do not have any Scud missiles and I don't know why they were fired into Kuwait.'

---

* This is a true story: During the 1940 Battle of Britain every trick in the book was used in a bid to put fear into potential German invaders. The other great lie was that the British had a secret means of setting fire to the English Channel once German invasion craft began to approach the shore.

294

On a separate occasion, when asked by a Western journalist if Saddam was still alive, he answered, 'I will only answer reasonable questions.'

His press briefings were so outrageous and so obviously false they developed a cult status. Even President Bush became a fan and would interrupt meetings to watch the latest instalment. The President told an NBC interviewer: 'He's my man, he was great.'[131]

Sahaf was quickly nicknamed 'Baghdad Bob' by the Americans, following the nickname given to a Vietnamese broadcaster, 'Hanoi Hannah', in that earlier conflict. To the press pack he became 'Saddam's Optimist' or 'Comical Ali' – a play on the nickname given to Hassan al-Majid, the author of poison gas attacks on the Kurds and better known as 'Chemical Ali'.*

Even as US tanks rumbled into Baghdad, Sahaf continued to preach a bewildering message of defiance. Holding a press conference at the Palestine Hotel, he denied the journalists' claims with his trademark cheeky, confident smile and the pronouncement: 'No! There are no tanks.'

Just a matter of a few hundred yards away the crackle of small arms fire almost drowned him out, but he continued nonetheless: 'Baghdad is safe. US soldiers are being slaughtered in their hundreds. They pushed a few of their armoured carriers and some of their tanks with their soldiers and we besieged them and we killed most of them and I think we will finish them soon. My feeling, as usual, is that we will slaughter them, all of these invaders – their tombs will be here in Iraq.'

---

* On the subject of nicknames a brief mention should be made of Huda Salih Mahdi Ammash, AKA 'Chemical Sally', an Iraqi scientist better known to the United States government as Mrs Anthrax. Then of course, the pièce de résistance, the Iraqi leader himself, Saddam Insane.

One correspondent pointed out to the minister that US armour was by the River Tigris. Sahaf retorted, 'There is no presence of American infidels ... at all.' When another said he had seen television pictures of tanks in the city, Sahaf countered, 'That was filmed somewhere else.' Even when coalition forces revealed that the Iraqi Ministry of Information building had been taken, Sahaf was still in a state of denial. Secretly working from a radio van, he replied to a question on the capture of his ministry with the words: 'Absolutely not true. I can tell you that because I am here, at the ministry.'[132]

With the sound of battle coming closer and chaos in the Palestine Hotel when a stray American tank round hit the building, BBC journalist Paul Wood thought the Information Minister was becoming increasingly detached from reality.

'Isn't it time you surrender?' Wood asked.

'They are going to surrender,' Sahaf replied. 'Or be burnt in their tanks.'

'You are not frightened?'

'Not at all. We are going to tackle them and destroy them.'[133]

When the end finally came on 9 April, Sahaf tried to reach the media centre at the Palestine Hotel but turned back after he saw American troops. Instead he worked from a transmitter van. When one journalist saw US tanks thundering past he asked the Information Minister about them. Sahaf said: 'No, no, no, maybe there are two or three tanks, but they will go.'

But he wasn't completely stupid – he was no Joseph Goebbels, killing his family and himself when his beloved Führer made himself extinct. No way. Muhammad Said al-Sahaf ditched his black beret, concealed the rank markings on his epaulettes, and wrapped a red and white kaffiyeh scarf around his head. He ordered the radio station to keep broadcasting a speech by Saddam Hussein and then made his bid for freedom out the back door of the studio. Three hours later US soldiers arrived.[134]

After fleeing, Sahaf stayed with his aunt in Baghdad. Towards the end of April a story emerged that he had given himself up to the Americans but that they had released him after questioning.[135] The Americans denied this; but Safah was not among the 55 most wanted Iraqis famously printed onto the backs of decks of playing cards and distributed to US troops.

To conclude this tale, the last word – as ever – should go to Sahaf. Here are some of his prime quotations from the war:[136]

'I speak better English than this villain Bush.'

'The midget Bush and that Rumsfeld deserve only to be beaten with shoes by freedom loving people everywhere.'

'We will slaughter them, Bush Jr and his international gang of bastards!'

'They are superpower of villains. They are superpower of Al Capone.'

'Yes, the American troops have advanced further. This will only make it easier for us to defeat them.'

'They are trapped in Umm Qasr. They are trapped near Basra. They are trapped near Najaf. They are trapped everywhere.'

'They are retreating on all fronts. Their military effort is a subject of laughter throughout the world.'

'They are not in Baghdad. They are not in control of any airport. I tell you this. It is all a lie. They lie. It is a Hollywood movie. You do not believe them.'

'We are winning!'

SAVING PRIVATE JESSICA

THE United States countered Comical Ali with a 'good news' story of their own – the 'Saving Private Lynch' story. In the long term, this story turned into a complete fiasco – a classic example of a PR stunt blowing up in a government's face.

An American servicewoman, Jessica Lynch, was captured on 23 March 2003 after the vehicle she was travelling in took a wrong turn, somewhere near Nasiriyah. Eleven of Lynch's comrades were killed and Lynch was posted as MIA (Missing in Action). Surviving the attack she was taken to the local hospital, which was reportedly teeming with fedayeen fighters. Acting on a tip off, on 1 April US Special Forces soldiers raided the hospital, found Lynch and airlifted her to safety. The US military filmed the entire stunt – sorry ... mission – and then fed an edited five-minute video of the rescue to the story-hungry 24-hour news media.

A number of claims were made about Jessica Lynch's capture. Firstly she was said to have fought bravely to the last round. It was then alleged that she had stab and bullet wounds. A biography of her claimed that she had been raped and otherwise sexually assaulted by her captors. Lynch's own recollection of the affair was vague. Suffering from amnesia, she did recall that her gun had jammed before she fired even a single shot and that she surrendered, but after that she could give no details.[137]

Although grateful for her rescue Lynch was critical of the military for using her for propaganda purposes. She was particularly unhappy about the release of false information relating to her capture and she also queried why her rescue had to be filmed. 'They used me as a way to symbolize all this stuff. It's wrong,' she told an ABC interviewer. As for her reported heroics before capture she revealed: 'I'm not about to take credit for something I didn't do ... I did not shoot – not a round, nothing. I went down praying to my knees – that's the last thing I remember.'[138]

When interviewed, the doctors in Nasiriyah claimed that they provided the best treatment possible for Lynch under difficult circumstances. They described her injuries as being in line with a road traffic accident. They were limited to a broken arm, a broken

"At last, a decent script!"

Cartoon by Patrick Blower in the Evening Standard, *2 April 2003. (The British Cartoon Archive, University of Kent, © Solo Syndication/Associated Newspapers)*

thigh and dislocated ankle, all of which could have been caused when the vehicle she was travelling in crashed. There were no signs of injury from a weapon and her clothes appeared intact, indicating there had been no sexual assault.

Perhaps the most interesting claim is that the Iraqi doctors actually tried to help Lynch escape to American lines in an ambulance, but that when they approached a checkpoint, American soldiers opened fire on them. Instead Lynch had to wait for the dramatic, televised rescue two days later, which an Iraqi doctor described as being like a scene from a Jackie Chan movie.[139]

It then emerged that certain photos of Lynch had been purchased by Larry Flynt, the high-profile owner of the *Hustler* magazine. Flynt claimed that the photos showed her topless and cavorting with fellow soldiers. The soldiers selling the photos said they were doing it to prove that Jessica Lynch was 'not all apple pie'.[140]

A well-known opponent of the Bush regime and the decision to go to war, Flynt claimed he bought the pictures to 'protect' Lynch and had locked them in a vault for safekeeping. His reasons for doing so were that Lynch was being used by the White House as a pawn.

From good news to bad news – the Lynch story turned into 'a monster' that White House myrmidons wished would quickly go away.

EQUATORIAL GUINEA COUP

Perched on the West African coast, Equatorial Guinea is slightly smaller in size than the US state of Maryland. A former Spanish colony, Equatorial Guinea won its independence in 1968 and in 1979, President Teodoro Obiang Nguema Mbascogo took power in a military coup, deposing and executing his uncle, the President.

The population is less than half a million strong, consisting mostly of poor subsistence farmers eking out a living in the tropical heat with a life expectancy well below what one would expect in the West – which is strange considering that Equatorial Guinea has the second highest per capita income in the world after Luxembourg![141]

You see, not so long ago someone discovered that Equatorial Guinea was sitting on a stupendously large off-shore oil field – possibly amounting to as much as 10 per cent of the entire planet's reserve. When oil company ExxonMobil made this discovery, President Obiang was thrust onto the international stage. His importance as a 'player' was only strengthened by the subsequent discovery of an equally large natural gas field.

But while Obiang and his entourage lavished money on fast cars and everything the finest Parisian shops have to offer, very little – if any – wealth filtered back into the country and its people. Although Equatorial Guinea is technically a democratic state, Obiang's regime has been one of the most corrupt, oppressive and anti-democratic states in the world. All in all, it is as if the country is being run by a Bond villain. Witness the following pronouncement made on the state radio show *Bidze-Nduan* in 2003:

> He can decide to kill without anyone calling him to account and without going to hell because it is God himself, with whom he is in permanent contact, and who gives him this strength.[142]

In 2004 President Obiang's country hit the world stage for other reasons, when a group of mercenaries were foiled attempting a coup. The fallout from this botched attempt to remove and possibly kill Obiang came to rest on an British ex-soldier and the son of a former British Prime Minister. It caused quite a scandal.

On 7 March a Boeing 727-100 touched down in Harare airport, Zimbabwe. On board the jet were the pilot, co-pilot and 64 mercenaries – mostly veterans of civil wars in Angola and Mozambique. While the plane was refuelled, it was supposed to pick up a cargo of weapons including AK-47 assault rifles, RPGs and grenades provided by Simon Mann, a well-known British ex-SAS soldier, who had been involved in 'security' work for a number of years in South Africa.

The plan was to take off and land in Equatorial Guinea's capital, Malabo, in the early hours of 8 March. An advanced team of 15 men led by South African Nick du Toit were already in the city. Their job was to escort the team of mercenaries to capture President Obiang, take him back to the airport and fly him off to exile in Spain – either that or shoot him in bed. In the meantime an exiled Opposition leader, Severo Moto, was scheduled to land 30 minutes behind the mercenaries and take power.

Unfortunately for the plotters, the 727 never got the chance to leave Harare. The trouble was that the coup had become common knowledge in certain circles and apparently President Obiang was warned to watch out for a coup by the South Africans.

The Zimbabweans separately became suspicious of Simon Mann's activities and his attempts to purchase weapons from the Zimbabwe Defence Industries. When the mercenary 747 landed in Harare it was impounded and the 66 crew and passengers were arrested on immigration charges. Mann was also arrested and told the Zimbabweans that the group were security personnel destined for a contract guarding diamond mines in the Democratic Republic of Congo.

This story held until Obiang revealed the capture of the 15 men already in Equatorial Guinea. During interrogation – du Toit later claimed that he was tortured – the full story of the coup began to emerge.

Simon Mann was jailed in Zimbabwe's maximum security Chikurubi prison and held in solitary confinement. Under interrogation he revealed how he had been introduced to Moto by Ely Calil, a Lebanese multi-millionaire businessman. Meeting Mann in Madrid, Moto asked for help in a coup bid to topple Obiang. Moto asked Mann to get him into the country in time for an uprising of local people against the President. Mann agreed to help.

Having admitted as much, Mann knew he was in big trouble, especially if he was extradited to Equatorial Guinea, where he would probably face a firing squad – something that was being threatened against du Toit. While in his cell Mann wrote a letter to his wife Amanda on scraps of paper, asking that the financial backers behind the coup use their influence and 'wonga' (slang for money) to get him released. It concluded:

This is not going well. I must say once again: what will get us out is MAJOR CLOUT. Once we get into a real trial scenario we are f****d.[143]

Unfortunately the note was intercepted by the South African intelligence. It made mention of two men, only referred to by their nicknames 'Scratcher' and 'Smelly'. Piecing together the evidence, South Africa's elite anti-fraud unit, the 'Scorpions', believed that 'Smelly' was Ely Calil and that 'Scratcher' was Sir Mark Thatcher – Mann's neighbour and son of the former British Prime Minister. If correct, this note would provide damning evidence against the two men.

Thatcher was arrested on 25 August 2004 and charged with providing logistical support to the failed coup. Although he pleaded his innocence, the South African authorities found it suspicious that his Cape Town residence was up for sale and his bags appeared to be packed ready to leave at the time of the arrest.

The story was quickly propelled onto the front pages around the world. Not only was Thatcher in trouble with the South Africans, who take a very hard line against mercenaries operating in their backyard these days, but Obiang wanted Thatcher delivered to Equatorial Guinea for trial. With reports that a German linked with the coup had died under torture in Obiang's notorious 'Black Beach' prison, Sir Mark was advised to plea bargain his way out of trouble.

It appears that Sir Mark invested in a company called Air Ambulance Africa or Triple A Aviation, which in fact provided the helicopter that took Severo Moto to Mali on the eve of the coup and would have been used to ferry him into Equatorial Guinea if the mercenaries had been able to leave Zimbabwe. On 13 January 2005 Sir Mark pleaded guilty after admitting he knew the helicopter was going to be used in mercenary action. He was fined 3 million rand and given a four-year suspended sentence for his part in the plot. The Scorpions have also revealed that Sir Mark had notified them of his willingness to provide future cooperation.

In Equatorial Guinea, Nick du Toit received a 34-year sentence, having been spared the death penalty. Opposition leader Severo Moto received a 63-year sentence *in absentia*. In Zimbabwe Simon Mann was found guilty of illegally buying weapons, he got four years plus the threat of possible extradition to Equatorial Guinea.

THE DEVIL'S OWN

IN October 2004 a stir was created when the British Royal Navy gave its blessing for one of its servicemen to formally register as a practising Satanist. In light of the mania for political correctness, and particularly after the UK government put 'Jedi Knight' on the list of practised religions in the 2001 annual census, it was only a question of time before the first devil-worshipping serviceman came out of the shadows.* Serving on board the frigate HMS *Cumberland*, naval technician Chris Cranmer, 24, had been a practising Satanist for nine years since coming across a copy of *The Satanic Bible*, written by Anton Szandor LaVey, who established the Church of Satan in San Francisco in 1966. In 2004 he approached Captain Russell Best and asked to be registered as a Satanist. Knowing of no official reason to deny Cranmer his request, and after having consulted with the ship's chaplain, Captain Best granted it.

Mr Cranmer was thenceforth excused from attending all religious ceremonies and was given a space where he could carry out Satanic

---

* See the 2001 UK census (www.statistics.gov.uk/census2001). 'Jedi Knight' is listed as religion 896. Although not officially recognized as a faith, in terms of numbers of followers the Star Wars creed came fourth in declared religions, behind Christian, Muslim and Hindu in the UK. In New Zealand, Jedi Knights were the second largest religious force (no pun intended) in the country, while in Australia in 2001 more than 70,000 people declared themselves believers. As alluded to in George Lucas' first instalment of his space-faring double-trilogy, some people are easily led.

rituals. If killed in action the navy undertook to contact the Church of Satan to provide a service, or, if this was not possible, to provide Mr Cranmer with a non-denominational funeral.

Mr Cranmer was relieved at the decision and later said, 'I didn't want to feel I couldn't get out my Satanic Bible and relax in bed.'

News of this irregular arrangement came about when Cranmer wrote an article on his quest for acceptance in the magazine *Rule Satannia*. As journalists began to probe the story further, the Royal Navy put out a statement saying that it was an equal opportunities employer and did not stop anyone from expressing freedom of worship. Furthermore the decision had been taken by the captain on the basis that it did not in any way interfere with the operational effectiveness, safety or security of the ship, or Mr Cranmer's colleagues.

The news was greeted with widespread incredulity and was considered 'utterly shocking' by Conservative MP Ann Widdecombe. A well-known practising Catholic, Widdecombe said that the navy should not permit Satanists on board its ships. The argument continued when Admiral Sir Sandy Woodward, the former British naval commander in the Falklands War, greeted the news with the memorable line: 'Good God, what the hell's going on?'

The ship's captain endorsed Cranmer's right to practise religion freely and thought of him as a good worker, saying, 'Nobody is suggesting there is anything at all dark about this.'

However, the last word must go to Mr Cranmer's mother, Catherine, a member of the Church of Scotland, who said of her son, 'He does not have an evil bone in his body.'

SWISS PLEAS

THE land of chocolate, cuckoo clocks, multipurpose pocket knives and secret bank accounts, Switzerland has a reputation for peace, stability and picture-postcard scenery. However, in 2006 the country was rocked by the murder of a former champion ladies' skier, Corinne Rey-Bellet, by her estranged husband. In addition to shooting his wife days after they separated, Gerold Stadler also killed his brother-in-law and badly wounded his mother-in-law with the gun before turning it on himself.

Apart from the celebrity of the principal victim, the case was notable because it lifted the lid on Switzerland's unusual practice of keeping military weapons at home. Stadler was a reservist army captain and he had used his army pistol to commit the crime.[144]

A confederation made up of German-, French- and Italian-speaking cantons, Switzerland has remained neutral since 1815 when it was freed from French control at the end of the Napoleonic Wars. Since then, anyone daft enough to attempt invading the country would find it very hard going.

In modern times, although the Swiss standing army is just a few thousand strong, within hours of the alert, around half a million trained men would be in position to defend the country. Add to that the mountains and narrow Alpine passes one would have to negotiate, invading Switzerland is just not worth the hassle.

Since the Second World War, all Swiss men fit for military service have been obliged to do national service and report for training each year as reservists. As part of their ongoing commitment to defence, all Swiss reservists keep their uniform, an assault rifle or pistol, and a box of 50 cartridges at home in case the alarm is sounded.

As well as the required assault rifle, many Swiss men keep additional firearms for recreational use. Speculating on how many guns there might be in Swiss homes, estimates vary at anything from 1 to 3 million weapons. Although these weapons must, by law, be contained in a secure metal box, there are no checks on gun ownership, nor are gun owners licensed.

Despite the existence of a strong gun lobby, the Rey-Bellet murders at least seem to have provoked a call for gun licensing. A similar question was raised about the suitability of military assault rifles being stored in people's homes.

Studies revealed that more than 300 people are killed in Switzerland every year by army guns and that the country has one of the highest gun-suicide rates in Europe.[145] It is commonly known that the majority of murder victims know their assailant, but in Switzerland 58 per cent of victims are murdered by members of their own family. Ever understated, the Swiss refer to such killings as 'family dramas'.[146] Dramas? Catastrophes more like.

Explaining this phenomenon, experts believe that the well-ordered Swiss are so used to things being correct and punctual, that they have a low tolerance level when things go wrong. The male of the species has a particular inability to cope with unexpected reversals of fortune. The sudden onset of stress and the close proximity of an assault rifle in the home are clearly a recipe for disaster.

Despite the continued deaths and petitioning by many women – the principal victims of domestic gun crime – the conservative Swiss are unlikely to change their habits over gun ownership any time soon.

AFTERWORD

COMING now to the end of our journey through the history of military misdemeanour we can look back on a collection of stories, some tragic, some curiously amusing.

No doubt there are many more instances in military history that could occupy us further, and you may at this time be wondering why such and such a figure has avoided the scrutiny of our irreverent gaze. There may even be some among you who now breathe a sigh of relief that these instalments have passed you by – for now. One thing is certain, that as surely as the summer gives way to autumn, scandal will continue to haunt the progress of military history no matter what politicians might say.

But before we bid goodbye, indulge us this parting warning: every day our newspapers and TV news channels report on civil wars, disputes, ethnic tensions and genocides taking place in the world around us. While global leaders belatedly chase after the bandwagon of climate change to hitch a ride to Votesville, you get the impression that there is nowhere near the same enthusiasm to tackle issues like the proliferation of arms in the Third World.

It is estimated that war costs Africa $15 billion in lost revenue per year. Although no one is saying that stopping the flow of arms will put an end to wars, it might make them shorter and less costly. Although not in Africa, the example of Afghanistan demonstrates this point well enough. People have been fighting in Afghanistan pretty much non-stop since the Russian invasion of 1979. How on earth do people manage to get their hands on so much ammunition? Who sells it to them? Where do they get the money from?

With the break-up of the Soviet Union and the end of the Cold War, a lot of surplus material came on the market in the early to mid-1990s. This was extremely fortuitous for some, because, with the eerie stability of the Cold War gone, there was now a huge demand for weapons of every kind.

Apparently, post-Soviet Ukraine was an arms dealer's paradise. When the Russians withdrew their forces, no one was quite sure what the Ukrainian armed forces had or were supposed to have in the way of weapons and equipment. It became a free-for-all. A supposedly secret report by the Ukrainian government estimated that 32 billion dollars' worth of military assets vanished between 1992 and 1998. That's an awful lot of AK47s.

More recently, in 2006, there were reports that a shipment of 200,000 AK47s had vanished en route from a US base in Bosnia to the fledgling Iraqi security forces. Reports indicate that the Moldovan airline used to ferry the arms had been stripped of its licence by the United Nations after being caught illegally supplying arms to Liberia. No one is quite sure what happened to the 200,000 assault rifles, except that they are not in the hands of the Iraqi authorities. In fact, it seems most are resigned to the fact that the guns are probably in the hands of the insurgents, al Qaeda or both.

One of the chief culprits behind this illicit arms trade is said to be a former KGB officer, named in a United Nations report as Victor Anatoliyevich Bout.[147] Known in Africa as the 'Merchant of Death', Mr Bout has been blamed for providing arms to numerous African conflicts including Sierra Leone, the Democratic Republic of Congo and Angola. The rebel groups purchase the weapons with 'conflict diamonds' from the mines they control. Once these diamonds are polished and put on the market they are almost impossible to trace.[148]

But forget about the 'illegals' – they are dealing in tiny amounts compared to the big boys of the arms industry. The arms trade is not just about unscrupulous, small-time, gun runners, but is a vast global industry involving the richest nations. For instance, the current top five countries profiting from the sale of arms are the five permanent members of the United Nations Security Council: the USA, the UK, France, Russia and China.

How does this sit with the Security Council's primary responsibility – the maintenance of international peace and security?*

Much of the big five's trade is with so-called developing nations.[149] Although they might not deal directly with the worst culprits, there are always middlemen who can facilitate an uncomfortable business proposition for a slice of the profits – which are always considerable.

And the reality of our charity to the developing world? While G8 leaders smile for the cameras and pledge their millions in aid, their arms dealers are busy lining up to offer them arms to spend their money on. Every year the West makes far more from the developing world in arms sales than it gives in aid. In any language, that *is* scandalous.

Money: it's the root of all evil.

---

* Visit the Security Council website on: www.un.org/Docs/sc/. Equally, next time you wonder where your taxes are going, look at the amount being spent on your defence. Figures quoted by the Center for Arms Control and Non-Proliferation show that the 2005 United States military budget was a staggering $522,000,000,000, well over double the combined budgets of the other four UN Security Council permanent members: China ($62.5 billion), Russia ($61.9 billion), the UK ($51.1 billion) and France ($41.6 billion).

ENDNOTES

1. Aubrey de Sélincourt (trans.), *Herodotus: The Histories* (Harmondsworth: Penguin Classics, 1972), pp.517–18.
2. Alexander Thomson (trans.), *The Lives of the Twelve Caesars by C. Suetonius Tranquillus* (London: Henry G. Bohn, 1855), p.34.
3. Ibid., p.32.
4. Ibid., p.34.
5. This account relies on G. T. Crook (ed.), *The Complete Newgate Calendar Volume II* (London: Navarre Society, 1926), pp.272–3. Fuller details of the testimony given are available at *The Proceedings of the Old Bailey,* Ref: T17190115-49 (www.oldbaileyonline.org/).
6. Brian Laverly, *Nelson's Navy: The Ships, Men and Organisation 1793–1815* (London: Conway Maritime Press, 1989), p.118.
7. David Hannay, *A Short History of the Royal Navy: Volume II 1689–1815* (London: Methuen & Co., 1889), p.143.
8. Crook, *The Complete Newgate Calendar Volume III*, pp.236–7.
9. This account relies on Hannay, *A Short History of the Royal Navy: Volume II,* pp.148–58 and *The 1780 Edition of The Newgate Calendar – Part 2 (1741–1799)* available at www.exclassics.com.
10. The story of the Chevalier d'Éon is told in Edna Nixon, *Royal Spy – The Strange Case of the Chevalier d'Eon* (London: Heinemann, 1966).
11. A full transcript of the trial is available at *The Proceedings of the Old Bailey* Ref: T17720715-22 (www.oldbaileyonline.org/).
12. Rictor Norton (ed.), *The Trial of Robert Jones, 1772, Homosexuality in Eighteenth-Century England: A Sourcebook*, 19 December 2004, www.infopt.demon.co.uk/jones2.htm>.
13. Baron Étienne d'Hastrel, *Mémoires (1766–1825)* (Paris: Librairie Historique F. Teissèdre, 1998), p.82.
14. Evangeline Bruce, *Napoleon and Josephine: An Improbable Marriage* (London: Weidenfeld & Nicolson, 1995), p.384.
15. Christian Tortel and Patricia Carlier, *Bonaparte de Toulon au Caire d'après 19 lettres de François Bernoyer témoin participant chef de l'atelier d'habillement de l'Armée d'Orient* (Montélimar: Armine-Edicylture, 1996), p.124.
16. Somerset de Chair, *Napoleon on Napoleon* (London: Cassell, 1992), p.107.
17. Joseph-Marie Moiret (trans. and ed. Rosemary Brindle), *Memoirs of Napoleon's Egyptian Expedition 1798–1801* (London: Greenhill Books, 2001), p.124.

18. See Gonzague Saint-Bris, *Desaix le sultan de Bonaparte* (Paris: Perrin, 1995), p.158. Believe it or not, in other versions the language used is much, much stronger.

19. Marmont, *Mémoires du Maréchal Marmont duc de Raguse, de 1792 à 1841, Volume I* (Paris: Perrotin, 1857), pp.410–2.

20. Tony Linck, *Napoleon's Generals: The Waterloo Campaign* (Chicago: Emperor's Press, 1994), p.81.

21. *Memoirs of the Court of St. Cloud* (London: The Grolier Society, 1904). See book 6, letter X, Paris, September, 1805. The 'ballerinas' description comes from J. R. Elting, *Swords Around a Throne* (London: Weidenfeld and Nicolson, 1989), p.161.

22. Marmont, *Mémoires*, p.411.

23. Ibid., p.411.

24. William James, *The Naval History of Great Britain, from the Declaration of War by France in 1793 to the Accession of George IV – Volume II* (London: Richard Bentley, 1837), p.102.

25. Ibid., p.103.

26. Hannay, *A Short History of the Royal Navy: Volume II*, p.384.

27. This account uses Roger Knight, *The Pursuit of Victory – the Life and Achievement of Horatio Nelson* (London: Allen Lane, 2005); and Laura Foreman and Ellen Blue Phillips, *Napoleon's Lost Fleet* (London: Discovery Books, 1999).

28. Elizabeth Longford, *Wellington: Years of the Sword* (London: Weidenfeld & Nicolson, 1969), pp.201–2.

29. The original manuscript version of *Childe Harold's Pilgrimage* (Canto I) given in *The Poetical Works of Lord Byron Volume I* (London: John Murray, 1839), pp.29–31.

30. Longford, *Wellington*, p.214.

31. Figure is supplied by IRINnews.org, UN Office for the Coordination of Humanitarian Affairs.

32. John Keay, *India – A History* (London: HarperCollins, 2000), p.419.

33. Keay, *India*, pp.436–7.

34. Article: 'A Few Words from the Khyber,' *Blackwood's Edinburgh Magazine*, Vol. LXXXII July–December, 1857 (William Blackwood & Sons, Edinburgh 1857), pp.610–1.

35. Excerpts taken from *Report on the Sanitary Condition of the British Army*. Quoted in *The Atlantic Monthly*, Vol. 10, No. 60, October 1862.

36. *Report on the Sanitary Condition of the British Army*.

37. *The Times*, 12 October 1854, www.timesonline.co.uk.

38. *Report on the Sanitary Condition of the British Army*.

39. See Bill Gallop, *The Gray Ghost's Raid on Fairfax* (www.ospreypublishing.com); www.mosbysrangers.com; and Charles Wells Russell (ed.), *The Memoirs of Colonel John S. Mosby* (Boston: Little Brown & Co., 1917).

40. From *Harper's Weekly*, 1 August 1863, p.494. The full *Harper's Weekly* report can be found on a number of websites and is well worth a read.

41. For a summary of the Belknap Affair see the website of the US Senate (www.senate.gov). For Custer's involvement see Stephen Ambrose, *Crazy Horse and Custer* (Garden City, NY: Doubleday, 1975).

42. Taken from: 47th Congress, Senate Report No. 926, 16 January 1883.

43. Adrian Greaves, *Rorke's Drift* (London: Cassell Military, 2002), p.184.

44. Thomas Packenham, *The Scramble for Africa, 1876–1912* (London: Phoenix Press, 2001).

45. Cited in Trevor Royle, *The Kitchener Enigma* (London: Joseph, 1985), p.133.

46. Ibid., pp.137–8.

47. Leading article, *The Times*, 10 June 1891. From www.timesonline.co.uk.

48. R. J. Rowan, *The Story of Secret Service* (London: John Miles Ltd, 1938), p.402.

49. Ibid., p.407.

50. *L'Aurore*, 13 January 1898. Author's translation.

51. Bernard K. Mbenga, *The Role of the Black People of the Eastern Transvaal in the South African War of 1899–1902*, p.138; article appears in *Mpumalanga – Reclaiming the Past, Defining the Future* (ed. Peter Delius), available from www.mpumalanga.gov.za/.

52. Royle, *The Kitchener Enigma*, p.192.

53. H. D. Davray, 'Souvenirs sur M. Krupp à Capri' *L'Européen* (29 November 1902).

54. Peter Batty, *The House of Krupp* (London: Secker & Warburg, 1966), p.111.

55. Scott Lively, *The Poisoned Stream* (Oregon: Founders Publishing Organisation, 1997), p.24.

56. Ibid., pp.19–20.

57. Review on Washingtonpost.com of Simon Levay *Queer Science – The Use and Abuse of Research into Homosexuality* (Massachusetts Institute of Technology Press 1996).

58. Much of the information in this section is taken from an information leaflet 'Homosexualität: Skandale' by the Centrum Schwule Geschichte (Gay History Centre) in Cologne.

59. Rowan, *The Story of Secret Service,* pp.461–8.

60. *News D'Ill* (Strasbourg: No.67, January 2003), p.14.

61. Gerard may have confused 'squarehead', or *tête carrée* in French, with an old insult originating in Lorraine and dating from American colonial times. Squarehead was originally a derogatory term used against the British. It indicates excessive formality and a lack of civility. The term is better known when applied to Germans. *News D'Ill,* p.14.

62. James W. Gerard, *My Four Years in Germany* (London: Hodder and Stoughton, 1917). The Zabern Affair is dealt with in Chapter IV.

63. Barbara W. Tuchman, *The Guns of August* (London: Robinson, 2000), p.40.

64. See www.edithcavell.org.uk for more information.

65. The full text of the telegram can be found in the author's *The Enemy Within* (Oxford: Osprey Publishing, 2006).

66. For these and similar tales of narcotic-induced scandals see Marek Kohn's delicious *Dope Girls – The Birth of the British Drug Underground* (London: Lawrence & Wishart, 1992) pp.34–5.

67. From *Time* magazine (23 March 1925).

68. *Time* magazine (23 March 1925).

69. Roger Wilkes, *Scandal. A Scurrilous History of Gossip* (London: Atlantic Books, 2003), pp.140–2.

70. See Gill Bennett, *A Most Extraordinary and Mysterious Business: The Zinoviev Letter of 1924* (Great Britain: Foreign and Commonwealth Office, 1999). This work is available online at www.fco.gov.uk.

71. Joan Miller, *One Girl's War: Personal Exploits in MI5's Most Secret Station* (Dingle, Co. Kerry: Brandon Book Publishers Ltd, 1986).

72. Nigel West (ed.), *The Guy Liddell Diaries Volume I: 1939–1942* (Abingdon, Oxfordshire: Routledge, 2005).

73. MI5 Release of Files to the National Archives, 4 September 2006. *Lady Howard of Effingham* (KV 2/2387-2388). Additional reporting by: Michael Evans, 'Society "Tart" who Evaded the Clutches of Wartime Intelligence' (*The Times*); Ben Fenton, 'Penniless "Spy" who Slept Her Way to the Top' (*The Telegraph*); Richard Norton-Taylor, 'Life and Loves of Peer's Wife Suspected of Being War Spy' (*The Guardian*), all 4 September 2006.

74. This piece relies on Frederick D. Parker, *A Priceless Advantage: U.S. Navy Communications Intelligence and the Battles of Coral Sea, Midway, and the Aleutians: United States Cryptologic History: Series IV, World War II, Volume 5* (Washington, DC: Center for Cryptologic History, National Security Agency, 1993).

75. Conversations are recreated from accounts given in D'Este and Charles M. Province's *Unknown Patton* (e-book edition, 2002), p.26.

76. Dwight D. Eisenhower, *Crusade in Europe* (London: William Heinemann Limited, 1948), pp.198–201.

77. This 'slapping' account relies mainly on Carlo D'Este's outstanding *A Genius For War* (New York: HarperCollins, 1995).

78. Andy Dougan, *Dynamo: defending the honour of Kiev* (London: Fourth Estate, 2001).

79. Nina Shandler, *The Strange Case of Hellish Nell – The Story of Helen Duncan and the Witch Trial of World War II* (Cambridge, MA: Da Capo Press, 2006), p.40.

80. Ibid., p.3.

81. Quotes from: *How Journalism Saved One Man, and the Rest of Us, from McCarthyism.* An interview with Radulovich by Michael Stoll for *Grade the News* (www.gradethenews.org), 20 February 2006.

82. Soviet perspective comes from Alexander Orlov, 'The U-2 Program: A Russian Officer Remembers', from CIA journal *Studies in Intelligence* (Winter 1998–99).

83. John Hughes-Wilson, *The Puppet Masters* (London: Weidenfeld & Nicolson, 2004).

84. This account of the Profumo Affair is based on the accounts given in Roger Wilkes, *Scandal – A Scurrilous History of Gossip*, Anthony Summers and Stephen Dorril, *Honeytrap: the secret worlds of Stephen Ward* (London: Weidenfeld and Nicolson, 1987).

85. Most of the factual details relating to *Ranch Hand* can be found in William A. Buckingham Jr, *Operation Ranch Hand: The Air Force and Herbicides in Southeast Asia 1961–1971* (Washington DC: Office of Airforce History United States Airforce, 1982).

86. Figures are from: United States District Court Eastern District of New York court judgement, 10 March 2005. Jack B Weinstein, Senior District Judge, Brooklyn, New York. p.19.

87. Buckingham, *Operation Ranch Hand,* p.199.

88. Figure from Vietnamese Red Cross, reported by BBC News on 10 March 2005.

89. Thomas Hauser, (with the cooperation of Muhammad Ali), *Muhammad Ali: His Life and Times* (London: Robson, 1991), p.143.

90. Ibid., p.145.

91. US Supreme Court, Clay v. United States, 403 U.S. 698 (1971) from supreme.justia.com.

92. Hauser, *Muhammad Ali,* p.167. This eventually got boiled down into the apocryphal quote: 'Ain't no Vietcong ever called me Nigger!'

93. Ibid., p.180.

94. An incomparable account of this contest is given in Norman Mailer's *The Fight* (Boston: Little Brown, 1975).

95. www.whitehouse.gov.

96. Simon Reeve, *One Day in September: The Story of the 1972 Munich Olympics Massacre, a Government Cover-up and a Covert Revenge Mission* (London: Faber, 2000). See also the 1999 documentary film this book accompanies, *One Day in September* directed by Kevin Macdonald, and the 2005 film *Munich* by Steven Spielberg.

97. Peter Beaumont, 'Argentine Commander Casts New Light on Falklands War Controversy' (*The Observer,* 25 May 2003).

98. Press release: *State Department Opens Files on Argentina's Dirty War – New Documents Describe Key Death Squad under Former Army Chief Galtieri* (National Security Archive Electronic Briefing Book No. 73 Part I, ed. Carlos Osorio, Washington, DC, 2002).

99. Lucy Ash, *The Living Disappeared* (BBC News, 19 August 1998).

100. See www.nuncamas.org.

101. Ash, *The Living Disappeared.*

102. For an excellent account of the affair see the website: www.greenpeace.org/international/rainbow-warrior-bombing/spy-story.

103. This sentiment was expressed by Professor Alexander Gillespie to the BBC: *Eyewitness: Rainbow Warrior Sinking* (7 July 2005).

104. Stephen Hoadley, *New Zealand and France: Politics, Diplomacy and Dispute Management* (Wellington: New Zealand Institute of International Affairs, 2005), p.42.

105. Kathy Marks, 'Bordeaux to Spies in Greenpeace Killing' (*The Independent,* 24 March 2001).

106. Hervé Gattegno, 'Le rapport secret de l'amiral Lacoste sur l'attentat contre le Rainbow Warrior' (*Le Monde,* 9 July 2005).

107. Catherine Field, 'We Were Betrayed Says Rainbow Warrior Agent' (*New Zealand Herald,* 9 October 2006).

108. Catherine Field, 'Saboteur Spills the French Beans' (*New Zealand Herald,* 8 April 1999).

109. See *The Oliver North File: His Diaries, E-Mail, and Memos on the Kerry Report, Contras and Drugs* (National Security Archive Electronic Briefing Book No. 113, 26 February 2004).

110. Unless cited otherwise this piece is based on the findings found in Independent Counsel Lawrence E. Walsh's *Final Report of the*

Independent Counsel for Iran/Contra Matters – Volume I: Investigations and Prosecutions (Washington, DC: United States Court of Appeals for The District of Columbia Circuit, 4 August 1993).

111. Data from Rear Admiral William M. Fogarty, *Formal Investigation into the Circumstances Surrounding the Downing of Iran Air Flight 655 on 3 July 1988* (Washington, DC: Dept of Defense, 1988).

112. Piers Morgan, *The Insider – The Private Diaries of a Scandalous Decade* (London: Ebury Press, 2005), p.110.

113. George Stephanopoulos, *All Too Human – A Political Education* (London: Hutchinson, 1999), p.74.

114. Susanne Höll, 'Die Saga von den fliegenden Kühen' (*Rhein-Zeitung*, 1 May 1997).

115. *Statement on the Inadvertent Bombing of the Chinese Embassy* by Bill Harlow, Director of Public Affairs, 10 April 2000.

116. *The 9/11 Commission Report: Final Report of the National Commission on Terrorist Attacks upon the United States* (Washington, DC: National Commission on Terrorist Attacks upon the United States, 2004), pp.140–1.

117. Chidanand Rajghatta, 'Coffins Were Not Meant to Carry Kargil Martyrs' (*The Times of India*, 13 December 2001).

118. Report by Alistair Lawson in New Delhi for the BBC.

119. Rajesh Ramachandran, 'Kargil Coffins Bought at Twice US Price' (*The Times of India*, 7 May 2002).

120. 'Coffin Scandal Rages in India' (BBC News, 12 December 2001).

121. 'Indian Defence Minister Row Goes on' (BBC News, 29 November 2001).

122. Interviewed on BBC2 *Horizon Special: What Sank the Kursk?* (Screened on 8 August 2001).

123. Terri Judd, 'Commander Wined and Dined as his destroyer headed for Catastrophe', (*The Independent*, 12 September 2003).

124. 'Courts Martial Verdicts on Grounded Destroyer' (*Navy News* 12 September 2003).

125. 'Warship Accident was "Worst Feeling"' (BBC, 8 July 2002).

126. 'Navy Sailors Used Gov't Credit Cards to Hire Prostitutes' (Associated Press, 8 October 2002).

127. GAO-02-863T (17 July 2002).

128. 'Latest Round of Financial Mismanagement Uncovered at the Pentagon: Air Force Personnel Charge Online Gambling and Cruise Tickets to Government-Issued Credit Cards' (Press Release for US Representative Jan Schakowsky; 20 December 2002).

129. United States General Accounting Office Report to Congressional Requesters *Purchase Cards: Control Weaknesses leave the Air Force Vulnerable to Fraud, Waste, and Abuse* GAO-03-292 (December 2002).

130. Report: GAO-03-298.

131. 'Saddam's Mouthpiece "Seeks Surrender"' (BBC Online, 29 April 2003).

132. Lara Marlowe & Jim Mcbeth, 'The master of smoke and mirrors has an interesting line in insults' (*The Scotsman*, 8 April 2003).

133. 'Americans Extended Control' (BBC *Newsnight*, 9 April, 2003).

134. 'Saddam's Information Minister Stayed Loyal to the Last' (BBC Online, 5 May 2003).

135. 'Saddam's Mouthpiece "Seeks Surrender."'

136. There is a website dedicated to his messages: www.welovetheiraqiinformationminister.com.

137. Interview with CNN International, 8 November 2003.

138. *War Spin* (BBC2, 18 May 2003).

139. BBC News, 15 May 2003.

140. CNN International, 12 November 2003.

141. Country details from the CIA's very handy *World Fact Book*.

142. Reported by BBC News: 'Equatorial Guinea's "God"', 26 July 2003. The broadcast was delivered in the language Fang – which is spoken by about 80 per cent of the population.

143. Cited in Fred Bridgland, 'Coup Plot Conviction Increases the Pressure on Mark Thatcher' (*The Scotsman*, 28 August 2004). The asterisks shown here were used by Mann. He was writing to his wife, after all.

144. Imogen Foulkes, 'Domestic Killings Shock Swiss' (BBC News, Geneva, 9 May 2006).

145. A study led by the Swiss criminologist Martin Killias, reported in Gregor Poletti, 'Armeeschusswaffen: Jedes Jahr 300 Tote' (*Berner Zeitung*, 16 December 2006).

146. Ruth Elkins, 'Skier's Murder Prompts Swiss Women's Campaign for Ban on Guns in the Home' (*The Independent*, 22 October 2006).

147. Owen Bowcott and Richard Norton-Taylor, 'Africa's Merchant of Death' (*The Guardian*, 23 December 2000).

148. For more on this subject, visit: www.un.org/peace/africa/Diamond.html.

149. For US sales see: Richard F. Grimmett, *U.S. Arms Sales: Agreements with and Deliveries to Major Clients, 1997–2004* (Congressional Research Service, The Library of Congress, 29 December 2005).